FORTUNE'S FAVOURITE

Franz Lehár ("Fortune's Favourite")

Fortune's Favourite

The Life and Times of
FRANZ LEHÁR

W. MACQUEEN-POPE
and
D. L. MURRAY

But, what is more than woman and wine,
The happy land of music is mine,
And all is always well
Where the music-makers dwell. . . .
Paganini (Act I)

HUTCHINSON
Stratford Place
London

Hutchinson & Co. (Publishers) Ltd.
London   New York   Toronto
Melbourne   Sydney   Cape Town

First published 1953

Set in eleven point Monotype Garamond
one point leaded

Printed in Great Britain
by The Anchor Press, Ltd.,
Tiptree, Essex

To That Gracious Lady
"The Merry Widow" who entranced us
the "Sonia" who captured our hearts
and who waltzes forever in our memories
LILY ELSIE
this book is offered in grateful homage
for the beauty which she gave us

Contents

List of Illustrations

Foreword

THIS study of Franz Lehár is the work of two Englishmen who wished to pay a debt they felt they owed to the great Viennese composer for the many hours of happiness he had given them in their lives. It does not claim to be a full-dress biography; for that Mme Maria von Peteani's book, *Franz Lehár; Seine Musik, Sein Leben*, must remain indispensable to all students of the subject, and we have to thank her for the permission to make use of material contained in it.

Since our aim is an English tribute, we do not feel that any apology is needed for the prominence we have given to the history of Lehár's works in this country. All nations have their own Lehár, and each loves him for some special quality. We have been concerned in particular with his impact upon the English Theatre and the people of England. This is not such a narrowly insular view as it might seem, for the London which Lehár took by storm at the beginning of this century was a world centre. Nor have the most famous interpreters of his operas over here been all English. It was an American actor who powerfully aided the triumph of *The Merry Widow* on its first production in London. The English version of *Gipsy Love* had for its stars a Hungarian singer and an artist who, though English, was born in Paris and received much of his musical education in Vienna. Lehár's later operas, *Paganini* and *The Land of Smiles*, were introduced to the British public by Richard Tauber, not a native of England, though he made his final home with us and became an English citizen.

Franz Lehár, in fact, enlarged the boundaries of the English Theatre. That is one of his many gifts to us that should not be forgotten.

Besides the biographies and other works given in the Bibliography at the end of the book, the authors wish to record a special debt of thankfulness for the information and material kindly supplied by Mme Emma Papházay, the sister of Franz Lehár; by Dr. Otto Blau, Director of the Glocken-Verlag, which publishes the music of Lehár; by Herr Paul Knepler, one of Lehár's principal librettists and his lifelong friend; and by Frau Mizzi Günther, the original exponent of the "Merry Widow".

We are also indebted to Dr. J. P. Hodin for permission to utilize unpublished notes of his on old Vienna.

The lines quoted on the title page are from the English lyrics to *Paganini*, by kind permission of the authors, Sir Alan P. Herbert and Mr. Reginald Arkell, and Messrs. Chappell and Co. Ltd.

W. M. P.

D. L. M.

The Overture

In a sitting-room in the Carlton Hotel, London, one summer's afternoon in 1931, three men sat awaiting the gentlemen of the Press. These had been invited to meet one of that trio, who was paying a rare visit to London. They were a very assorted trio. One of them, short, rubicund and bright-eyed, sat quietly, no doubt revolving what was coming and how to deal with it, in his mind. His name was Heilbronn; he represented a great firm of international dramatic and musical impresarios. His real reason for being there was to interpret, if necessary. The second man was large, cheerful and genial. To him this meeting with the Press had no terrors. It was his job; he was doing it every day. The men and women who were coming were to him "the boys and girls"—he knew them all. His only wish was to get the best out of the "story" he was handling at that moment, and as he knew the story was a good one, he was easy in his mind. He chatted from time to time with the other two, but he concentrated on the one who was about to take the stage, giving him hints as to what he was likely to be asked, putting into his mind the most suitable answers and the statements likely to get into the papers, not doing it in an authoritative way, but by means of gentle hints in conversational tones—but he knew he was being understood.

That third man was the Important Personage—a Very Important Personage indeed—a King in his way—a King of Light Music—he was Franz Lehár. He was the man who had composed *The Merry Widow* and so many other delightful musical shows. He was the man who had composed the waltzes to which the tempo of the world moved in the early portion of the present century. He was the man who could bring the true spirit of the romance of Vienna to the dingier atmosphere of London. At that moment one of his melodies was all the rage—it was being sung nightly at Theatre Royal, Drury Lane, and it was called "You Are

13

My Heart's Delight". Was being sung nightly? That was the trouble.
A tenor bound to that composer by many ties had come to Drury Lane,
had triumphed—had immediately been absent from the cast—had returned—had gone again—and had even gone back to Vienna. That tenor
was Richard Tauber. And Lehár the composer had brought him back,
had done so personally, had returned with the prodigal singer under his
watchful eye, and that very night was going to see that he resumed singing
at Drury Lane, and, what is more, was going to conduct the show in
person. So it was an occasion. Hence the Press Conference to meet Franz
Lehár. So it seems as good a time as any for those interested in him to
meet him as well. . . .

The ladies and gentlemen of the Press arrived, in their own leisurely
fashion. They were introduced. They saw a middle-sized man of no great
distinction to the quick glance, well dressed in a suit of excellent quality
but foreign cut. He gave the impression of squareness and of integrity
the moment one met his eyes. The grey hair and the close-clipped grey
moustache on the upper lip were both so well trimmed that they were not
apparent. Here was no artistic composer with flowing locks to match his
flowing melodies, with large bow tie or untidy appearance, which the
uninitiated think is the correct wear for genius. Here was a dapper man,
very much alive, very precise, quick and decided in his movements, erect
of carriage, direct of gaze, who moved rapidly, and who was extremely
courteous and polite. At times the uniform of a soldier seemed to peep
out from beneath the lounge suit. The casual observer might well have
taken this man for an officer in mufti, and they would have been right, for
Lehár had served for years as a Regimental Director of Music—and once
a soldier, always a soldier. So it was with him. At each introduction he
shook hands, clicked his heels, and bowed from the hips. Middle Europe
was all round him. Never once was he off his guard, never once did his
attention stray, never once did he relax. He was on parade—and used to it.

But he did not, as the central figures usually do on such occasions, just
sit back in a chair and prepare to be questioned. He was here, there and
everywhere. Before questions start at these Conferences, there is as a rule
a period of waiting until the full quota are present; some have to be a bit
late, through no fault of their own. So there is chatter—and refreshments.
During this interim period, habitually the man or woman they have come
to see, these Press people, just sits, smiles and has a desultory chat with
such as speak to him. Usually the Press let him alone until the man in
charge declares the ball open.

Lehár did not do that. He hurried about amongst them; he placed
chairs for them; he himself assisted the waiters and the Publicity Man not
only in pouring out, but in serving the drinks. He carried these round

himself—he handed cigarettes. He was anxious to be of genuine service; he was anxious to make those who had done him the honour of coming to see him do so under conditions of comfort. A crowd turned up, chairs ran short. A comfortable chair had been placed for Lehár's own use; with a charming smile he pushed it forward to a lady journalist. Other chairs had to be fetched. Seldom, if ever, has a man who has had to undergo the ordeal (for, however experienced you may be, it is still an ordeal, especially in a foreign country and a strange tongue) of facing a Press Conference done as did Lehár on that summer afternoon. He did what he did because he wanted to; it was his idea of how a gentleman should behave in such circumstances; he did not do it with any desire to gain favour—after all, he was Lehár and it never crossed his mind. He just did what his natural instinct prompted him to do. And had he been rehearsed carefully, he could not have done better. A feeling of the utmost friendliness was in the air.

At last the time was ripe, everyone who mattered was present. Lehár then, at the request of the Publicity Man, sat in his appointed chair—another comfortable chair had been fetched for him in place of the one he had surrendered. The Publicity Man said a few words of general introduction and the Conference was on. Usually one Press man or woman takes the lead and asks an opening question of a general nature. Lehár did not wait for that. He twinkled at them, and he began talking. It became clear that the interpreter would have an easy job. He was called on, it is true, to elucidate when the not very large stock of English ran out, to add a bit after some rapid words in German. But Lehár, with a smile which lit up his face and centred in his eyes, told them himself why he was there. He made them laugh too. They all got along very well. Questions began and the answer was always ready—and to the point. Everything about Lehár was direct. One man insisted on referring to the composer as "The Master". The Master acknowledged the compliment with a bow—but he did not like it very much. In the midst of the talk, the door opened.

A tall, elegant young man stood on the threshold. He wore a top hat, a morning coat, a grey tie, sponge-bag trousers and shiny boots to match the hat. He stood and looked around. The Publicity Man went to him: "Can I help you?" he asked. The young man gazed around: "I'm from *The Times*." The Publicity Man bowed. "Would you like to meet Herr Lehár?" he asked. "Is that he?" queried the elegant gentleman, nodding in the direction of The Master, and he was told he was right. "Ah," he said, and gazed for a few seconds. Then he ran his eye round the room, had one more look at Lehár, bowed to the Publicity Man and vanished. The next morning the leading newspaper of this land carried a most excellent description of the whole affair, and a very well-written and carefully assessed story of Lehár, complete as to his appearance. It just shows what can be done. . . .

Lehár told them stories of his shows, especially of *The Merry Widow*. He recalled coming over for the first night of that production. He had much of interest to say—and he said it. He answered every question properly and without waste of words.

He was asked about his next work, his next operette. He shrugged his shoulders. The libretto was the difficulty—they were so hard to find. The man who had called him "Master" jumped in. Would The Master allow his journal to try and find him a libretto—not to commit him to it, naturally, but to start a search through this country which might produce just what was wanted, and so be of help, and also gain some glory for British librettists? For one moment Lehár's eyes sought those of the Publicity Man. That official gave an imperceptible nod. And Lehár assured the gentleman of the Press that he would be delighted.

He laid down the rules, he expressed clearly what he wanted. Romance must be the main ingredient; there must be a touch of sentiment, a touch of dramatic incident, plenty of comedy—but in the main Romance. The setting? That did not really matter—naturally Vienna was as good a spot as any—but what did he care? There was as much romance in London as anywhere; he found it a most romantic place, he said. He had spent the morning looking out of the window as London swept by. He was enchanted by the rush of the traffic, by the scarlet buses, by the colour and the speed of it all—and he found it had rhythm in it. Yes, he did indeed like London. It always surprised him, and he liked being surprised. So it did not matter—London, England, Spain, Italy, New York, South America, France—so long as the story was right, so long as it was capable of inspiring him and making his mind move with music—that was what he wanted.

The Conference came to a close. He bade them all farewell separately, bowing to all as he shook hands with the men and kissed the hands of the ladies. They went away feeling they had met a friend. It was a most successful occasion—and the reason for the success was Lehár. When the last one had gone, Lehár turned to the Publicity Man and raised his eyebrows. He received the Publicity Man's sincere and heartfelt congratulations. They had met before over *The Merry Widow* years ago; but the Publicity Man was not of much account then; not that he mattered very much this time either. But they were friends—and they remained so. . . .

The night came and Theatre Royal, Drury Lane, was packed to suffocation. Tauber was to sing once more and Lehár was to conduct.

There was something else of major importance too, which Lehár had been told, but which, according to regulation, had been a closely guarded secret. Their Majesties, King George V and Queen Mary, were to be in the Royal Box. So it was a real occasion.

That wonderful theatre looked its best. There were the tail coats and the white ties, the gleam and colour of the women's dresses; there was the glow of the lights on its noble staircases and vestibules, and amongst the smartly dressed crowd of notabilities the powdered-haired footmen moved about in their Royal Liveries. The pit and gallery were crowded with excited, enthusiastic playgoers. And Lehár came into the front of the house from backstage. He had been presented to the King and Queen. He was very pleased. But he was quite self-possessed. In those eyes was a beaming twinkle. He still looked the soldier in his full evening dress. He gave no suggestion of the master musician, the man who had set the world singing his melodies, and dancing to his waltzes—the man who had given such genuine pleasure to so many thousands. But there was that head of his, so well shaped, with such a brow, and so well placed on his shoulders; there were those quick, artistic hands—never still, always moving, the sure sign of a creative mind—and above all there were the eyes.

The eyes were dominant in Lehár. They looked the world in the face, but they saw below the surface; they were pools wherein those melodies of his gathered and then flowed into his brain. For all their directness, their activity, there was a dream behind them, something which was not apparent to a quick glance but all the same was always there. They were the eyes of one who was at the same time a man of action and a thinker, a man of quick decision and also a dreamer, the eyes of a man of the world, and a poet who composed his poems instead of writing them.

He wanted to ask the Publicity Man a few questions. He did it. They shook hands again and Lehár went through the pass door, went down the stairs and vanished for the moment under the stage. The house was buzzing, as theatres do in the last few minutes of waiting. Then the orchestra, already in their places, rose to their feet and applauded, as is the custom, by tapping on their various instruments. And, from behind the conductor's stand, came Franz Lehár. He got into the chair. The house rose at him. Applause echoed round the theatre, clapping, cheers and many Bravos. He bowed from the waist, stiffly. He bowed to the orchestra too. And then the power of the man became apparent. Here, in his conductor's chair, he was a King on his throne—a King of the Land of Melody, master of it all. There was no doubt about it. He might not be big and impressive to look at; but Franz Lehár exuded power when at his work as he exuded charm when out of it.

B

He stood up, he took his baton. Into the Royal Box came the King and Queen. And the first beat that Lehár gave was that which started the National Anthem. Everyone stood to attention. Then, loyal and warm applause. Their Majesties seated themselves. The house did the same. And Lehár, glancing to his right and his left, gathering his men around him, began to conduct the overture.

The magnificent orchestra at Drury Lane played superbly. Lehár conducted with as little fuss and as few tricks as have ever been seen. It was the beat of the leader of a military band, but it was supreme in the knowledge of what was wanted. He might have been in the bandstand of an Austrian town, playing selections with his regimental musicians. No *bravura*, no movement of the body, but a beat which got everything out of the music and showed a complete understanding of the value of every note he had composed. The orchestra finished, the overture was over, the applause rang out again, and again Lehár bowed. A red light flickered by his side, the house dimmed down, the footlights glowed, and Lehár again gathered together his orchestra. His baton raised, he waited a second— and then—the great curtain swept up on *The Land of Smiles*. . . .

And so let the curtain rise on the story of the man who filled the world with his music—music which knew no barrier of nationality, music which will be for all time beloved, conceived behind those magnificent eyes in the creative brain of Franz Lehár. . . .

CHAPTER ONE

Under the Double Eagle

IN 1859 the 5th Austrian Regiment of Infantry was serving in Italy, and with it was a Band Sergeant-Major named Franz Lehár. This regiment belonged to that Army of the ancient Austrian Empire which George Meredith watched and hated as it filled the captive cities of Lombardy with the ponderous thud of its marching, the rumble of its guns and the glory of its martial music. In his novel *Vittoria* he drew a picture of it at Milan, in its medley of nationalities, Italians and Magyars, Croats and Serbs, Czechs and Germans, all polished to uniformity in the "clean tight military array of Austria":

> "It gleamed down the length of the Corso in a blinding sunlight; brass helmets and hussar feathers, white and violet surcoats, green plumes, maroon capes, bright steel scabbards, bayonet-points,—as gallant a show as some portentously magnified summer field, flowing with the wind, might be; and over all the banner of Austria—the black double-headed eagle ramping on a yellow ground."

In this polyglot array, the most strictly "professional" army in Europe, united only by loyalty to its Kaiser, and by its memories of many defeats and a few victories borne with equal stoicism, Band Sergeant-Major Lehár represented the Moravian stock. He came of a family of glass-workers in Schönwald near Neustadt, who had a tradition, with the ring of romance rather than history, that their name derived from a French officer of noble birth called "Le Harde", who, after capture by the Russians in the Revolutionary Wars, had escaped into Moravia and married a peasant maiden there. Franz Lehár the elder went through the campaign of Magenta and Solferino against the French, which saw the Austrian Army forced out of Lombardy, and reduced the Kaiser Franz

Joseph's holding in Italy to the province of Venetia. Lehár stayed on in garrison after the war in the land of sunshine and music, learnt to play every instrument in the band, and at the early age of twenty-five became Bandmaster (*Militärkapellmeister*) in the Regiment of the Grand Duke of Baden.

Life in Italy must have been a daily inspiration to Lehár, for one surmises that it was the musical rather than the military side of his profession that appealed to him. Certainly in his photograph it is the head of a musician rather than a soldier that looks out with its dreamy eyes and long hair over the stiff collar of the uniform. When the Austrian Kaiser was again at war in 1866, this time against Prussia and Italy, it is said that Lehár's Colonel found the strict black-out ordered for the regiment, as it lay close to the enemy lines at Peschia, violated by a single gleam. It was his Bandmaster, diligently composing by the light of a feeble taper. A few days later Lehár was present at the victory over the Italians at Custozza, and composed, on the spot where his regiment had been posted, the "Olioso March", which was to become a favourite in the repertory of Austrian military bands.

But Custozza could not save Austria, crushed by the Prussians at Sadowa, from losing the last of her Italian provinces, and while the politic Franz Joseph laboured to throw off the last shadowy trappings of the Holy Roman Empire, and to reconstruct his still enormous family heritage as a "Dual Monarchy", evenly poised on Budapest and Vienna, Bandmaster Lehár was transferred in 1868 to Komorn in Hungary. Here he married Christine Neubrandt, of a family originally German, but now completely Hungarian in character and sentiment, and on the 30th April, 1870, she bore him a son, who was named after his father Franz Lehár, and was to make the modest Bandmaster's name famous throughout the world.

The child's first days were passed in the ancient and picturesque town of Komorn, with its mixed Hungarian and Slovakian population, its grim memories of strife and rapine in the wars with the Tartars and the Turks, its store of legends and fairy tales, and its pervasive atmosphere of Slovak folk-song and gypsy fiddling. Here, too, had been born the famous Hungarian novelist, Maurus Jókai, one of whose tales, *The Gypsy Baron*, gave Johann Strauss the subject for a celebrated operette. Favourable influences hovered over the cradle of little Franz, whose life at first, however, was to be the life of the Army, still the sole real cement of the Monarchy, and the only imperial institution that included not only all the races of the Empire but all grades of society. In its highest posts were archdukes, princes and counts; among its corps of officers were to be found cultured foreign soldiers of fortune, like Meredith's Wilfrid

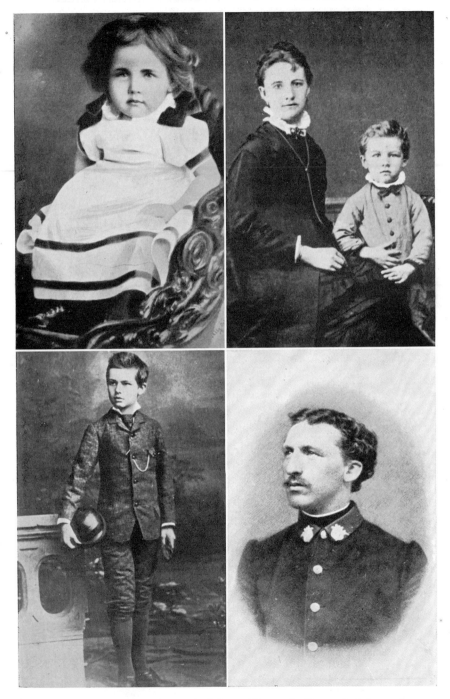

Top left: Franz Lehár at the age of three. *Top right*: Franz Lehár at the age of five, with his mother. *Bottom left*: Franz Lehár at the age of ten. *Bottom right*: Franz Lehár, senior (father of the composer), in 1870

Top left: Franz Lehár as Naval Bandmaster, 1894. *Top right*: The young Lehár, now free of the Army, immerses himself in work for the Theatre. *Bottom left*: A great combination of librettist and composer, Victor Léon (*standing*), part author of *The Merry Widow*, and Franz Lehár, its composer, just before this operette was produced. *Bottom right*: Lehár as he looked when *The Merry Widow* came to London

Pierson; in its ranks the barely literate peasantry of remote and primitive provinces.

It was a world within a world, ever on the move from posting to posting, having (not unlike Kipling's Anglo-Indians) its own habits, its own cooking recipes, its own idioms, and almost its own language— "Army German" (*Armeedeutsch*), a composite dialect of all the nationalities it embraced. Life was Spartan in the Bandmaster's family, with its travel-worn furniture and constant need for economy in living on the slender Army pay. But little Franz's mother knew how to cook delicious Hungarian dishes, and while she cooked she would tell him the legends and sing him the folk-songs of her country—lessons never to be erased.

Other lessons, those taught in school, did not come so easily to the gay and thoughtless child. An early preceptor of his declared that Franzi was "one of the most charming feather-brains and one of the most feather-brained charmers" he had ever had to deal with. In a photograph taken with his mother when he was only five years old there is a tinge of melancholy in the sensitive face, and a hand is laid upon her silk dress, as if for reassurance. About now he is said to have composed his first song; it began, "I feel a pain deep down within me". Yet, for all his gentleness, "Lanzi" (as he childishly mispronounced his name "Franzi") showed a quiet but indomitable obstinacy. Neither scolding nor even slapping could silence him one day in a public park when the sight of some better-dressed children provoked him to cry out again and again, "I want white breeches too!"

Something more important than a taste for smart clothes awoke early in Franz. There was one kind of lesson that did not bore him—the music lesson. At six years old, as we have seen, he was making little tunes by ear on the piano, and when he was ten and the regiment at Klausenburg he saw a sight that he never forgot. The aged Liszt, his fellow-countryman, came to conduct a concert in the cathedral. To do him honour, Bandmaster Lehár offered his services as a violinist in the orchestra. At the end of the performance Franz, who had been listening from the choir stalls, saw his father bending low, as he took his leave, over the hand of the silver-haired visitor. It was a first glimpse to childish eyes of the majesty of the musician's calling. A sacredness seemed to enhalo it, as the boy gazed upon the almost legendary figure of the celebrated Abbé in his ecclesiastical costume. Music, then, was a vocation! Franz Lehár would never lose sight of that guiding light amid all the intoxications of waltz time.

With this vision to sustain him, a lazy schoolboy in the famous Piaristengymnasium in Budapest scribbles musical notes all over his atlas during the geography lesson; he is sent off to Sternberg in Moravia so that he may learn to speak German properly and not only his native Hungarian; and then at the age of sixteen comes the first decisive turning-point in his career. He sits for a scholarship at the Prague Conservatorium of Music . . . and wins it. When Lanzi's will is set on something, already nothing can turn him from his path; to train as a musician he will even work at his books. At the famous Conservatorium in one of the narrow streets of the Prage Neustadt Franz Lehár worked hard both at the theory and practice of music, and especially at the violin. He lived in lodgings on a tiny allowance, and knew what it was to have an empty stomach. Sometimes he even turned faint and giddy in the street from hunger. He tried to keep his half-starved condition a secret from his parents; even his mother, when she paid him a visit, was deceived by his air of gaiety— until, just as her train was going out of the station, a cry he could not repress of "Mother! Mother!" betrayed for an instant his misery. In a moment he was cheerfully waving his handkerchief in farewell, but his mother had understood.

His endurance was rewarded; for unexpectedly his father was appointed to a regiment in Prague, and Franz again had a home and good food . . . the favourite maternal cooking. He was now winning golden opinions from his teachers both at the violin and at the piano. Once at a school concert he was accompanying a fellow-pupil in a violin concerto. The violinist faltered, lost his memory, was on the point of a break-down; but Lehár at the piano, improvising imperturbably, hinted the theme he had lost, and all ended well. Meanwhile in private Franz was still composing, and still brimming with courage and audacity. When the Director of the school took him to visit Dvořák, Franz took advantage of the introduction to send the formidable Master some of his compositions and ask for an opinion. Dvořák glanced through them, and growled. "Not bad! . . . My boy, you'll make a composer!" Soon afterwards Lehár dared to invite the criticism of a greater man still, Brahms himself. He received in return a card of introduction to the Secretary of the Vienna Society of Music-Lovers, on which Brahms had written in his own hand, "The enclosed specimens are a further recommendation." But this priceless testimonial was never presented. Lehár the romantic could not bear to part with the autograph of Brahms. He kept the card to the end of his life among his treasures. As always with him the ideal was greater than the reality.

But he would have been a more than human youth if he had not been elated enough by such praises to beg leave from his father to abandon the violin and devote himself entirely to composition. The sage old campaigner, however, shook his head. "Stick to the fiddle, my boy! There's always a living in that. Composing? I've tried it myself." Franz sighed, but saw the sense of it. He went back to the fiddle, and at eighteen passed out of the Conservatorium with credit.

At once the problem of earning his living presented itself. He could not, even if that had been his way, look to his father for support, for the Bandmaster was at the moment in Vienna without a post. Franz took the first job that offered; it was poorly paid, but exciting enough. The Joint Municipal Theatres of Barmen-Elberfeld in the Rhineland had advertised for an orchestra leader and chorus-master. Lehár applied and was accepted, at a salary of 150M a month, and in this fashion passed through the dusty doors of that glamorous Theatre world in which he was to reign as King.

It was an inestimable benefit to him thus to learn the Theatre early, and to learn it practically, the hard way. There were two theatres to be served, both Opera and operette to be rehearsed and played: the hours of work were endless. As Mme Peteani remarks, it was truly a case of "Figaro, here! . . . Figaro, there!" Lehár made acquaintance with the ill-temper of managers, the temperament of singers, the jealousies and petty plots of colleagues, the ingratitude that is ever the lot of the man who does the real work. . . . Compensations? Yes, there must have been such. Laughter and flirtations with the pretty chorus there doubtless were, and above all the mounting sense of enchantment as the work took shape in melody and colour, banishing the drab realities of boards and ropes and pulleys. But there was one disadvantage that outweighed the magic of the footlights. For the orchestra leader and chorus-master there was no time left for composing. The ruled sheets of music paper lay blank in his lodgings. It was clear that this would not do, and while Lehár brooded over his difficulties came the sudden news that his father had been appointed Bandmaster to the 50th Regiment in Vienna and would be glad to have him as his First Violin. In Vienna!

With his usual smiling optimism Franz applied for release from his contract at Barmen-Elberfeld. The answer was a chilling douche. He must find a suitable deputy, or else stay at his post. Otherwise he would be liable for breach of contract. Franz's brow puckered—but not for long. After reflection he telegraphed to his father. Back came the reply in the shape of a call-up notice from the authorities for his yet unfulfilled military service. Such a summons cancelled any contract, and Franz Lehár, no doubt still smiling, stepped into the train for the Austrian capital. Even at this age he was not easily to be balked when his heart was set upon a thing. . . . It had once been white breeches; now it was Vienna.

CHAPTER TWO

Kapellmeister Lehár

V IENNA, when Lehár arrived there in 1890, was at the height of its renown as the capital of pleasure. As early as the 17th century a French traveller had declared, "If you cannot spend your life in Paris, then by all means spend it in Vienna," and at the end of the 19th century it was still the only city in Europe that could compete with Paris in gaiety, charm and *savoir vivre*.

In the glittering façade there might indeed be ominous cracks. The divergent races of the Dual Monarchy were seething with nationalistic passion; the crumbling of Turkish Power made the Near East an explosive problem for Austro-Hungarian diplomacy; the aged Emperor, patiently shouldering his dynastic burden, had grievous trials and scandals to hide in the imperial family. His lovely wife the Empress Elizabeth, beset by the mental eccentricity of her stock, had practically abandoned the duties of her station, to lead a roving life and indulge her love of horses—even of circus-riding; his only son the Crown Prince Rudolf had come to a violent end the year before in the still unsolved horror of Mayerling.

Yet the outer show remained glorious. Its background was either the ancient city, tightly packed within the circle of the former walls, with its quaint medieval lanes, its painted stucco house-fronts, its bulbous towers and sombre Gothic cathedral, its churches and palaces of richly sculptured baroque, and its fountains spraying the limbs of marble nymphs; or else the ponderous magnificence of the engirdling 19th-century Ringstrasse, with its plutocratic mock-Renaissance lavishness. The pavements resounded with the feet of well-dressed dandies and idlers, with the clinking spurs of Hungarian officers in tasselled boots and shakoes crowned with aigrets, with the stiff tread of Austrian officers in pairs, each duly per-

24

fumed, monocled and corseted. The innumerable cafés, as padded and comfortable as London clubs, were crammed with cigar-smoking possessors of the divine gift of leisure, each sipping his favourite brand of coffee, *braun* or *mocca*, Turkish or *kapuziner*, which the waiter should know without being asked. The main Avenue of the Prater—the Hyde Park of Vienna—gleamed with rare horse-flesh and brass-studded harness, as one of the most apparently secure aristocracies in Europe drove, rode and exchanged greetings and gossip; while the grand balls they gave at the Rathaus or the Sophiensaal were the chief events of the season, including always the splendid cotillion, the *Damenwahl*, in which the ladies chose their partners.

That faint sense of doom in the air was shrugged off light-heartedly by a population of mixed blood, drawn from all the nationalities of the Monarchy. In Vienna they yawned at politics and smiled at racial furies. Their passions were inflamed by very different things, by the theatre and by music. Vienna was, and had always been, a theatre town, just as Paris was a town of painters. "The best actors in the world, either for tragedy, comedy, history, pastoral. . . . Seneca cannot be too heavy, nor Plautus too light." Whether for Grand Opera, or its naughty step-daughter, operette, whether for poetic tragedy or satirical revue, whether for dignity or impudence, production and acting in the Vienna theatres were a pattern. Nowhere was Shakespeare played with more zest and understanding than in the stately Burgtheater, nowhere could richer and more unctuous interpreters of the humour of Falstaff be found than among the Viennese comedians.

They were on their mettle, for the Viennese population was genuinely theatre- and music-minded. To the medley of races composing it, says V. Tissot, Italian Opera artists, Hungarian and French singers, English ballet girls had added their own spice of effervescence. The photographs of the popular actresses filled the shop-windows in the Graben, and even the lower orders knew not only the pieces played at the popular theatres, but also the chief Operas and dramas. Actors, conductors, singers and their voices were eagerly discussed, for they were experts, the men and women in the standing-room at the back of the stalls or in the top gallery. They were a critical, a most formidable, audience, but once conquered they never forgot their favourites.

Sensuous as Italians, sentimental as Slavs, with a Parisian sense of colour and wit—such, it has been said, was the theatre-going public of Vienna.[1]

Equally keen was the appreciation of music. It was said that a new waltz had for the Viennese the same importance as a victory for the

P. Wertheimer, *Alt Wiener Theater.*

French. Wagner, when he visited the country, had been astounded at the effect which waltz music had upon the Viennese.

"This demon of the Viennese folk-spirit," he wrote, "quivered at the beginning of a new waltz like the Pythian Sybil, and a veritable whinny of pleasure, which actually came more from the music than from the drinks that had been consumed, raised the excitement of the intoxicated auditorium to a height that was frightening to me."

Ever since the moment when Carl Maria von Weber at the beginning of the 19th century sent out the dreamy strains of his "Invitation to the Waltz", down through the days of Lanner, the Strausses, father and son, of Millöcker and Suppé, it could be said that the history of the waltz was the history of the Viennese spirit.

This gay, careless and gregarious people lived in public, and the life and movement of its streets went to the continual sound of music. Every day in the courtyard of the Hofburg, the huge imperial residence at the heart of the city, there was military music for an hour during the changing of the guard, when the Kaiser would appear at one of the windows. The lilt of the Radetzky March and the other popular military airs accompanied the brilliantly uniformed regiments through the streets; there was music in the cafés, in the beer-cellars, in the little wine-shops and garden restaurants of the outskirts, where trios and quartets played, and where folk-singers and zither-players from the streets wooed the customers with the *Fiakerlied* and other popular melodies.

Many of the city restaurants too during the summer months erected wooden terraces outside, adorned with trellises and flowers and awnings, where tables and chairs were set, and small orchestras played to the diners. And at one such open-air café, the Grand Pavilion in the Vienna Town Park, the band of the 50th Infantry Regiment, which was, like all the Austrian military bands, a symphony orchestra and not merely a brass band, and which counted among its First Violins Leo Fall, the future composer of *The Dollar Princess*, was now sometimes conducted by its leader, the son of the *Kapellmeister* Lehár, a trim smiling figure in blue uniform, rejoicing already in one of the thick, up-curled moustaches known in England as the German Kaiser type, with underneath it a jutting and resolute chin.

He would conduct, and sometimes lay aside the baton to take up his violin and play a solo in the gypsy mode. He would play with all his heart to the women of Vienna seated behind the slender beer-glasses at the tables around him, those women of Vienna whom he was one day to glorify in his music:

Wiener Frauen, blond und braun,
Edelsteine sonder Zahl,
Herzerfrischend anzuschauen,
Seid gegrüsst viel tausendmal![1]

Who indeed could be swifter than Franz Lehár to take fire from the presence of these women of whom Tissot had written:

"The purity and grace of their outlines would arouse the envy of a Greek statue. Their cheeks have the delicate shades of a tea-rose, in their eyes are the deep shadows of the Orient."

There, as the Strauss waltzes melted with their suavity and soft melancholy into the trees behind the gay fairy-lights, Lehár saw before him the arched feet of the gracefully stepping Hungarians, the marble skins and great black eyes of the Slav strain, the slim, mysterious Jewesses. If the mothers tended to heaviness in maturity, the daughters, the typical girls of Vienna, were delicate as porcelain, friendly, dancing through life with the crucifix hung on their necks.

All this, it might be thought, would be as an earthly Paradise to the young Lehár. How came it then that after only ten months he snapped off his music under the Vienna stars and went as Regimental Bandmaster to a remote Hungarian town?

A romantic reason has been suggested. He left Vienna, it is said, to cure a broken heart after an unhappy love affair with the daughter of a titled lady, who was herself infatuated with the handsome young band-leader. A red rose laid on his music-desk had been misinterpreted. The thoughtless Franzi, true to his old schoolmaster's account of him, expended his charm in thanking the daughter, not the mother who had really sent the flower, and thence came a jealousy that wrecked his romance. . . . The tale has at any rate the material of a Lehár operette in it.

But perhaps the chief, perhaps the only, reason for his turning his back upon the delights of Vienna was that he set ambition before enjoyment. There was a vacancy for a bandmaster in a regiment posted at Losoncz, a small Hungarian town north of Budapest, with some 9000 inhabitants. Lehár was just twenty, and when he was appointed was the youngest *Kapellmeister* in the Army. It was a step on the upward path, but what a stony one!

---

[1] Vienna women, dark and fair,
Un-numbered jewels, rich and rare,
O heart-refreshing sight to see,
A thousand-fold your welcome be!

Losoncz, by a remote railway junction, was little more than a large village, built around its ancient church. It had a garrison and was also a small mineral spa. Its houses were mostly one-storied—mere white-washed cottages, or, the better-class ones, painted in crude reds and greens and blues. Under the eaves the inhabitants would sit of an evening on benches, contemplating, without repining, the emptiness of existence. There were few pavements, and in the muddy main street families of swine routed at will. Only on market days did any life flow through the stagnant ways of the little town. Then peasants, with their animals for sale, peddlers and merchants collected under the trees in the market-place; where, also, the military band would play on the greater holidays, and there would be song and dances. Lehár, with his Hungarian blood, would have taken pleasure in the *czardas*, that dance drama of love and jealousy, accompanied by fiddles and cymbals, and in the picturesque costumes of the dancers: the braided jackets and tight trousers of the men, the bright-bordered aprons and high scarlet boots of the women. But otherwise life at Losoncz must have been dreary in the extreme.

Lehár, however, reminded himself that he had come to this place at the world's end to forward his career, to study music, to compose at leisure. Losoncz had at least the advantage of a number of good families living on their estates in the vicinity, and soon the *Kapellmeister* began to make the remote little town music-conscious. He gave concerts, founded quartets for chamber music, organized Masses and oratorios in the church, became, with his smart uniform and curling moustache, a leading figure in the place. Yes, he had come there to work, only . . .

His Colonel's daughter wished to learn singing. Her father passed her to the Bandmaster; voice production must be part of his duties. Lehár knew nothing of it, but in the Army, when a command is given to do something, one does not wait to ask whether one can do it or not. The *Kapellmeister* wrote for text-books from Vienna; he worked hard with his attractive pupil; the result, says Mme Peteani, was that "she lost her voice, he his heart, but by a miracle the Colonel did not lose his confidence in his Bandmaster".[1] It was never easy to be angry with Franz Lehár.

The young officers of the garrison must have revelled in the tale. They had plenty of time for gossip and flirtation. These, with drinking and card-playing, dancing and skating, were their only relief from boredom. This happy-go-lucky gaiety appealed, no doubt, to one side of Franz Lehár's nature. He was a good companion, but one night during a party at the Officers' Casino he asked himself where he was going . . . where his pay had gone. The others laughed at his resolve to reform his ways. They

[1] *Peteani*, p. 30.

The Merry Widow is born in Vienna and these are the original players.
Top: The male members of the cast at Theater an der Wien, December
1905. *Bottom left*: Louis Treumann, Mizzi Günther, the original Danilo
and Widow. *Bottom right*: Mizzi Günther

George Edwardes, "The Guvnor," who gambled on *The Merry Widow* in London wagered him it would not last a week. He took the wager, and swore to give up all amusements, to abandon the dance-floor even, and hang up his skates. It should all go, until he had composed something worthy . . . an Opera perhaps.

He kept his word, poured out a stream of compositions—marches, waltzes, mazurkas, songs—but all the time kept in front of him the ideal of creating an Opera. But now he found himself at the beginning of the trouble that was to pursue him all his life, the difficulty of finding a suitable libretto. The first that was offered him, called *The Cuirassier*, was the work of one of the local railway officials, but he could make no headway with it. Then he found that one of the regimental officers had written a one-act piece, a robber-drama called *Rodrigo*. Lehár decided to set it to music, not without doubts; but the Duke of Coburg-Gotha had instituted a prize for the best one-act Opera and the idea of competing was a temptation. Lehár worked on the score; his bandsmen loyally rehearsed it; and from the mien of these practised players he could tell when they approved and when he had failed.

In spite of all, however, *Rodrigo* did not win the ducal prize, which was carried off by another composer with a piece called *The Rose of Pontevedro* —one of the first of those echo-auguries that meet us in Lehár's early life. He could not know what that name would come to mean to him. Meanwhile there was still hard work (he had won his wager) in drab surroundings; there was—it could never be otherwise with him—another love romance, an ideal and platonic affair, it would seem, with another Baroness's daughter, from among the local gentlefolk; and then once more a sudden squall.

It has been said that it was never easy to be angry with Franz Lehár; but he did not find it so difficult to be angry when he felt himself ill-used. In the Casino at Losoncz, as at the Grand Pavilion of the Vienna Town Park, Lehár was used, when he felt in the mood, to flatter his audience by taking his fiddle and going round among the tables, gypsy-fashion, playing, as the phrase was, "in their ears". One night, after he had handed over his baton to the deputy conductor while he had his supper, a superior officer, a Staff Major, entered and sent a peremptory order by the waiter to the *Kapellmeister* to come and play at his table "in his ear". Lehár's quick temper flamed out. "Tell the Major I'm not a gypsy minstrel!" he ordered the waiter. Such a message from a Bandmaster to a Staff Major . . . and sent by the mouth of a waiter! The matter had to be taken up, and apologies were demanded from Lehár. He preferred to resign his post; and so, after four years, with the sympathy of his brother officers and escorted to the station by half the town deeply grieving, Lehár—surely not too heart-broken?—left dusty, uncivilized Losoncz behind him, and

the slow train wound its way with him out of the desolate plains towards
new destinies.

To his family at least these did not appear brilliant. They could not
share Franz's light-hearted view of his prospects. His father, quartered at
this time with the family in far-away Sarajevo, not yet marked with its
bloody sign for Europe, reflected gloomily on his eldest son's mutability.
Franzi had thrown up Barmen-Elberfeld; he had thrown up Vienna; he
had thrown up Losoncz . . . what was to come next?

What actually did come next was a surprise to all, and showed who was
Fortune's darling. The Austrian Navy had a single fortified base, Pola,
and a single naval band of 110 performers stationed there. The post of
bandmaster was at the moment open, and tempting enough for there to
be 120 applicants for it. Franz Lehár beat them all, and became the one
and only *Marinekapellmeister* of all Austria, at a far higher salary than the
Army ever paid. A photograph of the period shows him in the sober
naval uniform, his moustache trimly waxed at the ends and lacking its
flamboyant military curl. Indeed Pola had altogether a very different
atmosphere from Losoncz. With its great harbour and naval barracks, its
17th-century castle, its chain of protecting forts on the hills behind, it was
a fortress of first-class importance. The old town was picturesque and rich
in historic monuments. There was a cathedral, an ancient Franciscan
monastery, a 13th-century Town Hall, a Roman Amphitheatre. It was an
inspiring environment, and the new *Kapellmeister's* handling of his
magnificent orchestra soon spread his fame through the port and the
province, indeed to all corners of Austria in the world of officers and
officials and their families. The word went round, "There's a marvellous
Navy conductor at Pola these days—and all the girls are in love with him!"
Yes, it must have seemed a happy life by the sparkle of the sun-lit Adriatic
waves, and it is not surprising that there flowed from his pen an "Adriatic
waltz", an elegant trifle, but, as Mme Peteani says, not yet fired with the
true Lehár quality. It was, as she says, only an essay in the idiom of the
moment, and a Lincke could have composed it.[1]

Another piece of good fortune that befell him was the sending of an
Austrian squadron to Kiel for the opening of the great naval Canal by
the German Kaiser Wilhelm II. Lehár was attached to the mission with
a section of his band, and on the voyage to their destination he saw the
Mediterranean coast, the Riviera, Tangiers, Morocco, Spain, the very
scenes of operatic romance with their costumes and their dances. The
fruits of this experience, so potent for his imagination, were to show
themselves years later in Lehár's work.

[1] *Peteani*, p. 38.

For the present, however, he had still to seek that missing Opera libretto. Once more a brother officer came to his rescue. Captain of Corvette Felix Falzari was a poet, and in the course of long walks along the shore and among the palm-trees beneath the glowing Southern sky he and Lehár hammered out the idea of an Opera of which Falzari wrote the book under the title *Kukuschka*. Lehár worked on the score with enthusiasm; the Russian colour appealed to his love of folk-music. He always considered it his first serious work . . . and it was given an amateur performance, without scenery or dresses, by the officers of the garrison! This was a compliment, but not what its composer had dreamed of. But how could one conquer the operatic boards of the world from distant Pola? It was Losoncz all over again. The bonds of discipline seemed more irksome than ever. The splendour of his position at the head of the great naval orchestra paled. "I'm no good for the Services," he confessed. "I've too much self-respect." And once more he resigned. His career as *Kapellmeister* was drawing to its close.

CHAPTER THREE

"Wiener Frauen!"

FRANZ LEHÁR had thrown himself again upon the world; his prospects seemed truly precarious now; but Fortune never found it in her heart completely to forsake him. The score of *Kukuschka* was published by Hofbauer and copies sent to various Opera Houses. Almost at once it was accepted for performance at Leipzig, and Lehár was triumphant. "Will you not," he wrote to his parents, who were in Vienna once more, "forgive your child if he finally puts an end to his servitude? I cannot serve any longer; I must have freedom." Such a claim, as Ernst Decsey says, did not sound well in ears for which military service had always spelt not servitude but honour. His father however studied the score, and with his usual artistic integrity confessed that it contained very fine music; it appeared too that the stage production was going to be magnificent. Yes, the old man had hopes of a success . . . but what would happen then? Nobody understood less about business than his son; he was a child in such matters:

> "His habit is to throw money (which he has never had) out of the window; not to spend it on necessary things, oh! no, but only on noble passions, in which he is exploited on all hands. It is always other people who line their stomachs, while he is made the fool. One shouldn't be egotistical, no doubt; but one needs to have money to burn to behave as he does."

Kukuschka was produced at Leipzig on the 27th November, 1896. The audience, cold and reserved at first, began to yield as the evening proceeded. Such choral numbers, Decsey tells us, as "See how the Volga shimmers!" and "Leaving the gold-tipped mountain tops" aroused growing enthusiasm, while the lovers' final duet, "Think of me when the swallows pass!"—the titles have the real Lehár ring—was acclaimed with delight and calls for the composer. Franz's brother, Lieutenant Anton Lehár, afterwards to be a General in the Austrian Army, had come to Leipzig for the *première*, and when the excitement was over the two brothers sat together in a café, building those "castles in the air" that were to be celebrated one day in some of Franz's most yearning and gossamer-like music.[1] But Anton did not know that Franz had had to pawn his watch and rings to meet the expenses of the occasion.

In fact the success was (as Father Lehár had foreboded) artistic rather than financial. The Press was excellent, though it is amusing to find one critic blaming Lehár for introducing no national dances into the piece, indeed an odd neglect on his part; but the composer's takings were poor. Lehár made about 51 *gulden* in royalties—but he had spent 170, besides pledging everything he possessed. His mother, when he came to see her (and give her 10 of his hard-earned *gulden*), was shocked at his shabby appearance. He looked a real artist, she complained, in a letter to Anton, with his cloak, and necktie out of place . . . no tie-pin, no watch-chain! In spite of his exultation at his success, she couldn't keep her eyes off his crumpled clothing. "I had imagined the envied lot of the artist somewhat otherwise," she concluded pitifully.[2]

In fact Lehár's position soon became desperate—as desperate as that of his own Count of Luxembourg! In spite of his Leipzig *succès d'estime* he could not induce any other Opera House to put on *Kukuschka*; his publisher, too, set the Managers against him by his tactless handling of his affairs. Once again actual hunger stared him in the face. There was nothing for it but to accept the bitter lessons of parental wisdom, swallow his pride, and re-engage himself as an Army Bandmaster. The former proud conductor of the great naval orchestra with its 110 executants became a mere *Kapellmeister* in an infantry regiment again. And, what was worse, his regiment was soon moved from Trieste to Pola, the very scene of his former reign! The pale satin blue wavelets of the Adriatic must have seemed to mock him; but Franz's smile and his underlying toughness carried him through the trial. His moustache again took its upward military twirl—a defiance, it might seem, to the passing slights of the jade Fortune.

In 1898 a heavy blow fell upon the affectionately united Lehár family. Besides Franz and Anton, six years his junior, this had included a sister Emmy, twenty years younger than Franz, who is still living; an elder sister Mariska, who died while Franz was in Pola; and two boys who died in early childhood. Now the old *Kapellmeister* passed

---

[1] Viscount Camille de Jolidon's song in Act I of *The Merry Widow*.

[2] If Lehár really presented himself to his mother in Bohemian disarray, it must have been the only time in his life that he appeared so. He was always, and to the end, of a military neatness and precision in his clothes.

C

away in Budapest just after his retirement. Franz, called with Anton to
his death-bed, softly played the melodies of *Kukuschka*, which his father
had been eagerly studying so long as he had strength, to ease the moments
of his passing.

As he had been planning before he died, his son Franz took over his
place in Budapest. Fortune indeed could not be angry with her favourite
for long. With the money he inherited from his father he was able to buy
back the rights in *Kukuschka* from the troublesome publisher, and in May
1899 it was produced in Budapest with complete success. The happy
composer was entertained at a banquet after the fall of the curtain, and the
news that an Opera by a local bandmaster was to be given that evening
had even percolated to the table of the Kaiser, who was staying in
Budapest. The next morning the Bandmaster of the 3rd Bosnia-Herze-
govina Infantry Regiment, after so much celebration, was absent from
early parade. He hastened to make his excuses to his Colonel, who replied
sardonically, "It's a pity, *Herr Kapellmeister*. For the Emperor himself was
on parade and asked for you by name. . . ." Years afterwards when the
world-famous composer Lehár was being discussed at Court the aged
Emperor remarked with a chuckle, "Yes, yes . . . I know him well. . . .
That's the Lehár who overslept himself in Budapest!"

All this meant a taste of success, but it was not the "break through"
that every composer and every author who seeks fame desires. Lehár
began to feel as if somehow his efforts were misdirected. What was
wrong with him? One night, when he had taken refuge from a shower
in a café, an acquaintance who had come over to his table said to him,
"I am surprised that you have never written an operette. Surely, it would
be the very thing for you?" It was a casual remark but it sank deep
into the hearer. Lehár did not perhaps remember that years before
Offenbach had suggested to Johann Strauss that he should give up
composing waltzes merely, and write an operette; history was repeating
itself.

An operette? Yes; but the old difficulty at once raised its head: where
was the libretto, light, topical and witty, to come from? Not from
Budapest, with its essential provincialism, its grim memories of the past
and of Turkish oppression, its passion for nationalism, power and political
intrigue. No; operette could only be created in the place where it belonged, in Vienna. There it had had its origin in the 18th century, when,
amid all the stateliness of the baroque era, the booths of Hanswurst, the
South German Punch, and the other buffoons of the *commedia dell arte*
had been fearlessly set up in the market-places, and their popular songs
and topical jests had been tolerated even by the severely reforming
Emperor Joseph II. Its spirit had gleamed and laughed upon the stages

of the *Vorstadt* theatres, the suburban "minors" of Vienna, the Leopold-stadtertheater, later the Carl Theater, the Theater an der Wien, the Josefstadt Theater, where in the early 19th century comedians of renown, often in their own persons actors, managers and dramatists, such as Carl, Nestroy, Raimund, mirrored the humours of the Viennese people.

For a time the torch of operette seemed to pass to Paris, with the triumph of a group of brilliant composers, Hervé, Lecocq, Planquette and Offenbach, and it seemed as if in the middle years of the century the native Viennese operette would be lost in the popular *opéra bouffe,* in the triumph of *Chilperic, Orphée aux Enfers, La Grande Duchesse, La Fille de Mme Angot* and *Les Cloches de Corneville.* But, whatever the enchantment of these Parisian masterpieces, the population of Vienna had too much of a soul of its own to be permanently satisfied with foreign wit and sentiment. Johann Strauss in 1871 wrote the first real Viennese operette, *Indigo,* to be followed by the classic *Die Fledermaus* in 1874 and *Der Zigeunerbaron* eleven years later. He too became the centre of a galaxy: Carl Millöcker, composer of *Der Bettelstudent*; R. Genée, who wrote *Der Seekadett*; and Franz von Suppé, known today still by his operette *Boccaccio,* and even more widely by his exquisite overtures, *Poet and Peasant, Light Cavalry* and *Morning, Noon and Night in Vienna.* Vienna was the birthplace and home of Austrian operette; thither, Franz Lehár realized, he must return—and without delay—if he was to make his name in this style. But that would mean yet another resignation—his seventh! While he hesitated came the news that the Bandmastership of the 26th Regiment was vacant . . . and in Vienna!

His feet were now on the right path, but the end of the journey was not yet. While he still sought for a subject and a text for his operette he took pains to win the favour of the Vienna public by the fine concerts of military music that he arranged. Once again the handsome conductor with the fine moustache and the vigorous personality began to make an impression. Whispers went round the audience, "It's the man from Pola!" Lehár was becoming one of the personalities of the capital, and soon a March of his, *"Jetzt geht's los!"* ("Now we're off!"), was being hummed and whistled everywhere.

In the last year of the 1800's Princess Metternich, that fabulous Pauline Metternich, whose wit and *diablerie*, whose *chic* and cigar-smoking, had turned all heads at the Tuileries when she was Austrian Ambassadress at the Court of Napoleon III, Pauline Metternich, who could never grow old, and had survived, ever gay and ever the last word in smartness, the fall of crowns and the wreck of empires, gave a great fancy ball in the Sophiensaal with the *motif* "Gold and Silver". Kapellmeister Lehár composed a special waltz for the occasion, called the "Gold and Silver

Waltz", which was played under an artificial heaven of silver-grey muslin decked with golden stars, amid the shimmering spangles of the fashionable dancers. The composer had considered it a trifle, and had sold it for a song, but from that night it has never ceased to be applauded, and is today one of the most celebrated waltzes in the world. It was another bright feather in Lehár's cap . . . and it came to him, as it were, from the hand of an Ambassadress. He perhaps found no omen in that, at the time.

Meanwhile the petty affronts and the monotony of military life continued. About this time too he was balked of a fine opening—which might well have ruined all his future. The post of Conductor of the Vienna Municipal Orchestra fell vacant, and he put in for it. He was rejected largely on the judgment of Professor Richard Heuberger, himself a composer of operettes, of which *Der Opernball* was the best known. "This Bandmaster," said he sagely, "conducts classical stuff well enough, but he hasn't any idea of waltzes." One day Lehár was to play a return match with Heuberger; but he probably did not realize what the Professor had saved him from. Then Fate cut short his hesitations. His regiment was ordered to Raab, and Lehár had made it a condition of his engagement that he should not be forced to follow them out of Vienna. So at last (and not by his own mutiny) he was free of the uniform, never to put it on again.

Already the ex-*Kapellmeister* had received several offers of engagements. He chose the one now that seemed most in line with his ambitions. On the bank of the tiny tributary of the Danube known as the River Wien, just beyond the line of the ancient fortifications, stood the most celebrated, if not quite the oldest, of the Vienna *Vorstadt* theatres, the Theater an der Wien. It had been opened in 1801 by the actor-author-manager Emmanuel Schikaneder, the librettist of Mozart's *Magic Flute*, which received its first performance here the year after the opening. The Theater an der Wien in its original form, with its five tiers, and its stage with eighteen wings, and doors that allowed it to be extended at the back into the courtyard before the House of the Jesuits, had been reckoned the largest and most comfortable in Vienna. In it Beethoven's *Fidelio* was first played as well as Schubert's *Rosamunde*.[1] In time it became in M. Gaston Knosp's words "the grand temple of Viennese operette", where the principal works of Suppé, Millöcker and Strauss, including *Die Fledermaus* and *Der Zigeunerbaron*, first saw the footlights. Many of these were helped to success by the most famous performer in the history of operette, the comedian Alexander Girardi. He was still appearing there when in 1902 Franz Lehár took up his duties as "conductor of light opera" in the

---

[1] See *Die Wiener Vorstadtbühnen*, by Rudolf Holzer, pp. 34–72.

Fred Farren, who arranged the dances for *The Merry Widow* at Daly's Theatre, including the famous Waltz

J. A. E. Malone, first lieutenant to George Edwardes and Stage Director of Daly's Theatre

W. H. Berry, the famous comedian, who made a great success in *The Merry Widow*

George Graves, the great comedian, whose performance as Baron Popoff was a triumph. He is seen here in *The Little Michus*

historic house, externally unimpressive among the neighbouring blocks
of flats, except for its elegant little classical portico in honour of Schikaneder, whose statue in the role of Papageno stood over the doors, and its
squat octagonal tower above the tall scene-dock. . . . Yet the new conductor may have gazed with most interest at the place in the orchestra
where, many years before, his own father, not yet an Army bandsman,
had sat among the horn players.

Lehár now determined upon a bold step. He sent the score of *Kukuschka*
to the librettist Victor Léon, with the suggestion that they might collaborate. Victor Léon was an important personage in the world of light
opera. He was the chief stage director of the Carl Theater (formerly the
Leopoldstadtertheater) the oldest of the Vienna *Vorstadt* houses, dating
from 1781, and the keenest rival in operette of the Theater an der Wien,
and he had collaborated as librettist with the great Johann Strauss himself.
He therefore made polite excuses to the audacious beginner.

But he was not to find it as easy as that. For Léon had a charming
blonde daughter, named Lizzy, only a child about thirteen years old, but
she had lost her heart to the handsome young *Kapellmeister*, whom she
had seen on her visits to the skating rink. There it had been part of Lehár's
duties to conduct his band, in an uncomfortable Pavilion, where he was
roasted by a red-hot stove at his back and frozen in front. Occasionally,
for the fun of the thing, he had slipped his skates on and taken the child
for a round or two on the ice. . . . And now Lizzy heard that her idol
wished to compose the music for one of her father's operettes! Léon had
no more peace at home. When pleas and arguments failed, his child took
to playing the score of *Kukuschka* on the piano all day. Perhaps in order to
hear Lehár's music no more, or perhaps with a curiosity to hear more of
it, Léon at length sent for the composer and handed him the Prologue to
a new operette, entitled *Der Rastelbinder* ("The Tinker"). He could try his
hand at it, if he cared to. Should the result satisfy Léon, then Lehár might
be given the rest of the piece to set.

Lehár was delighted with the text, for it turned on a Slovakian folk-
tale, such as he used to hear in his babyhood, and Victor Léon, after seeing
his first specimens, had no hesitation in asking him to do the whole score.
It seemed as if the longed-for opportunity had arrived at last. . . . Then
followed a complication which anybody less unworldly than Lehár must,
one would think, have foreseen. *Der Rastelbinder* was being composed for
the Carl Theater; the Carl Theater was the historic rival of the Theater
an der Wien; Lehár had been engaged as conductor at the latter. That he
could not be on both sides was promptly made clear to him by his
Managers. They were Karl Wallner and Wilhelm Karczag. Wallner was

an ex-actor who, thanks to his wife's fortune, had been able to go into management; he was conventional in his ideas and hidebound by the maxims of the "old professional". Karczag, a Hungarian, had been a journalist and had scribbled pieces. He too possessed a useful wife, a light opera soubrette of renown. He was, in distinction from Wallner, quick-witted and versatile, with a smiling mouth under a thick black moustache and lively little dark eyes. Capable (we shall see) of terrible mistakes, he was also quick to learn, and became one of the most successful Managers of his time.

On this point, at any rate, the partners were quite at one. If Lehár wished to compose operettes for the Carl Theater, he must resign his position with them. There could be no argument about that. After an embittered discussion, Wallner picked up the libretto of *Der Rastelbinder* and announced that he would return it with his own hand to Léon. Followed in melancholy procession by Lehár, he sought out Léon at his accustomed café, where the latter without a word took the book back from him. He understood.

But Franz Lehár did not. The situation was intolerable. After a week of struggle he went to Léon's house; "Please give me back *Der Rastel-binder*," he pleaded. Léon smiled. "I expected you," he said, and one surmises a new note of respect in his voice. "Take it, and resign your post as conductor." Resign again! Lehár knew too much about resignations, but then . . .

Wallner and Karczag showed themselves inexorable. They accepted Lehár's resignation as conductor, his only sure means of livelihood at the moment; then, as he was leaving the room, the astute Karczag remarked, "Go on with your other work for us, all the same!"

What was this other work? Some time before, two authors, Emil Norini and Otto Tann-Bergler, had put into Lehár's hands the libretto for an operette to be called *Wiener Frauen*. The title must have thrilled Lehár like a violin. Who better than he could treat that subject—its enchantment, its gaiety, its melancholy?

> *Wiener Frauen, blond und braun,*
> *Edelsteine sonder Zahl. . . .*

It had seemed made for him . . . but now "The Tinker", with its folk-colouring and passion, its evocation of his own childish memories, seemed to have come between him and this slighter, more typically light operatic theme. Thus early the struggle in Lehár's soul between his deeper and his more superficial gift made itself felt. And there was another cause for uneasiness. It was a condition of *Wiener Frauen* being put on at the Theater an der Wien that it should contain the right sort of part for the great Alexander Girardi, the fifty-year-old prince of comedy character actors, who was still the leading man of the company; it was no light task to satisfy the exigencies of such a star, especially since the composer by some odd chance had never even seen Girardi act! However, he would do his best, as always.

Wiener Frauen was produced in November 1902. It has a thoroughly conventional plot about a piano-teacher, played by Girardi, who steals the heart of his well-born pupil with a wonderful waltz he has composed, and then wanders off to America; only to return on the eve of her marriage and, in the disguise of a piano-tuner, enter her house and awake the past with the sound of the fatal waltz. The "uncommonly elegant overture", as Lehár's biographer terms it,[1] with its inserted piano solo and its softly swelling harp and flute *motifs*, at once gripped the audience. "This is the coming man!" a well-known critic cried at the end of it, and success was soon assured. But the hit of the evening was neither waltz nor love theme. It was a comedy number that Girardi had asked Lehár to put in during rehearsals, "to give him a chance", and it became in a short time known all over Austria as "the Nechledil-March", from the name of the character:

> *Nechledil, du schöner Mann*
> *Du hast es allen angetan.*
> *Jede seufst: O Nechledil,*
> *Du bist meiner Wünsche Ziel!*[2]

The verve of it was irresistible; Girardi had never had anything that better suited his peculiar genius. Thus Lehár's first stage triumph was a comedy march—it was one more arrow pointing towards the future!

Immediately afterwards he had to turn his energies towards the production of *Der Rastelbinder*, which had been fixed for a week or two later just before Christmas. But at the Carl Theater the atmosphere was hostile. Léon, who now believed fervently in the composer he claimed to have "discovered", could not prevail against the scepticism of the Manager, Leopold Müller. He had only consented to put the piece on as a stopgap before a new operette *Madame Sherry* should be brought out in January, and he was not going to spend money or time on rehearsals for a predestined failure. "I think nothing of Bandmasters," was his answer to all remonstrances—in which he voiced a common musical opinion of the day, which in order of merit set first the real composers, then the

---

[1] *Peteani*, p. 60.
[2] Oh! Nechledil, you lovely man!
Tell all you do to us who can?
Sighs every maid, with heart on fire,
" 'Tis Nechledil, my soul's desire!"

orchestral conductors, *Kapellmeister*, and then, in the lowest depths, the
Militärkapellmeister. In vain Léon protested that the piece could not be
produced without proper rehearsal, and demanded a postponement. The
reply was that he could postpone if he liked, but that nothing on earth
would prevent *Madame Sherry* being put into the bill on the 6th January.

Lehár set great store by this operette. It was rooted in his own experience. It was, says Mme Peteani, "Komorn and Losoncz music"—the
music of his birthplace and his formative years. He must have chafed
under the difficulties that were being put in his way, and not least when
his principal actor was warned that it would mean professional ruin if he
appeared in the rôle allotted to him of the wandering old Jewish tinker,
Wolf Bär Pfefferkorn. This actor was the thirty-year-old Louis Treumann,
who had already made a brilliant success of personality on the light
operatic stage, but who could, as yet, have no dream of the fame Lehár
was one day to bring him. No doubt the "d—d good-natured friends"
who had warned him of an anti-Semitic storm if he played the Jewish
tinker also shook their heads at his appearing in an old man's part, he
the most charming tenor of the time!

Luckily Treumann was not intimidated by these threats nor Léon by
managerial wiles. *Der Rastelbinder*, a romantic story of a child-betrothal
in a Slovakian village, followed inevitably by the separation of the
engaged pair as soon as they grow up and taste the life of Vienna, was a
triumph not to be chilled by a frigid Press. . . . Folk-music and sophisticated Viennese charm: it was a blend that was to serve Lehár well again
and again. Louis Treumann, as the ragged old tinker who twists and
untwists the threads of the plot like a presiding wizard, won encore after
encore, and was well rewarded for his courage in sticking to the part. As
for *Madame Sherry*, so irrevocably fixed for the following January, it was
not wanted at the Carl Theater for two years. . . .

Now there was a new constellation in the world of Viennese operette.
Lehár and Léon: they were the triumphant partnership. From now on
Léon kept in his study a photograph of Lehár with the inscription, "To
my discoverer". Lehár had not learnt the art of ingratitude in the tide of
success. True, his next two works, *Der Göttergatte*, the tale of a god's
wooing in human form, which seemed to hark back to the classical
parodies of Offenbach, and *Die Juxheirat* (*The Mock Marriage*), a modern
musical farce, with Girardi as a *chauffeur* (at that date, like Bernard Shaw's
" 'Enry Straker", a character sounding the last word in novelty) were of
slighter importance. But they fortified his position, which, if not yet one
of world celebrity, was very different from any that the struggling
Militärkapellmeister had so far enjoyed. He was sought after; he was

"news"; and—one of the surest signs of his altered status—he passed his summers now at Bad Ischl.

This delicious little Alpine spa in a setting of forests and lakes, six hours distant by train from the capital, was the favourite summer resort of Vienna Society. Here the Kaiser Franz Joseph had his residence during the hot weather, where he loved to lay aside all that a Hapsburg could of etiquette, and to walk among his subjects without ceremony, as their father rather than their sovereign. There was a charming little theatre, of Biedermeier design, regularly attended with the minimum of formality by the old Emperor; and, while fashion inevitably followed where the Court went, Bad Ischl became also during the summer months the chosen haunt of the theatre world.

It was in particular the H.Q. of operette, being known as the *operetten-küche* (the light opera kitchen). Johann Strauss had had his villa in Ischl, and most of the other famous composers of operette had stayed there, besides such august visitors as Brahms, Meyerbeer, Bruckner and Hugo Wolf. As a coming man Franz Lehár could not afford *not* to afford a house in Ischl (if only on lease), and there he did much of his work, matching his music to that of the laughing mountain streams and the soft sighing of the wind in the pines. From time to time he would break off and look through the window of the house opposite, where, framed in *her* window, there appeared from time to time a ravishing Titian blonde with a peach-blossom complexion. Her name was Sophie Paschkis and it did not take Lehár four seconds to fall in love with her, though it took him four years to win her for his wife after the dissolution of her first marriage to a Herr Meth; and then he was to stay faithful to her until the end. . . .

It was on a day in the summer of 1903 that he was driving through the town in a one-horse cab when he met a lady and her young daughter, acquaintances of his. The girl was his future biographer, Maria von Peteani. Lehár at sight of them dismounted from his cab, and with his usual courtesy offered to drive them to their lodgings on the outskirts. As he took leave of them on the pavement outside their house with the usual ceremonious hand-kissing and gallantry of the epoch, he suddenly uttered a cry, "Where is she? . . . Lost! . . . I've left her in the cab!" and turning he dashed in pursuit.

The ladies could not imagine who he meant. But "She" was destined within a very short time to be on everybody's lips. She was a lady whose name would differ on the different play-bills of the world, but whose character would stay ever unchanged. She was the "Merry Widow", the half-finished score of whose life-story had been carried away by the clip-clop of the one-horse cab. . . .

CHAPTER FOUR

Birth of a Famous Lady

IT is one of the impish twists of stage history that the composer of *The Merry Widow* was very nearly *not* Franz Lehár. The origins of the most famous of all operettes are complicated. Henry Meilhac, the prolific French farce-writer and librettist of Offenbach, had written a comedy called *L'Attaché*, from which Victor Léon and a frequent collaborator of his, Leo Stein, part-author of *Der Göttergatte*, took the central idea and worked it up into the book of an operette. They considered this sufficiently their own to put their names to it with only the vaguest allusion to a "foreign source" for the main idea. (But they were to hear more of this some day!) They entitled it *Die Lustige Witwe* and gave it to Richard Heuberger to compose the score. This was that Heuberger who had said that *Militärkapellmeister* Lehár knew nothing about waltzes, and had prevented him from getting the post of conductor to the Vienna Municipal Orchestra. Heuberger set to work at once upon the love story of the yet unknown widow, called in the original "Hanna Glawari", and the Balkan princeling, her suitor, for whom the authors from the first had Louis Treumann in view.

But now it was the turn of Professor Heuberger to find that waltzes could be a headache . . . anyhow he could not find the inspiration he needed for this tale of high society in Paris, with its under-current of Balkan passion. Both Léon and Treumann were disappointed when they heard his first numbers, and he himself did not seem very well pleased with what he had done. Léon walked away from the audition in a gloomy mood, to consult with the Managers of the Theater an der Wien. In the theatre he met the Secretary Steininger, a shrewd and practised judge in such matters, and told him his trouble. Steininger immediately pointed out the obvious: "Send it to Lehár!" After long and anxious consultation —surprising, it must seem, in the circumstances, but then Lehár's greatest success, so far, had been in folk-operette—the authors decided to give him the book to read. He sat up all night with it, and in the morning was round at Léon's: "Please give me *The Merry Widow*; I simply *must* do it!" . . . And on the evening of that very day he rang up Léon, and, placing the mouthpiece of the telephone near the keyboard, played him the first number he had composed for the new piece. It was the duet, *Dummer, dummer Reitersmann!*; in the English version, "Silly, silly cavalier!"

All through that summer of 1905 Lehár worked at the score in Vienna and in Ischl, and everything went flowingly . . . except that he did not like the title. Nor did anybody else to whom he told it; nor, afterwards, did anybody in London, where he was to be assured that plays about widows were notoriously unlucky! And so for a while it seemed again on the cards that Lehár's fame would never be associated with the words "Merry Widow". But nobody in Vienna then, or in London later, could think of anything better, and so in this detail also Destiny fulfilled itself.

By the autumn Lehár was ready to play the whole score to Wallner and Karczag on the piano. Léon was present, too, and as Lehár exerted himself, with all his unrivalled verve and enthusiasm, at the keyboard, and the music that all the world would soon be singing poured out from the piano, the two Directors listened . . . with faces that grew longer and longer. With its deep feeling, and its outbursts of barbaric fury, this music was something absolutely new in operette. Something new . . . that was enough! According to a famous story, Karczag drew the librettist aside, and twisting his black moustache in anguish murmured, "What were you thinking of, my dear Léon? This isn't music!" (*Das ist ka' Musik!*) By this saying the normally astute Hungarian, Karczag Vilmos, has gained himself an unwelcome niche in history.[1]

The rehearsals of *The Merry Widow* were as disheartening as the first audition; it was the story of *Der Rastelbinder* over again. Apprehensive—if not convinced—that they had a failure on their hands, the Managers were resolved to risk no money on it. A harp for the orchestra? Ridiculous! Costumes? Anything vaguely Balkan that could be disinterred from the existing wardrobe must be made to do (which ultimately turned the characters into Montenegrins, and caused trouble). Scenery? Good heavens! Weren't there enough ancient back-cloths in stock? Léon had actually at the last moment to run out and buy paper lanterns to lend a touch of glamour to the Widow's Parisian garden fête! The rehearsals dragged along so listlessly that Léon had at last to come down to the theatre with a lawyer and threaten to withdraw his piece. The reply was

[1] But it has been suggested that the crafty Manager knew better. He was a music publisher as well as a theatre Manager, and had it in mind to issue the score of *The Merry Widow*. It was not for him to run up the price. Nevertheless . .

disconcerting. "By all means, withdraw it!" cried Messrs. Wallner and Karczag, smiling for the first time for weeks. . . .

One person, however, was not despondent—the composer. At the conductor's desk Lehár carried on the rehearsals imperturbably, confidently, indefatigably. Singers and orchestra might be ready to drop from exhaustion. He never tired, and was never satisfied; the iron hand of the military Bandmaster underlay his graciousness and charm. And he had two powerful allies. Both his principals believed in *The Merry Widow* as fervently as he did himself. Each was a favourite of the Vienna Theatre. The Widow, Mizzi Günther, had already appeared in Lehár's *Der Göttergatte*, and was then, like a rich flower in bloom, at the height of her full-bosomed, blonde beauty. A sound judge, after hearing her sing, had urged her to train for Grand Opera, but she had decided that her destiny did not lie that way. She had too much temperament, too much exuberance, too much of the spirit of Vienna, too much of what was not yet known as "sex appeal", to find her home anywhere else than in operette. Her lover, "Count Danilo Danilowitsch", was (as has been noted) that Louis Treumann who had played the old tinker in *Der Rastelbinder* with such art, but who had in the Balkan prince a part far more ideally suited to his slim, dark grace, his skill as a dancer, and the extraordinary seduction that he exercised over the feminine element in his audiences.[1]

Both these stars lamented loudly at the notion of withdrawing *The Merry Widow*, or even postponing it. To make up for indecision and delays, they offered to rehearse at night after the ordinary performance in the theatre was over. Only let the show go on! And so from eleven at night until three in the morning they continued to work.

The date of the dress rehearsal arrived, and just as it was about to begin, Ludwig Karpath, the music critic of the *Neues Wiener Tagblatt*, thrust his head inquisitively through the doors. Karczag hastened to drive him out. "Nobody is admitted to the rehearsal!" he declared. "And besides, nothing's going right. Only look at the composer. . . . Hasn't finished his score *yet*! *He* doesn't suffer from nerves, anyhow!" In fact, Lehár, at the conductor's desk, was calmly scribbling additional bits of music, to be snatched from his hands, as he wrote them, by anxious copyists. . . . Had he no nerves? At least he could keep them in control.

Meanwhile Karpath had coaxed permission out of Karczag to stay and watch the rehearsal. He took a seat in the dreary void of the stalls and

---

[1] The diary of a Vienna lady, quoted in *Wiener Vorstadtbühnen*, p. 637, says of Treumann: "His voice, his acting, his movements, his mannerisms, everything about him has a magnetic effect on me and puts me in his power. . . . Other actors vanish beside him. Only he remains, to speak, to sing, to act. Louis, what have you done to me? You are a dangerous man." Poor Treumann! All Hitler's passion for *The Merry Widow* did not save the first, and possibly the greatest, of Danilos from starving in prison for his Jewish blood.

The Merry Widow at Daly's Theatre, 8th June, 1907—that wonderful first night. The Finale to Act II. *Left to right*: V. O'Connor as Khadja; Elizabeth Firth as Natalie; George Graves as Popoff; Robert Evett as Jolidon; Lily Elsie as Sonia; W. H. Berry as Nisch; Joseph Coyne as Danilo

Lennox Pawle, who played Cascada

W. H. Berry as Nisch and Fred Kaye as Novikovich in *The Merry Widow*

prepared to listen. . . . After a while he could no longer restrain himself. "*Bravo!*" he shouted out of the dimness of the empty house, and again "*Bravo!*" Franz Lehár turned round at his desk, and smiled at the first person in the world to applaud *The Merry Widow*. . . .

The last quarter of an hour before world-fame breaks, those final moments during which Fortune seems grudgingly to count out the full price of success, are often peculiarly hard upon her favourites. Lehár must have felt that when on the morning of the 31st December, 1905, he read the Press notices that followed the scenes of the evening before.

For there, in the great, pillared auditorium of the Theater an der Wien, it had been triumph . . . Danilo and the Widow . . . the Widow and Danilo . . . Treumann and Günther . . . Günther and Treumann . . . all the way. Nobody had bothered about the shabbiness of the production; those Embassy guests arrayed in white cotton gloves and hired evening suits, not one of which fitted, as Lehár's sister, who was present as a child, well remembers; or those cheap paper lanterns which Victor Léon himself had rushed out to buy at the last moment, to give some brightness to his millionairess's Fête. The audience had not been put off by the novelty of the whole thing, a coherent story and strong characterization, so startling in operette; they had responded eagerly to the freshness of the music, the clashing barbaric strains and the surging waves of passion that, as the plot deepened, replaced the carefree gaiety, like bubbling champagne, of the Paris ballroom melodies; above all they had broken out in enthusiasm over that seductive slow waltz, then heard for the first time, that was to prove the hallmark for ever of this masterpiece among light operas:

> *Lippen schweigen,*
> *'s flüstern geigen.* . . .

There had been no music of this power or colour before in operette, and there was no half-heartedness about its welcome. The "calls" at the end had been repeated, and among them one had been taken by the Directors, Wallner and Karczag, in glittering evening dress, eager to claim the recognition due to their far-sightedness. . . . Nevertheless, when long afterwards an illustrated souvenir was being prepared in honour of the 300th performance of *The Merry Widow*, Léon was sardonically to propose that the head of the composer should be encircled, as by a wreath, with the words, "This isn't music". . . .

Yes, it had been a happy and excited audience that had streamed away from the Theater an der Wien through the Schikaneder portico and under the laughing Papageno group. They had departed into the bitter winter night with a clatter of hoofs and wheels and only an occasional hum of automobile tyres. They had gone in their broughams and their carriages drawn by high-stepping pairs, in the luxurious Viennese *fiaker*, with their curtains and mirrors and their bowler-hatted drivers full of joviality and repartee, in the humbler one-horse droshkys, and on foot to their various cafés, to whet the appetite, surely, of the rest of Vienna for this new, delightful musical fare? . . . And now the morning after! This hesitant Press, friendly, and even appreciative, but scarcely rapturous, and decidedly sarcastic about the faults of the libretto! No one could possibly gather from these notices that a historical event had taken place the night before at the Theater an der Wien, that the old playhouse had witnessed a new birth, a stage in the development of operette.

And there was worse to follow. The public, influenced, no doubt, by the coolness of the critics, hung back from the box-office. The house had to be cleverly "papered" that the fiftieth performance of *The Merry Widow* might be reached. . . . Fifty performances, and that might have been the end of it! But the Manager of the Neue Wiener Stadttheater (now the Volksoper) a remote suburban house, a sort of park theatre, far from the centre of the town, finding he had a vacant month, made a bid for the whole production to fill the gap. Here the box-office began to talk, and Wallner and Karczag began at last to get a glimmer of what they possessed. They decided to reopen in the autumn with *The Merry Widow* again.

In September, Wallner, who was taking a holiday with his family at Marseilles, began to open his eyes at the staggering figure of the returns forwarded to him week by week. . . . He wondered if there were, as we should say, some "funny business" going on. . . . Yes, that must be it! They wanted to keep him out of things, relaxing at Marseilles, while they lulled him with fabulous figures, and in his absence got on with . . . well, whatever the little game might be. He threw himself, in agitation, into an express train, and reappeared, unannounced, in Vienna . . . only to find that it was all true, that *The Merry Widow* was the draw of all time, and that there would be no need to worry about a new show for the spring!

The Widow was more than a theatrical success; she was a furore. The 600th performance was attained in Vienna . . . and the Widow was still waltzing! Nor did her conquests end with the capital. She was applauded in all the theatres of Austria-Hungary, and soon her dancing feet carried her over the frontier. The operette had been accepted for Leipzig on the night of its first performance in Vienna; it was a resounding success in Hamburg; and the Hamburg production was, with much hesitation, engaged by the Manager of the Berlintheater for a season there. "I fear

... I fear empty houses," he wrote lugubriously to Mme Peteani's father. The answer to his forebodings was a run of 600 performances.

Meanwhile in Vienna the Widow's triumphal course continued, and one night there was a slight stir of excitement amongst the staff and management of the Theater an der Wien. It was occasioned by the fact that two men—foreigners, yet well known to the management—were sitting in the best box. Their presence meant nothing to the audience which had gathered to see *The Merry Widow* on that particular evening, but it meant a good deal to those who were interested in the play. The conductor would glance up at those two men from time to time, and doubtless the principal members of the cast would also let their eyes stray to that box, and perhaps bestow a bow upon the occupants. A few of those interested in the future of *The Merry Widow* watched them keenly. For these two men were important. Their judgment and their verdict would mean much to many people, but most of all to Franz Lehár.

The two were somewhat alike in appearance. They were both large and portly. They both had fresh complexions and greying hair. And they were both unmistakably British. In those things they resembled each other, and also in the fact that their interests were very much the same, and that they were both extremely powerful men in the world of the Theatre and of Music. There the resemblance ended, for their methods and their characteristics were quite unlike each other's. But tonight they had common cause and both were working towards the same end.

To everyone connected with the stage abroad, especially the stage of light music, these two men were of vital importance, for their power was international. But the greatest thing about them was that they represented London. And if a continental light opera got a production in London under their aegis—well, fame and fortune on a world-wide scale usually resulted. For London then was the centre of the world, and these two men were the centre of theatrical and musical London. They were William Boosey and George Edwardes: one the greatest music publisher of his time; the other the greatest theatrical Manager, perhaps, of all time.

William Boosey, adopted by his uncle John Boosey, director of the music publishing firm which bore his name, had been educated at Charterhouse and was destined by his uncle to carry on the firm. He did that with great success for years, and then became Chairman of Messrs. Chappell and Co. Ltd., world-famous then as today. William Boosey was also a great force in the theatre world, for he would publish the scores and selections of the musical plays presented by his friend and colleague George Edwardes. Mr. Boosey was also a director of the Gaiety Theatre, of which George Edwardes was Manager and Managing Director, and the Chairman of which was Sir George Dance.

William Boosey was responsible for Edwardes being in the Theater an der Wien on that particular evening. Ever on the look-out for musical plays (as well as all sorts of music) all over the world, he had been told about *The Merry Widow*. He had been asked to get hold of the rights of an old German comedy entitled *Peace in War* with a view to turning it into a musical play. He had communicated with his friend Sliwinski, a very famous agent in Berlin, about this, and when he went to Prague to see a production of Léoni's *Ib and Christina* Sliwinski met him there. He explained to Boosey that *Peace in War* had already been acquired—for the same purpose as Boosey wanted it—by Rheinhardt, a Viennese composer of eminence, so Boosey was too late. But he said he had a couple of shows, of which *Peace in War* was one, being produced in Vienna that autumn. The other was called *The Merry Widow*, by Franz Lehár. Would Boosey come and see them—and bring George Edwardes? If so, Sliwinski would hold the performing rights until then.

Boosey said he would do his best and returned to London. In due course *The Merry Widow* was produced, as has been told. In London, Paul Rubens, the composer of so much delightful music, who was at the time deeply interested in the Apollo Theatre, heard from a friend of his, Lord Kilmarnock, an attaché at the Embassy in Vienna, that *The Merry Widow* was worth having. Rubens went at once to Boosey, who was, he knew, going to Vienna, and asked him to secure the play for him. But Boosey had to tell him that he had already given the first refusal—in so far as it was his to give—to George Edwardes. But he made haste to go to Vienna. He went to Edwardes and told him to come along too. Edwardes was very busy and very worried. He was having a rather bad time—things were not going well—one of those inexplicable but recurring changes in public taste was apparently in progress, and Edwardes, who sensed these things, was exercised in his mind just what to do next, how to get in first on the new market. He did not want to go to Vienna, he was most unwilling to leave London; but at last he agreed.

So there they were, in that box at the Theater an der Wien. They had seen the Rheinhardt musical play the previous night—the night of their arrival—and found it was no use to either of them—not suitable for the English market. So this, the second evening of their stay, found them watching *The Merry Widow*. They knew its strange history; they knew its early struggle; and they watched with expert eyes, and listened with expert ears. No doubt Boosey kept his attention glued to the stage, and also drank in the melody. It is probable that Edwardes watched the audience as much as he watched the show—for it was by audience reaction that he judged things—he could absorb a show while hardly glancing at it. It was the effect—and the music—which mattered to him.

He knew that if he bought the piece he would re-create it to suit his public. And he found that this was just the sort of show on which he could bring his magic to bear and make it a success. Both men made up their minds that the *Widow* would be all right for London, but of the two Boosey was the most enthusiastic.

The next day Edwardes was on the point of leaving for Budapest. The agent Sliwinski rushed to Boosey at the Hotel Bristol, almost with tears in his eyes. Was the great George Edwardes not going to secure *The Merry Widow*? Was such a terrible thing as that going to happen? Boosey went to Edwardes and talked to him. And just before he left for Budapest "The Guvnor", as everyone called him, bought *The Merry Widow*—almost at the very last minute. Boosey had told him that if he did not snap it up, there were plenty of others who would. So Edwardes bought it—and it is very significant, in view of what happened, that he bought this play for and on behalf of the Gaiety Theatre Company Ltd. But, at any rate, he had bought it, and a new and amazing chain of events had begun to be forged. . . .

D

CHAPTER FIVE

George Edwardes

IT is necessary, at this juncture, to look backwards for a short time, and to get not only George Edwardes into proper perspective, but also the conditions ruling in London and the London Theatre at the time of the production of *The Merry Widow*. For all that has a bearing on the wonderful success this work of Lehár's achieved.

During the closing epoch of the Victorian Age in this country, the Theatre had assumed an importance and stability which it had not known before. It was passing from the long years of suspicion as to its respectability, or even its mere desirableness in general, to the position of a recognized and appreciated form of art and culture. It was no longer a Vagabond amongst the Professions; it had become part of the general scheme of life. Queen Victoria had seen fit to knight an actor, Sir Henry Irving, and how far-reaching that was is not properly appreciated today. It was a tribute not only to the power of the actor but to the fact that he had raised the status of his calling and the art of the Theatre to the highest point it had reached up to then. Never before had an actor been knighted; it is said that David Garrick had expected the accolade, but he never received it. Irving had raised beauty of presentation to a very high level. Gone were the old, slovenly makeshift days of production and *décor*. Irving had lit a brighter light than even the beacons of Macready and Charles Kean had done. He, the actor-manager, carved the way which the great galaxy of actor-managers—Tree, Wyndham, Cyril Maude, John Hare, John Martin-Harvey, Charles Hawtrey, Lewis Waller and so many more—were to tread, and under the reign of those actor-managers the British Theatre reached its pinnacle.

Those were the days of Empire; and during those late Victorian years and the more tolerant but no less rich Edwardian days which followed them (the Edwardian era only ended in 1914 when the First World War shattered all established things) another Empire was being built up within the Theatre itself, quite apart from the "legitimate" stage trodden by the actor-managers. And this, within the Edwardian Empire, was the Edwardesian Empire, the Empire builder being George Edwardes himself. To build an Empire one must have courage, an adventurous spirit, keen powers of observation, tremendous knowledge of humanity and a pioneering and creative mind. George Edwardes, the son of an Irish country gentleman, educated at an English public school, had all those things.

He had a complete understanding of his job, and he had a flair which was a marvellous gift. He had learnt his business working in the Royal Academy of the D'Oyly Carte régime—the Gilbert and Sullivan operas. These were, and have remained to this day, a thing apart in the evolution of light opera. They originated in a revolt that took place in the mind of W. S. Gilbert against the burlesques of the eighteen-seventies (of which he himself had written several) and the adaptations of the French *opéra bouffe* that were then holding the London stage. He had come to realize that these were an obstacle to the development of his peculiar gifts as a writer, while they also increasingly jarred upon his susceptibilities as an educated gentleman of the upper middle class. In this latter feeling he was at one with an important section of his fellow-countrymen, who (as has been remarked above) had come more and more to look upon the stage as the "Vagabond among the Professions" and the theatre as a definitely disreputable place of resort. The Puritan condemnation of all forms of dramatic entertainment had gone deep into the blood of the respectable English middle class; and, even where this disapproval did not linger, the crudeness and lack of culture, as well as the vulgarity of much that was presented on the English stage, were narrowing its influence and diminishing its audiences.[1]

What Irving was doing for the serious drama at the Lyceum, Gilbert was anxious to do for the lighter stage. It is significant that he early associated himself with the entertainment called "The German Reed Gallery of Illustration", which was in effect an ingenious device of a Mr. German Reed to provide the middle class with dramatic performances as part of a programme that could not be called "going to the theatre". He interspersed comedies and comediettas among a miscellany of songs, recitations and other unexceptionable forms of entertainment, and gave his performance, which was, of course, of unimpeachable propriety, in a kind of concert hall. What Gilbert asked himself was whether the enthusiastic patrons of German Reed could not be brought into a real theatre,

---

[1] The ease with which free passes could apparently be obtained to the theatres at this period must strike any reader of the literature of the day.

if the real theatre were made as respectable as the Gallery of Illustration.

To this end he formulated certain principles which were to be the base of the operettes he planned to write with Mr. Arthur Sullivan, a rising young musician, then chiefly known for religious or semi-religious music, but who had, like Gilbert, worked for German Reed. These works were to be thoroughly English; they were to deliver our Theatre from Offenbach, *opéra bouffe*, and all continental enormities. They were to be rigidly respectable, and not a word was to be spoken in them which could not be uttered in a lady's drawing-room. As part of this campaign for propriety, Gilbert (in defiance of Shakespeare!) felt it necessary to lay down that no male character should be played by a woman, no female character by a man.[1] He was also resolved to woo the cultured class by dethroning the then omnipotent pun, and adorning his lyrics with allusions intelligible to those only who had had the benefit of a classical education.[2] Even in the presentation of the Gilbert and Sullivan operettes a touch of the "drawing-room" atmosphere was preserved; for, while it would be impossible to over-rate the subtle artistry of the leading players in the original productions, a certain stiffness and air of giving out a set recitation on the part of the juvenile leads was also inherent in the tradition. . . . And, of course, for the comedian who ventured to gag, there remained only "the big black block".[3]

It is beyond our task to enquire how far the triumph of Gilbert and Sullivan was a triumph for Sullivan, in whose enchanting scores there may be moments of melancholy, and even hymnody, but never any disturbing hints of passion. Nor does it require any great effort to judge how much success the excellent Gilbertian principles would have had if Gilbert had not been a genius—a philosopher of the absurd, a revealer of the insanity of logic, a master of words without equal in the long array of English humorists, and a poet with a lyrical movement that might have carried him very high had he not been bound to earth by the comic sock. But it is important to see exactly what was achieved by the Gilbert and Sullivan operas. It is not strictly accurate to say (as is so often said) that they "killed" *opéra bouffe*. It has been pointed out that almost contemporaneously with their appearance, *Les Cloches de Corneville*, *Madame Favart* and *Olivette* were enjoying comparable runs, and that as late as 1897, long after the great collaboration had effectively ceased, "*La Poupée*

---

[1] Yet the disguised male students of *Princess Ida* come perilously near a *travesti*.
[2] "One Latin word
One Greek remark
And one that's French."—as the Peers sing in *Iolanthe*.
[3] That is at least the legend, but Rutland Barrington got away with a good many quips of his own as Pooh-Bah.

took the liberty of running up five hundred and seventy six performances"
in London.[1]

In fact Gilbert and Sullivan opera was of too special a quality to sweep
all competitors off the stage; it made no attempt to offer much that the
greater public will always demand—the element of passion is an obvious
absentee. Nor, except for *The Mikado*, did it appeal outside the English-
speaking countries. Nor could it found a school, in spite of the gallant
attempts of Basil Hood and Edward German. Gilbert could have no
successor. But it has remained undying in its own right, continuing
through all vicissitudes of time and taste to pack English theatres whenever it is played; and his early association with it could not be without
its effect on George Edwardes. Those were his standards, and there were
none higher. He was inspired by the tireless energy, the never ceasing
care which D'Oyly Carte lavished on his work, and by the scrupulous
polishing which both Gilbert and Sullivan gave to their operas. And, as
Irving continued to lift the status of his side of the theatrical profession,
so did George Edwardes follow Gilbert in raising the status of the side
to which he devoted himself—that of musical plays and light entertainment. He did more than that, he invented an entirely new form, which
was to be the most attractive of all right from its inception, and which
remains so today. He invented Musical Comedy.

Such a man was not destined to work for others. Quite early in his
career he had formed his plans. And he watched what was happening in
the world of the Theatre. He watched failure, and found out the cause.
He watched success, and worked out the reason for that. Most of all, he
watched the Gaiety Theatre, just across the Strand. Already that place was
unique in the amusement world of London. John Hollingshead, its
creator, had struck out his own line. He had, after a time, made Burlesque
his great drawing card. In his own words, he "lit the sacred lamp of
Burlesque". But Hollingshead was no longer young, and his activities at
the Gaiety were taxing him. George Edwardes saw all that, and decided
that the Gaiety was the place for him. He considered that the "Sacred
Lamp" was perhaps running a little low, and that the flame seemed to
flicker. He judged that one of the reasons might be the great popularity
of the Savoy operas, of which he was then part. He had seen them compete successfully with the *opéra bouffe* imported from France, and he knew
why. It did not matter to him that Hollingshead called them "Burlesques
in Long Clothes". The old Manager had said that because in his burlesques
there was plenty of limb on view—tights, scanty clothing; it was all part
of the spirit of Burlesque.

But the watchful Edwardes saw that the amazing respectability of tone

[1] C. Hibbert, *A Playgoer's Memories*, p. 32.

and costume in the Savoy operas did not detract from their success. Hollingshead had already created the Gaiety Girl. Into George Edwardes's brain swam a picture of a new type of Gaiety Girl—a new phase for the Gaiety—he could create her, it was within his power. And so he became a partner of John Hollingshead—for a year. And then the older man retired. George Edwardes was King of the Gaiety. He set about putting his kingdom into shape. He made mistakes, of course, but he learnt by them. He realized that his new idea was not yet ripe. But he kept trying it on, each time getting a little nearer and nearer, until at last he took the plunge and gave the Gaiety a new type of show. It was *The Shop Girl*, which he called Musical Comedy. He chose exactly the right time, and he triumphed.

The basis of Edwardes's idea was always The Girl—the glorification of Femininity. As soon as he could, he made those girls as feminine as possible. Away went the tights, away went the semi-nudity. In its place was the shimmer of satin and silk, the whole armour of feminine attraction, which is concealment of actuality under the cloak of enticement. The girls in those skirts, those dresses, and that foam of lacy petticoats, had infinitely more enchantment than those wearing the semi-pantomime styles of the old Burlesque. Edwardes had created his new Gaiety and his new Gaiety Girl. He was the finest picker of feminine beauty and talent of his day—perhaps of any day.

And then something else happened. Edwardes had built a theatre for a celebrated American impresario named Augustin Daly. Maybe when he built it he sensed that one day it would be his. And that came to pass. Daly, despite splendid casts and splendid effort, could not make the theatre which was named after him a success. It passed into the hands of George Edwardes. Daly gave that theatre its name, which it retained until the end, but Edwardes gave that theatre its soul, in the form of Musical Comedy, musical plays of which the spirit was Romance. He was now King of both Daly's and the Gaiety, with manifold interests elsewhere, and productions in many other theatres. But those two, Daly's and the Gaiety, were the core of the Edwardesian Empire, twin capitals—like Buda-Pest—of it all.

He was a wise man. He never brought the two theatres into opposition. Both did musical comedies, but in very different style. The Gaiety, as its name implied, was lighthearted and sparkling. At Daly's Edwardes kept to a more solid type of show, not so far removed from Comic Opera, but always with Romance as its hard core.

He made that theatre, which had been built for an American and which bore an American name, a very English place indeed. This cannot be a history of delectable Daly's, but its stage must be set as a proper frame for the arrival, at the apex of the years of Empire, of the Viennese magician of music Franz Lehár. For he was indeed of the quality with which Edwardes had endowed Daly's—the same quality that Edwardes possessed himself—and it was at Daly's that the three greatest triumphs of Lehár were achieved.

Edwardes started at Daly's with an astounding run of success, a series of musical plays composed by an Englishman, Sidney Jones. Those formed of themselves a splendid chapter in the history of the British musical play. They were *An Artist's Model*, with which Edwardes opened his reign, *The Geisha*, *A Greek Slave* and *San Toy*. They laid the foundation of the magic of Daly's. And they were all big successes with long runs. *An Artist's Model* ran for 405 performances, *The Geisha* for 760, *A Greek Slave* for 352 and *San Toy* for 768. The public knew what they would get at Daly's, just as they knew what line of goods Edwardes sold them at the Gaiety. And at both theatres he had a team; he built up artists and kept them. Wonderful names: Marie Tempest, Hayden Coffin, Rutland Barrington, Gracie Leigh, Huntley Wright, Letty Lind, Fred Kaye, Willie Warde—those were the stalwarts; and as one or another dropped out, new people, to become just as popular, took their places. If the girls at Daly's were not quite so lovely and exciting as those of the Gaiety, still they were more lovely than elsewhere, and also, at Daly's, the accent was more on vocal power than was the case at the Gaiety. For the Daly's shows, as stated, still kept a link with the Comic Operas, and would have big vocal finales at the end of acts. The girls at Daly's had to be able to sing and to sing well.

Daly's was now a landmark of London, of deeper hue than the diamond of the Gaiety, but a gem of the first water all the same. It had the atmosphere which Edwardes always supplied—maybe he built it into the very bricks. It was an immensely smart house, more staid and sedate perhaps than the Gaiety, without the crowd of young bloods round the stage door, although Daly's stage door had its attendants too. But the whole thing was more solid, a rich satisfying burgundy against the champagne of the Gaiety, a ruby or a pearl against the diamond's brilliance—none the less precious however.

After that amazing cavalcade of plays by Sidney Jones, Edwardes moved a little nearer to Musical Comedy as it is generally understood. *A Country Girl* followed, in 1902, with the score by Lionel Monckton and extra numbers by Paul Rubens. Edwardes had observed the change which had taken place. The Boer War was over; the Victorian days had gone; the much swifter tempo of the days of King Edward VII had begun. Edwardes met it. *A Country Girl* was much lighter than its forerunners, though it still had touches of the old Comic Opera. But it was very much of its period. It was the most English of all his Daly's shows, a Devonshire setting for a Devonshire girl (or girls) with lovely tuneful music, lighter indeed than had been usual, and with plenty of comedy. It had a splendid cast, with Evie Greene at her superb best. It ran for 729 performances. It seemed that Edwardes could not do wrong at Daly's.

He followed that with *The Cingalee*. This time the setting was exotic, as compared with much that had gone before. True, we had been to ancient Rome, with success, to Japan and to China with overwhelming success. But somehow, despite the notable cast, the beautiful setting—redolent of the spicy breezes where every prospect pleased—*The Cingalee*, hailed by the Press as a masterpiece, ran for only 363 performances. Only 363? A long run then, but three of its predecessors had all notched over 700. Edwardes decided on a change. So, for the first time in the history of Edwardesian Daly's (save for an early experiment with *Hansel and Gretel* before he made the theatre his own), he went abroad for a play. And he chose France.

It seemed a good idea. So much that was popular had come from that country in one way and another—the *opéra bouffe* of Offenbach, for instance. France was then regarded by the British as a slightly naughty but very romantic country, where life was artistic, and where, in many respects, they managed certain things better than in this land. But the British, by and large, had no very high opinion of the French as a race, nor of any other foreign people. This country—their country—was the richest, the most powerful, the most prosperous in the world. They were quite ready to admit that they might not be an artistic race, but at the same time, when they chose, they could do things well—and they did Musical Comedy better than anyone else, as the shows at Daly's, the Gaiety and elsewhere witnessed. They exported Musical Comedy to America, and Musical Comedy was, in Britain, the most popular form of light entertainment with all classes. France might have her Offenbach—who was a German Jew by extraction anyway—and the others, but Britain had her Gilbert and Sullivan—and her George Edwardes. Still, France had her points when it came to music.

So Edwardes opened the doors of Daly's to a French invasion. He had plenty of precedent. The great actor-managers of the legitimate stage drew largely on French plays for their attractions. But they had them well adapted and made suitable for the British palate. In those days there were more plays of French origin holding the stage than there are American plays today, a point which should be borne in mind. Only, of course, the American plays are not turned into English and the French plays were.

Edwardes chose a French musical play, of a light but sentimental nature, by a composer named André Messager, adapted from the French of A. Vanloo and G. Duval by Henry Hamilton, with lyrics by Percy Greenbank. It was called *The Little Michus*. Messager was a composer not very well known in this country. He had had a failure which was called *La Basoche* at the Palace. He had had a failure at the Savoy in 1894— *Mirette*, presented by D'Oyly Carte, and the programme had announced that it was written expressly for that theatre. Despite a cast which included John Coates, Herbert Ralland, Courtice Pounds, Scott Russell, Maud Ellicott, Florence Perry, Emmie Owen and Rosina Brandram, it failed.

But another Messager score came to London. It was first produced at the Coronet Theatre, Notting Hill Gate, in 1903, by a French company. Edwardes saw it, acquired it, had it turned into English, and presented it at the Apollo Theatre in 1904. It was *Véronique* and it was a very big success indeed, one of the most delightful musical plays—or operettes— ever seen in London, as fresh, bright and gay as Paris on a spring morning. It was of a charming period; it had a wonderful cast which included Ruth Vincent, Rosina Brandram, Kitty Gordon, Maudi Darrell, Lawrence Rea (and later Hayden Coffin), Fred Emney, Aubrey Fitzgerald, and a rising young comedian, George Graves. It was produced for Edwardes by that pocket genius Sydney Ellison. Its music is popular today, and it ran for 495 performances. This success seemed to wipe out the two previous failures. Edwardes therefore had no qualms in taking a Messager play to Daly's for his first foreign venture there.

He gave the production his usual lavish care, and there were the prettiest possible stage pictures, representing Paris in Napoleonic days, a few years before Waterloo—a most attractive period for costume. There was a love story concerning two little girls named Michu, who were "sweet seventeen" and named Blanche-Marie and Marie-Blanche. But one of them was an adopted child, which led to complications, though all came right in the end.

With the change of type of play there was also a change in the old Daly's team. Very few of the Old Guard who had made those Daly's plays so successful were included in *The Little Michus*. Willie Warde was there; Huntley Wright was there, too, but he left quite early in the run, and was succeeded by James Blakeley. W. Louis Bradfield, a stalwart of the Edwardesian régime, was also in it, but he, too, left and was followed by no less a person than Henry A. Lytton, the Savoyard who eventually gained the honour of knighthood. Ambrose Manning, an excellent actor, played Père Michu, Amy Augarde was Madame Michu. There was a scene at a school and a wonderful bunch of school girls, which included Alice D'Orme, Nina Sevening, Doris Stocker, Ida Lytton, Agnes Gunn,

Alice Hatton and Freda Vivian. That was a bouquet of girls well able to challenge the Gaiety in beauty. The little Michus themselves were played by Mabel Green and Adrienne Augarde, two sweetly pretty girls of contrasted type yet sufficiently alike to be sisters—or to be taken for such. And the part of Madame du Tertre—not very much of a part—was played by a lady named Lily Elsie. There was another newcomer, too, who was destined to play a great part in the story of Daly's Theatre— Robert Evett, a Savoyard with a fine tenor voice and considerable acting ability. He was to uphold the banner of Daly's and the Edwardes tradition, in years to come, against great odds and to find, in times of stress, a great success in *The Maid of the Mountains*. But that was in the mists of tomorrow.

That great comedian and actor Willie Edouin played the comedy part of General des Ifs. But he left the cast too—*The Little Michus* company underwent many changes during the run—and in his place came a young actor who had only recently won his spurs in town, but had won them under the Edwardesian banner. He specialized in comic old men, and his name was George Graves. He had made a hit in *The School Girl* and another in *Véronique*. And when he joined *The Little Michus* he made yet another. He had adapted a style which he made his own. He was a great gagster. Indeed, so good was he in impromptu vein that they told Arthur Roberts, the king of all gagsters, that he must look to his laurels. Arthur, an ageing man, snorted in disgust. "What—me afraid of a man who uses nose-paste?" he said with scorn. But in Graves he had a foeman worthy of his steel.

The Little Michus was produced at Daly's on the 29th April, 1905. It ran for 401 performances. That looks well on paper, but it never really made the grade. It was not a true Daly's show; it was charming, tuneful, colourful enough, but not really in the Daly's tradition. At the Apollo it might have repeated the financial success of *Véronique*, but at Daly's it lost the Guvnor money. It was a bad title, and titles are important. Nobody knew what it meant. The piece never settled down. The many changes in cast did not help; Huntley Wright's leaving the theatre where he had made his name and assisted in so many successes was most unfortunate, despite the cleverness of Jimmy Blakeley. Edwardes, as always, tried everything. At one time he imported Madame Adeline Genée herself to give a solo dance, putting in a special part for her, Mlle St. Cyr, described as a famous dancer of the period. Fred Emney succeeded Ambrose Manning. But still *The Little Michus* did not pack the theatre. None of those alterations or additions helped.

What did help, however, was young Mr. George Graves. He presented a completely different General des Ifs from that portrayed by

Willie Edouin, classic though it was. The General, in the hands of Mr. Graves, developed a lot of curious traits, among them a habit of commenting on passing events and of making dissertations on objects of interest hitherto unknown. Mr. Graves told the audiences at Daly's about the habit and manners of an odd little beast called the "Gazeka". The Gazeka became the rage. Mr. Graves was always finding out something new about it, and he would reduce audiences to tears of laughter. Gazekas were manufactured and put on sale. Everybody bought them. But a Gazeka, however popular, and even with George Graves as its sponsor, cannot make a success of a play any more than one swallow can make a summer. What it did accomplish was the solidification of the success of George Graves.

Despite that face-saving run, *The Little Michus* lost a lot of money for Edwardes. He was having a bad patch. So far, France had not conquered the very British atmosphere of Daly's. And Edwardes was having bad luck outside Daly's too. Things were tight, and Daly's was very much his own speculation. He knew he would get the money back on tour. He knew that the provinces were, for him, a gilt-edged investment. But all that took time. He had lost money often in town—*Kitty Grey* was an instance—and recouped it all, with a big profit, from the country. But that did not prevent things from getting tight at the moment.

He prepared the successor to *The Little Michus*, and once more he turned to France. Maybe he thought that, *The Little Michus* having broken the ice, this second French importation would be welcome. But he made a mistake—a curious one for him. He, who could pick a title for a play with as much skill as he could pick a chorus, allowed the new play to be called *Les Merveilleuses*. It was worse than *The Little Michus*. It was a bad mistake, and it seems extraordinary that Edwardes should have made it. *Les Merveilleuses* was a very difficult thing to say—and the British are shy of foreign words, especially those awkward to pronounce. He should have remembered the difficulty which the theatre called the Opera Comique— much easier to say than *Les Merveilleuses*—had experienced in its time, and how the public had jibbed at the seemingly straightforward title of *H.M.S. Pinafore*, strange as it may seem now. Some thought it was a foreign word and called it "pin-af-or-*e*". They could not believe that Gilbert meant that very ordinary garment, then so much used.

But Edwardes persisted in calling this play—which he labelled "A Comedy Opera", another mistake—by its almost unpronounceable name. The book was by Victorien Sardou, and the English version by Captain Basil Hood. Adrian Ross did the lyrics and Hugo Felix was the composer. *Les Merveilleuses* were, of course, the ladies of the French Directorate, who broke away from the austerity which had been imposed by the

Terror, adopted classical attire—very revealing classical attire—and contributed a period of lax morals much resembling the easy virtue of Restoration times, which had been, in this country, the reaction to the Puritanical rule. Not that the British Public of those days, in the bulk, knew anything about that, but George Edwardes saw fit to inspire an article explaining it all in the *Daily Telegraph* of the 24th October, 1906.

Les Merveilleuses was a very beautiful production indeed and had a cast to match it. That cast contained Robert Evett, now a regular at Daly's, W. Louis Bradfield, Fred Kaye, Willie Warde, Fred Emney, Scott Russell, Gordon Cleather, Mlle Mariette Sully, Denise Orme (who married into the Peerage), Elizabeth Firth, handsome woman and fine singer, some beautiful girls like Eleanor Souray, Nina Sevening, D. Dunbar, M. Erskine and E. Barker, and in the character of Lodoiska, Evie Greene herself, that woman of dark, burning beauty, high acting ability and a voice of pure gold.

There was also a newcomer to Daly's, who had made good for Edwardes elsewhere, and whose name was W. H. Berry. Edwardes brought him into *Les Merveilleuses* at rather short notice. W. H. (Bill) Berry was not quite sure, on the first night, of certain cues. So he wrote them on paper and put them in his hat. He was a most resourceful comedian, and when he had need of recourse to his aid to memory, he removed the hat and glanced inside, remarking as he did so, "For France." The other comedians, perforce, did the same, the "gag" got laughs, and remained part of the show.

But *Les Merveilleuses* was not a success. It created a vogue for Directoire costumes, it is true; but the public, in the mass, fought shy of it. Even when the name was changed to *The Lady Dandies*—not a good title either —and Gabrielle Ray was brought into the cast, to sing in her curious little voice and dance like a moonbeam, and Berry was transferred to the part played originally by Fred Emney, and Huntley Wright, the true comedian of Daly's, returned to the fold, to play the part which Berry had created, still it made no difference. *Les Merveilleuses*, or *The Lady Dandies*, did not attract. It ran for only 186 performances.

George Edwardes was very much up against it. His bad luck dogged him. *The Cingalee* had not been the smash hit of its forerunners; *The Little Michus* had lost him money; and *Les Merveilleuses*, despite his magnificence of staging and cast, was, by the Daly's standard, a flop, or as Edwardes himself called such things, a "nitter". He had been unsuccessful in ventures outside Daly's, also. Two plays at the Prince of Wales's, *The Little Cherub* and *See See*, had certainly not rung the bell of success. Even the Gaiety, with *The New Aladdin*, was not doing very well; it was saved by quick changes in the cast and interpolations, but it was not a money-spinner.

The real worry, however, was Daly's; there a successor was wanted and wanted quickly. There was no time to get a real Daly's home-made article ready in time. The Guvnor had not expected to have to do a new show so soon. He had acquired, in pursuance of his flair that romance from abroad would be in demand from the public, a musical play called *The Dollar Princess*, composed by that Leo Fall who had been a First Violin in the elder Sehár's band at Vienna, but there was no adaptation, no time to cast it, no time to complete the involved negotiations and get it ready by the date required. Edwardes was in a really tight spot, and he was very hard up. He never counted cost, he never spared money, he never worried about expenses; all he cared about was Quality. If he failed—as very naturally he did from time to time—it was never from want of care, never from want of trouble, never from want of good taste, of scenes, costumes and girls of beauty, or because there was a mistake in the casting. It was due to one of those odd stumbling-blocks in the way of producers which are either overlooked because unforeseen, or are quite impossible to guard against, because the public supply them out of their own minds and without previous warning. No great man's career is unmarked by a period when bad luck is in the ascendant, and this was the period when George Edwardes met his.

So here was the King of the Musical Theatre, harassed and worried, with a financial crisis on his hands, as well as the prospect of finding a successor for that theatre where success had reigned for so long, the theatre which was perhaps nearer his own heart than any other—Daly's. But despite all the worries and troubles, he was not caught napping entirely. That far-seeing mind had been at work. He had known at once that *Les Merveilleuses* was what he called a "nitter". He had changed many seeming failures into winners, and he had tried hard with this. But it was basically wrong. All he could do was gain time, and he needed time desperately. *The Dollar Princess*, in which he firmly believed, was out of the question for the moment. Very well, he would do another musical play, one which he had bought for the Gaiety, one on which he had been at work at intervals, both actually and in his own mind, one by a composer unknown to London save for some waltzes—notably that named "Gold and Silver"—a play he had bought at the last moment in Vienna. There was not a moment to lose; things were desperate. All right! He would close the gap at Daly's with *The Merry Widow*, composed by Franz Lehár.

CHAPTER SIX

The Widow Crosses the Channel

IT is probable, it is indeed almost certain, that never had George Edwardes, the Guvnor, been in such trouble or such low water financially as when he took the decision to stage *The Merry Widow* at Daly's Theatre. That choice made it certain that the sequence of shows at Daly's under his management—the whole theatre was under his sole control—would be unbroken, and that the theatre would not be closed down for a considerable period. But that was the only tension it relieved. One trouble cropped up after another. Fate seemed to be taking a hand, and it became quite clear later that Fate most certainly was. But at that moment Fate seemed to be against Daly's, whereas, in its own inscrutable way, it was working for the theatre's good.

Edwardes, having bought *The Merry Widow* for the Gaiety, had proceeded along his usual lines. He had sent his first lieutenant J. A. E. Malone over to see it. Malone had returned full of praise, only with the conviction that it was a Daly's, not a Gaiety, show. Well, it was going to be at Daly's now—and a further snag arose. Edwardes had not bought it from the Gaiety Company for his own use when he announced it for Daly's. That however was soon smoothed over. He was Managing Director and moving spirit at the Gaiety, too; but there were other directors there and shareholders, jealous of their rights.

That Edwardes had paid some attention to the play is certain; he was always preparing well beforehand for everything he put on; and that is why he was able to produce *The Merry Widow* as quickly as he did. Still with the Gaiety in view, he had had an English version made of the play by a man well known for his work in that field. When this version was given to Malone, that able and practical man of the Theatre thought it was impossible. He told the Guvnor so. This was indeed serious. Time was getting short. Somebody else had to be found in a hurry, and, of course, they found him in the person of Captain Basil Hood, a witty and polished writer of light opera books, who had endeavoured, not unsuccessfully, to carry on the Savoy tradition with pieces like *Merrie England* and *The Rose of Persia*. Hood went to work, and in a remarkably short space of time turned out the version of this story which London eventually saw.

But the original adapter was never told about the switch-over, or so the story went at Daly's. He was not called to rehearsals, but he was given seats for the first night. To his amazement he saw a play which did not resemble that which he had prepared at all, except in the main outline of plot. He recognized none of the words; this was not his work at all— what on earth had happened? As soon as the show was over he took steps, and he found out that his version, which had not been considered satisfactory, had been shelved and that of Hood's used.

They had wished to spare his feelings and to come to some amicable arrangement. The name of the adapter was not even on the programme! There was talk of a lawsuit, but the matter was settled. The author who had not written the Daly's version of *The Merry Widow* drew fees all through the run. Edwardes did not mind that very much; he wanted the best and he had got it. But it goes to show his state of mind at the time of production. Had he not been so driven, had he not carried such a load of care, he, with his wonderful diplomacy and tact, would have settled the whole thing on satisfactory terms—and even made the aggrieved author feel grateful to him. He often did things like that.

William Boosey had kept reminding Edwardes about *The Merry Widow*, in which he had great faith—far more than had the Guvnor. He would make suggestions as to cast, and one evening both men met at a First Night. It was at the Aldwych Theatre, and the play was *Nellie Neil*, a musical comedy with score by Ivan Caryll, in which Edna May appeared (it turned out to be her last professional engagement). Charles Frohman was the "presenter"—he invented that phrase—and in the cast was a young man from America. He was little known in London, although he had appeared there once before, six years previously, at the Duke of York's Theatre. On that occasion the play was *The Girl From Up There*, Edna May, again, being the leading lady, and Frohman the manager.

The night on which Edwardes and Boosey saw the young American at the Aldwych was the 10th January, 1907. His name was Joseph Coyne. He was a curious-looking fellow, with a round face and a pair of rather sad eyes, loose-limbed and with a habit of kicking out on each side with his feet as he walked. But there was something about him—there was that indefinable quality of charm. And there was individuality. Here was a man who could twist a woman round his finger without effort, by his simple, wistful appeal, and who also would be hail-fellow-well-met with the men; there was the smile and the lurking mischief in the eye, which peeped forth from time to time, to prove it.

So thought Edwardes, as he watched from the stalls. Those blue eyes of his saw clearly the possibilities in this young man, who could not sing at all, but who could certainly dance, and who could most certainly act. And above all that, Edwardes saw Coyne as a new type. His pioneering spirit was awake; here was a complete change from the rather stiff, if handsome and stagily dashing, young leading man whose voice, as a rule, made his success. This young man had no voice, but he had personality, he had charm, he had individuality. Here was a man who could play Prince Danilo in *The Merry Widow*, as Edwardes now thought it should be played, not as a romantic hero of the light operatic stage, but as a lover in real life with actual flesh and blood and feelings. In the interval Boosey spoke to him, and told him he thought Coyne would be ideal for the *Widow*. Edwardes replied that he thought so too.

He acted at once. He himself went round to Coyne's dressing-room and offered him the part. It was a habit of George Edwardes to do this, to go to the player instead of summoning the player to come to his office. It was just one of those things in which he showed his genius. The actor or actress so honoured were overwhelmed by the fact that the Great Man had actually come to them. The Guvnor always did it to those he really wanted. He did it to Ada Reeve, he did it to Connie Ediss, to many others. He offered Coyne the part then and there, and Coyne, flattered and delighted—and knowing nothing at all of what the part was like—told the Guvnor that he was under contract to Charles Frohman. Edwardes did not worry about that; he and Frohman were friends and often business partners. Probably Joe Coyne had one of the famous Frohman contracts, nothing at all in writing, just the Manager's word—which was never broken and was far more binding than any engrossed vellum agreement ever drawn up by lawyers. Anyway, it was arranged between Edwardes and Frohman that Coyne should appear in *The Merry Widow* when wanted, and if Frohman got any pecuniary benefit out of it, it does not matter, and is very unlikely.

Certain chroniclers have stated that Edwardes was not keen on Coyne playing Danilo. The reverse is true. It was Edwardes's idea and he stuck to it. He frequently told the tale of how he made Coyne do it. For when Coyne was shown the part he was horrified. He had never played a romantic hero—nor did he want to. He was a funny man, a comic, not a romantic maker of love and a singer of songs. He was frightened out of his life; he said he would not do it, he begged to be let off. But Edwardes was adamant. He told Coyne to leave it to him. "You are going to be an enormous success, Joe," he said; "you wait and see."

Some Daly's Personalities. *Top left*: Elizabeth Firth as Natalie. *Top right*: Robert Evett as Jolidon. *Bottom left*: Mabel Russell (afterwards Member of Parliament for Berwick-on-Tweed), who played "Frou-Frou" in *The Merry Widow*. *Bottom right*: Gertie Millar as Lady Babby in *Gipsy Love*, another Lehár success at Daly's Theatre

Top left: Gabrielle Ray, who followed Mabel Russell as "Frou-Frou" in *The Merry Widow* at Daly's. *Top right*: Louis Bradfield, a favourite Danilo in the Provinces. *Bottom left*: Elizabeth Firth and Robert Evett in Act II of *The Merry Widow* at Daly's. *Bottom right*: Robert Michaelis, who took Joseph Coyne's place for a time as Danilo at Daly's and afterwards starred there in Lehár's *Gipsy Love*

But Coyne was most unhappy. Even when he discovered, at rehearsals, that he was to play it in the way which suited his personality, that he was not expected to sing some of the more difficult numbers, that he was to let his own ability and charm carry him along, he was still afraid. This was not his line of country at all, this Ruritanian stuff; he wanted to be slick and modern and American, as those things were understood in 1907. Even at the dress rehearsal he was scared stiff. He told William Boosey that he was in for the failure of his life. Boosey told him that, on the contrary, he was going to make the biggest hit of his career and would establish himself as a real and lasting favourite in London. Coyne shook his head dolefully. But both Edwardes and Boosey were right, for as a result of Danilo Joe Coyne was to be a favourite with London audiences until the day he died.

Actors so often do not know when they are really suited—especially if they have to try a new line. The stage is terribly conservative in all respects. And most actors always see themselves as something quite different from what they actually are. They are apt to let what they want to do override what they really can do. The art of being a successful actor —or actress—is to do what you can do and do it at your very best. That may not be artistic, but it is good craftsmanship and good sense. But, despite his enormous success in the part, Coyne never liked playing Danilo, and when it was all over said he was glad.

He was an extraordinary man. All theatrical people are a little mad; otherwise they are no good in that crazy place, the Theatre. But Joe had slightly more madness than usual. He had strong likes and dislikes. If he did not like anyone, they knew all about it. If he did, they knew all about it too. It was a matter of extreme difficulty to get him to make up his mind about anything—especially if it was for his own good. One of the present writers had a long-drawn-out and weary task in persuading him to play in *Going Up* at the Gaiety, in which he made an immense success. He was very doubtful about it. But he did it.

He was of a very economical turn of mind. He believed in ready money, but had little faith in banks or investments. He liked to see his cash. For many years he kept his money in a safe deposit in the West End and would go down and count it. He said he would retire when it reached a certain figure. That figure never was reached because he was persuaded to make some investments—or speculations—also against his will, and he suffered for this departure from his custom by losing a lot of money in one of the Wall Street crashes.

That frightened him badly. Indeed, he imagined he was ruined. Even the sight of his own money failed to reassure him. He became more economical than ever. He lived in a top room at the Carlton Hotel, but he

E

did not have meals there. He said he could not afford them. He would wash his own "smalls" in his bedroom and dry his socks and handkerchiefs on the towel rail. It saved him money. He went out to tea most afternoons with his friend, one of the hotel linkmen, and they partook of this meal in a little dairy in the neighbourhood of St. James's Street. His one extravagance was ice cream. Of this he devoured quantities. He would go into the Coventry Street Corner House, at all hours of the day or night, and consume small mountains of it. He said he liked it, and that it kept him fit.

He took the greatest care of his clothes; many of his suits were years old and most of them he had worn on the stage—and acquired. Comment on his smart shoes, and, if he knew you, he would lift up his foot and show the metal "taps" still on the soles. Shirts, collars and ties—all came from the theatre, and he valeted himself with scrupulous care. He walked everywhere; he said it kept him slim and fit. It also saved money.

Despite all the charm he could be most obstinate and difficult. Under stress he would release a flow of invective which was as remarkable for its violence as its variety. He embraced the oaths of both hemispheres. On one occasion he fell out with the then manager of the Gaiety Theatre; it was during the run of *Going Up*. He met the writer of these lines in the Haymarket and, full of his grievance, began to tell his tale. He did so with noise and gestures; a crowd began to collect. So his friend edged him into a shop door, into the porch, as it were. The door stood invitingly open. Coyne continued to pour forth his story, and the swearing was of such a high order that his listener stood amazed. A shop assistant, whose ears it had reached, rushed forward to remonstrate—there were customers in the shop and ladies too! When he saw the source of the rich flow, he lost his head and hesitated. He, like everyone else, knew Joe Coyne. But he shut the door and held it fast, and his agonized face looked through the glass, full of reproach, until at last Joe's friend was able to draw him away. The worst of the storm over, they walked to the Corner House, and Joe was happy with ice cream again.

He appeared in a very ill-fated play at the Globe Theatre during the First World War. It was called *The Clock Goes Round*. He played a Pierrot, a member of a concert party giving their show at the end of a small-town pier. In the cast was an old friend of his from Daly's—Lennox Pawle. Joe had to wear a straw hat in the opening scene, and he was determined that it should be exactly right. He produced an old "boater" of his own—mature in age, but well looked after. He would not let the Property Master "break it down", as the process of mellowing or wrecking something is called backstage. He decided that the thing to do was to expose it to the elements and have it wrecked properly at first hand. So he put it on the roof of the theatre—the month was October—to let rain, fog and soot do their worst—or best. There came a day of high wind—and the straw hat was never seen again. Joe was furious and brokenhearted at the same time.

Although that play was a deadly flop, it was not without a sensation supplied by Mr. Coyne, who could, as said, be the most obstinate of men. The last scene but one showed the interior of a miserable little pavilion in which the troupe appeared. It was after the show, and everyone was full of depression. Joe had to enter with a candle stuck in a bottle and place this illuminant on the little cottage piano. He wore Pierrot's dress, white and with ruffle complete. Naked lights on the stage being taboo, except in special circumstances, an electric candle was fixed into the stone ginger-beer bottle, which looked just like the real thing, and all Joe had to do was to press over a tiny switch at the base. He hated this. He had a dislike for anything mechanical, and he never got the candle to work properly, although there was nothing at all the matter with it. He held the thing in detestation.

On the first night, he rushed on the stage, evading the stage manager, with a real candle, lighted and burning, of course, in a ginger-beer bottle, instead of the electric "prop". Nothing could be done about it. He put the bottle down on the piano and proceeded with his part. The Manager of the theatre was making the customary first-night tour in company with two Inspectors of the London County Council, those bowler-hatted and blue-suited men who are such regular First Nighters in the interests of the public safety, although the public does not notice them. On this occasion they entered the upper circle just in time to see Joe Coyne back into the candle and set his ruffle alight. As it began to flame, with presence of mind he got it off and trod it underfoot, but a great gout of smoke floated through the proscenium arch and into the auditorium. It so happened that the "Take Cover" sounded just then, which rather relieved the situation, so far as the Manager was concerned; but the incident took a good deal of explaining away, and Joe Coyne was made to own up to his misdoing. But all through the run—the very brief run—of that play, the Council Inspectors haunted the building. . . . That was in 1916, nine years after *The Merry Widow*. But at the point our story has reached Coyne was at Daly's, in 1907, with only two London appearances to his credit, going to play a lead at the famous theatre, and doing it against his will.

On the stage Joseph Coyne was unique. Few, very few, men had the mixture of charm, ability and talent which he possessed, and few, very few, ever stormed the hearts of the British Public as did this young American. London not only took him to itself but kept him. He was here so long, and so well beloved, that most people forgot he was an American altogether. He was a complete professional. He had learnt his business the hard way. He had been born in New York, in 1867; so he was forty when he played Danilo. He was of Irish blood, and had all the attractive charm of his race. There was not much money at home, and young Coyne, as a lad, got a job in a sculptors' studio—the job being to keep the clay moist for modelling. He had to work over week-ends to achieve this, when the sculptors were away. But he had a great love of the Theatre; he wanted to be an actor. He used to sneak off and watch shows instead of pouring or sprinkling water over the clay figures. In the end he managed to break a large statue which he had neglected, and he fled for his life.

He then answered an advertisement in a paper, which stated that 100 boys were wanted, but that they must be able to dance. Applicants had to apply at the stage door of Niblo's Garden Theatre. Joe went along and found hundreds of children waiting. Luck was with him. He was in the first twelve tried out, and being loose-limbed, and having a sense of dancing which was inherent, he was amongst the six lads who were chosen. He was part of the ballet in the big spectacular show called *Excelsior*, which was produced by those brothers of genius, the Királfys. It ran a year, and when it went on tour Joe Coyne went with it.

Next he teamed up with a friend, Frank Evans, and as Evans and Coyne they worked the Music Halls and anywhere they could get a job. They also became part of a circus, with blacked faces; Coyne played the drums as well. Then, when he was twenty, Joseph Coyne became a real actor. He joined a stock company, but it was just an appendage of a big circus. The Circus seemed to dominate Coyne. After that he joined another company, which specialized in visiting stars. This little crowd would rehearse a play, and then a visiting star would come and act the leading part amongst them for a week. It was hard and unrewarding work, but it was fine experience.

Fortune, however, was to find Joe Coyne, and it happened when he was playing a very cheap theatre in New York. Fate took the form of a queer little man, very reserved, with a shy but sweet smile, who came round such places to see if there was any talent about. He was a man of international fame, but he went out himself to look for talent. His name was Charles Frohman. He saw Coyne, and he knew he had discovered something, and from that moment Joseph Coyne had been upon the up grade, which had now landed him at Daly's Theatre to play a leading rôle for George Edwardes. And as, at rehearsals, he looked sadder and sadder, muttered to himself about his part, and dreaded the opening night, he had as little idea of the next trick of Fate as he had the night he stepped on the stage of that obscure New York theatre and caught the eye of Frohman.

So much for the Danilo—what of the Sonia, as she was called in the English version—the Merry Widow herself? George Edwardes had entrusted that rôle to a young lady named Lily Elsie. It was a big star rôle, but at that time Lily Elsie was not a big star—indeed, she was not a star at all. She was born of the Theatre, she had almost a lifetime of experience behind her, but she had not yet made a real impression. Yet the Guvnor cast her for Sonia.

She had been born at Wortley, near Leeds, in 1886, so she was only twenty-one when Fame came to her. She had made her first appearance at the age of eleven in *Little Red Riding Hood*, a pantomime, at the old Queen's Theatre, Manchester. She had lived in Salford since she was two, and she was not a strong child. Her parents did not encourage her to go on the stage, but they did not deter her either, for, from her earliest years, she had shown a considerable gift of mimicry. She went on the Music Halls next, as "Little Elsie". And there a young man saw her and thought her very good. He was only a struggling young actor himself at the time, but he knew Quality when he saw it and talked about this clever and pretty little girl to everyone. Little did he dream that, in the future, they would be associated in one of the most dramatic stories in the history of the stage, at one of the world's most famous theatres, Daly's. The young man's name was George Graves.

When Little Elsie had reached the mature age of fourteen years she joined a show called *McKenna's Flirtation*. That landed her in pantomime in London; if not in the West End, still at a very famous theatre—the Britannia, Hoxton, where she played Arielle in *King Klondike*. That was in 1898. She then went into musical comedy, in a touring company of Tom B. Davis's playing *The Silver Slipper*. In 1901 pantomime again claimed her, once more in the London suburbs, and she was Alice Fitzwarren in *Dick Whittington* at the Camden Theatre, and Morgiana in *The Forty Thieves* at the Coronet, Notting Hill Gate, in 1902. More musical comedy followed; on tour in *Three Little Maids* she played Hilda Moody's part, singing "She was a Miller's Daughter".

Now she received an offer for a show which was to go to Town. George Dance had seen her and asked her to play Princess Soo-Soo in *A Chinese Honeymoon*. Miss Lily Elsie, as she now called herself (her real name was Cotton), did not jump at it. She was rather afraid of the West End; she was not sure she was ready; she was only sixteen. But she took the part—after persuasion by Frank Curzon and the pressure of the already forceful Dance—and this lovely young girl, slim and graceful as a willow wand, with the direct gaze and complete unconcern about her beauty, made a big hit. Her song "Egypt, my Cleopatra" became very popular indeed.

George Edwardes now became aware of her. He wanted her for *The Duchess of Dantzig*, but Dance had a prior claim—subject to pantomime again at the Coronet, where she played Fatima in *Blue Beard*—and he wanted her for *Madame Sherry*. But she did eventually join Edwardes in *Lady Madcap* at the Prince of Wales's, where she served her apprenticeship for him, and afterwards he gave her Isabel Jay's part in *The Cingalee* on tour. He watched her and brought her along by degrees. He gave her a small part at Daly's in *The Little Michus*; he gave her a leading part in *The Little Cherub* at the Prince of Wales's in 1906; but in his own parlance, that show was a "nitter". So was Lily Elsie's next venture under the Edwardes banner, *See See* at the same theatre in the same year.

In the September of 1906 she opened at the Gaiety as lead in *The New Aladdin*. She looked delightful, she sang and danced delightfully; but the show was something of a throwback to the old tradition of burlesque; it was not true Gaiety. Moreover there had been a leading lady at the Gaiety who *was* the epitome of its spirit, named Gertie Millar, but who was not in *The New Aladdin* when it opened. In the end she came back, and Lily Elsie went out. She was not of the Gaiety either; she was of Romance, she was not of the champagne sparkle. And so Edwardes selected her to play the lead in a show which had been bought for the Gaiety but was not truly a Gaiety show, and had the luck to dodge the fate which would have befallen it had it been produced there. Neither Lily Elsie nor *The Merry Widow* were Gaiety, but both of them were essentially Daly's. The disaster at Daly's which let in the Lehár operette was Kismet for the play and its leading lady—and for its composer as well.

Edwardes was quite sure Lily Elsie could play Sonia. His assistants, in many cases, did not share his view. Nor did William Boosey. Edwardes packed Miss Elsie off to Vienna to see the play. She went, and she saw it twice. She did not understand German. She saw a lady of stately figure playing the part which Edwardes told her was to be hers, and playing it in a manner which was as foreign to Lily Elsie as the language of the play itself. It was not her line; she had done nothing like it. She could not play it, she said. Edwardes laughed at her, though his staff agreed with the actress. However, the Guvnor had made up his mind. Lily Elsie and nobody else was to be Sonia. . . .

But now things were growing difficult. Never had Edwardes been so hard pressed. His Edwardesian Empire was on the brink. It might topple. Money was so scarce as to be almost extinct in the Treasury. But the show had to go on. Edwardes, a born gambler, took the gamble. He would do his best with what he had. But this piece could only be a stop-gap. It might keep up the curtain; it might even tide things over; but they must press on with the show to follow it with all speed and at any cost. He must raise money for that, and meanwhile he must also present *The Merry Widow*, and, as it was a George Edwardes production, it must look like one, too.

He did not expect much. He told W. H. Berry himself that he thought they might get six weeks out of it. Consequently he would not spend much, and indeed he had not much to spend. For the first time in his career he utilized old scenery; the Garden scene was actually out of *Les Merveilleuses*, turned about a bit, touched up and repainted, and with the Pavilion added. Although Lucile and Pascaud made some of the dresses, most of the costumes were the work of the wonderful Mrs. Field, in Daly's own wardrobe, who did all those amazing dresses which Lily Elsie wore with such beauty. It was as quick and as cheap a job as ever Edwardes did. But his genius and his impeccable taste made it look a million dollars; his knowledge of technique and his magic touch achieved what would have been impossible for anyone else.

And so, in the summer of 1907, up to his neck in trouble, George Edwardes started rehearsals of his latest Daly's show, with two leading people who were not recognized West End stars, and an operette by a composer who was unknown in London in that capacity. *The Merry Widow*, in fact, was repeating her continental history. . . . That is how Franz Lehár came to London Town.

CHAPTER SEVEN

Crisis at Daly's

IN that spring and early summer of 1907, when there was a crisis in the Edwardesian Empire, what was happening in the Edwardian Empire itself? There was plenty going on, for the Age of Opulence was at its height. The speed of life was quickening. The vitality and humanity of the King who reigned and had given his name to the era had broken the shackles of the Victorian Age, but had not destroyed the leisure and grace, had indeed added to them. There was more open display, more entertaining in public, more travelling; and although the conventions were still strictly observed, still there was a tolerance which could not have happened under the austerity of the old Queen.

This country was fabulously rich and was the centre of the finance of the world. The rigid family life of the older days was relaxing, restaurants were more crowded and more numerous, and were the resort of both sexes. They were brighter, gayer, and orchestras played at meal time. That life moved more speedily was because the internal combustion engine was steadily ousting the horse—although that still held its place—and the first glimmer of the Age of Speed was dimly discernible away on the horizon. But it was a rich and happy world, and above all it was secure. It seemed likely to go on for ever. People talked of Progress; but the future to which that Progress was to lead—the wars of overwhelming magnitude—was not guessed at. Great Britain was still an island, unassailable and invincible; of that its people were quite sure.

In the year when *The Merry Widow* was to make her London début, much was happening all the world over. There was a terrible earthquake in Jamaica, assassinations in Russia and, as usual, disaster on the biggest scale in China. There was an enthralling Murder. William Whiteley, founder of the gigantic store in Westbourne Grove, the man who was called "The Universal Provider", was shot in his own emporium by a man called Rayner, who claimed to be his illegitimate son. It was a widely discussed and widely publicized piece of homicide, or patricide. Rayner was found guilty, sentenced to death, and reprieved. A British submarine blew up in Portsmouth Harbour. A French battleship did the same thing at Toulon, and caused much loss of life. The liner *Suevic* ran on the Shark's Fin Rock near the Lizard, in a fog. She remained upright, the rock impaling her. Everyone was saved, and eventually the ship was sawn in half, taken to dry dock in sections, joined together again, and continued to sail the seas. A French ship *Poictou* was not so lucky; she was lost with a casualty list of one hundred, and the s.s. *Santiago* foundered off Chile with great loss of life, too. The Great Eastern Railway steamer s.s. *Berlin* went ashore in a violent storm off the Hook of Holland and again lives were lost. The Prince Consort of the Queen of Holland worked at the rescue. But to counterbalance all that, the wonder ship s.s. *Mauretania* took the sea, won the Blue Riband of the Atlantic, and remained for years the best liner ever launched.

The Liberal Party was in power, swept into Government with a huge majority the previous year on the issue of Free Trade and Chinese Labour on the Rand. Sir Henry Campbell-Bannerman was Prime Minister. The Conservative Party, led by A. J. Balfour, who had been unseated in the 1906 election, but had got back again, preferred to call themselves the Unionist Party, being against Home Rule for Ireland. And already Labour was a growing power, for there were no less than thirty-six Labour Members in Parliament in 1907 (there was occasionally a confusing subtitle of "Liberal-Labour", or Lib.-Lab.). The group included such men as John Burns (who attained Cabinet rank), Keir Hardie, the first Labour M.P. ever to be elected, Dr. Macnamara, Will Crooks, Richard Bell, and G. N. Barnes. But the bulk of the people did not as yet take this movement seriously.

There was labour unrest also, bad strikes at Belfast organized by Jim Larkin, and on account of them the military took over, in field kit of khaki, to the astonishment of all that such things could be. There was some rioting in Trafalgar Square, too, occasioned by Municipal Reform. And there were also riots by women, the Suffragettes, at Westminster. The Feminist Movement was gathering momentum, although laughed to scorn. Women were challenging the men, and 1907 saw the first Women's Rowing Club on the Thames. The ladies wore high-necked sweaters, blue serge skirts and had their hair coiffured; they pulled two oars each. Moreover, they had a mere male as a cox. But there they were, all the same.

Death took its toll of celebrities all over the world in 1907. Lord

Kelvin, the great scientist, Sir Benjamin Baker, builder of dams, Viscount Goschen, famous banker and Chancellor of the Exchequer, and Lord Brampton, eminent lawyer and Judge, were amongst those who passed in this country. Lord Brampton, before his elevation to the Peerage, had been Sir Henry Hawkins, one of the deadliest of cross-examiners at the Bar. On elevation to the Bench he became a most severe figure and was called "the Hanging Judge".

Grieg, the famous Norwegian composer (of Scottish descent), and Joachim were two great figures in the world of music who died in 1907. In America, Theodore Roosevelt was President, a man of immense drive, who had fought in the field, been a rough-rider, and whose greatest claim to fame in this country was the fact that his nickname of "Teddie" was applied to the immortally popular Teddie Bear. There was another step in the evolution of the British Empire into the Commonwealth of Nations. New Zealand became a Dominion, a status already reached by Canada and Australia.

It was also the dawn of the Electric Age. Electric light was gradually ousting gas, and a great step forward in the development of electricity was the establishment at Glace Bay, in Canada, of the first Transatlantic Wireless Station, under the direction of Marconi. People spoke of it with wonder, but had not the vaguest idea of the marvels which would evolve from it—the marvels of Radio and Television, of Radar, of telephonic communication with ships at sea and planes in the air, and all the things taken for granted today. Electricity also challenged the growing dominance of the Motor Bus, for the London Electrobus put a vehicle on the road which was run by electricity and promptly christened by the Public the "Battery Bus", because it had frequently to be recharged. The petrol bus won.

Electricity challenged the motor-cars as well. The electric brougham did certainly gain a good deal of popularity amongst the wealthier classes, who could afford such things, for motors were then the prerogative of the rich and not the universal possession they are today. The leisured ladies with plenty of money found the electric brougham extremely smart for shopping expeditions and theatre-going. It resembled the brougham from which it took its name, but it was driven by a chauffeur who sat perched up on the box in front, much as the coachman did on a horse brougham. He drove and guided the car by means of a tiller. But he rather spoiled the effect, for he made the vehicle look top-heavy and liable to tip forwards. There was nothing in front of him to balance the line. When going downhill, in such streets as The Haymarket, this top-heavy look was most apparent. But the electric broughams were modern and smart and therefore esteemed by the members of what was then known as "the

Smart Set". They ran along swiftly and very silently. Also, of course, the car being like a brougham, the occupants were under cover.

But electric broughams did not last for very long, and the ordinary motor-car went steadily forward. In those days they were mostly open cars, with a hood to be drawn across the top in the event of inclement weather. They were increasing in size, in horse-power—the touring cars were mostly 25–30 h.p.—and in reliability. In 1907 there was another innovation. Steel-studded tyres became the rage. This was to prevent skidding and to give extra durability. There was a curious swishing noise, as a result, when the cars moved over the asphalt or wooden-blocked roads, as if they were either splashing up water or scattering dry leaves.

The motor was enthroned, not only as a means of transport but in the world of sport as well. It was the prime mover in the quickening tempo, and nothing shows this more than the fact that Brooklands, the great car-racing track, opened in 1907. There was a long parade of cars, of varied makes and sizes, all rather high at the back, and the drivers wore serge suits, stiff collars and caps. Lord Lonsdale, the Prime Minister of all sports, and Lord Carnarvon were in the cavalcade. And then S. F. Edge, at Brooklands, showed how far the car had advanced, for he did a non-stop run of 24 hours during which time he covered 1581 miles 1310 yards at the average pace of 60 miles an hour, the speed of the express trains of the day. Speed also was remarkable at sea, for the *Mauretania*, one of the finest ships the world has ever seen, with her four funnels and her "happy" disposition, at once secured the Blue Riband of the Atlantic. She did the eastward trip to New York in 4 days 17 hours and 21 minutes, and the westward in 4 days 10 hours and 51 minutes. When she was quite an old ship, at a time of need, she broke the record with an even faster speed. Her maiden voyage was in November 1907.

Men began to invade the air. A British airship flew from Aldershot to the Crystal Palace and caused much excitement. It was called *Nulli Secundus*. But it was wrecked by a gale whilst at its moorings. A French airship *Patrie* flew from Chalais-Meudon across Paris and back again, with Clemenceau aboard. A week later it became a total wreck. But a German airship flew from Tegel to Berlin and back again and was not wrecked then or later. Sport was of supreme importance, and produced some sensations. But the greatest sensation of all in the sporting world of 1907 was the theft of the Gold Cup at Ascot, which somebody stole from right under the noses of its custodians and with a big crowd of people all round. To this day how it was done or by whom is not known. The race for that Cup was won by Solly (S. B.) Joel, to whom a duplicate was given. The policeman who had charge of that Cup later joined the theatrical profession—or at least he worked in a theatre. He became a janitor at the

Palm Court at the London Palladium. But there is a link between that stolen trophy and George Edwardes, for he built the story of one of his greatest Gaiety successes, *Our Miss Gibbs*, around the episode.

In 1907 Orby won the Derby and Cambridge the Boat Race. The Grand National was won by Eremon, the Two Thousand Guineas by Slieve Gallion, the One Thousand Guineas by Witch Elm, the Oaks by Glass Doll, the St. Leger by Wool Winder, the Cesarewitch by Demure and the Cambridgeshire by Land League. Velocity carried off the City and Suburban. The Blue Riband of the Coursing world, the Waterloo Cup, was won by that famous greyhound Long Span.

J. Ball was the amateur golf champion and Arnaud Massy the Open Champion. Sheffield Wednesday won the F.A. Cup and Newcastle United the League Championship. Notts was the Champion County in cricket, and N. Brookes was Lawn Tennis Champion. Lieutenant Addison won the King's Prize at Bisley. There was road-racing for cars, too, for the Tourist Trophy was held in the Isle of Man. And the growing interest in aviation, not purely as a sport but as a thing of the future, was shown by the fact that the Aero Club held its first trial for model aeroplanes at the Alexandra Palace in 1907. These were not toys but actual experimental models.

Owners of motor-bicycles and side-cars today may be interested in the fact that there were such things in 1907, though very unlike the swift vehicles of the present. The so-called side-car was actually in front— slightly to the left of the driver, but ahead of him; the bicycle had two front wheels and one at the back, and the handle-bars were not handle-bars but a steering-wheel, as with a car.

Great Britain really ruled the waves, with a Navy larger than any combination which two other Great Powers could bring against her, and her Merchant Fleet was overwhelming—she was the carrier for the world.

King Edward VII and his beautiful wife, Queen Alexandra, were tremendously popular. He was called "Teddie" amongst the people, and although they thumped him on the back when he led in his Derby winner —he won that race twice—they would never have dared to take a liberty in his presence. For, although a man of geniality and charm, and nothing like the despotic disciplinarian which Queen Victoria had been, he was nevertheless every inch a King, and Royalty was held in the greatest respect. He understood his people, and they understood him. He was a sportsman, and that endeared him to everyone. He was also a very astute man indeed, and a remarkably able statesman and diplomat. Those were the days of Kings and Queens; Europe was full of them. And King Edward VII not only delighted to receive them as visitors but would go to foreign lands himself. He took the power of his Empire with him.

Queen Victoria had been for years a recluse. The King went about the world as he had gone about his own country. He saw for himself, he judged for himself, he was indeed a man of the world in every sense. Those visits did immense good. In 1907 he paid visits to France, to Ireland, to the Austrian Empire—to Vienna, indeed—and he even visited his nephew, the Kaiser, in Berlin. There was no love lost between these two and never had been. King Edward had expressed the opinion that his nephew Wilhelm was no gentleman, the most sweeping and damning condemnation of Edwardian times. But, to the outward eye at least, this visit of 1907 was a success. And these State visits made King Edward—called Edward the Peacemaker—very popular abroad, except perhaps in Germany, which gazed with envious eyes on the British Empire, hated the diplomacy which had brought about the *Entente Cordiale* with France —largely the King's work—and wanted, for its steadily increasing population, what it called "a Place in the Sun".

King Edward was very popular in Vienna, and he was very fond of the Austrians. He enjoyed his visit in 1907, and there was no shadow upon it. There had always been friendship between Austria and Britain. It did not seem conceivable then that a shot fired on Austrian soil, at Sarajevo —where Lehár's father had once lived—would, by killing an Austrian Grand Duke, cause that somewhat ramshackle Empire to fire the first shot of the carnage which started in 1914 and changed the whole world. No such cloud darkened the horizon in 1907, and the last seven years—seven is always a somewhat mystic number—of the old and secure world were entering upon their cycle.

King Edward VII knew and liked George Edwardes. The Gaiety was his favourite theatre; he and his Queen attended the first night of the New Gaiety when it reopened—a signal honour—and Edwardes very nearly missed receiving his Royal guest. But if Edward VII, as King and Emperor of his wide domains, knew no cause for anxiety, it was not so with George Edwardes in the Edwardesian Empire, which he himself had created. In 1907 that Empire was in straits, and there was trouble in one of its twin capitals, Daly's Theatre.

The events enumerated above did not matter, of course, to the people at Daly's. They were almost oblivious of the outside world, and, with true theatrical self-concentration, paid attention only to what went on inside the four walls in which they worked, although they took a little interest in what was happening in the other theatres. In 1907, what was going on? There was trouble in the world of the Music Hall. The newly formed Trade Union, The Variety Artists' Federation, was trying its immature strength against the managerial giants of the Variety world. There was a Music Hall Strike. The artists wanted a Standard Contract. They did not get it. So they struck. Nearly all the big stars supported the strike and came out. The whole thing was conducted as one would expect it to be by such a volatile and exuberant set of people. The public were solidly on the side of the artists and greatly resented being unable to see their favourites in such of the Halls as managed to remain open. Eventually a compromise was reached, but the artists got nearly all they wanted.

In the legitimate theatre the actor-managers still reigned. It was one of the very brightest epochs of the British Theatre. The leader of the Profession, since the death of Sir Henry Irving, was Herbert Beerbohm Tree. In 1907 he had taken his company from His Majesty's Theatre—as regal in appearance and in his method of conducting it as in its name—to Berlin. His presentation of the British way of staging and acting deeply impressed the Germans, and the visit was a resounding success. Tree himself was not so impressed—it took a lot to impress him—and his love of a joke broke out the moment he stepped from the train in Berlin and was received with much pomp and dignity, bowing and heel-clicking by the officials of that city and of the German Theatre. He responded with that grace which was his, that almost majestical manner, and with the greatest of courtesy; but he murmured, *sotto voce*, to one of his chief assistants, the late Stanley Bell, "Stanley, Stanley, what a lot of foreigners!" Berlin flocked to his season, special trips were run from distant cities, the Kaiser paid two official visits, and Tree was given the German Order of the Crown. Back in his own theatre he gave a series of classic revivals with magnificent staging and casts.

Actor-manager Seymour Hicks, with his wife, the delightful Ellaline Terriss, as lovely today as then, were at the Aldwych with a musical comedy *The Gay Gordons*, of which Hicks also wrote the libretto. At the Apollo was *Tom Jones*, score by Edward German, with Hayden Coffin, Dan Rolyat, Carrie Moore and Ruth Vincent in the cast. Theatre Royal, Drury Lane, had a tremendous drama, *The Sins of Society*, the company of which included Constance Collier, Albert Chevalier, Fanny Brough and Lyn Harding. The Haymarket staged *Sweet Kitty Bellairs*, produced by that brilliant American *metteur en-scène* David Belasco, with Eva Moore as the enchanting widow, supported by Henry Neville, Owen Roughwood and Louis Calvert. Gerald du Maurier was at the Hicks Theatre, now the Globe, in Shaftesbury Avenue, playing in *Brewster's Millions* (which has since been turned into a musical play under another title); Cyril Maude, who had just been able to get into his new managerial home, the Playhouse (rebuilt after its accident when a railway station fell on it), was appearing in *The Earl of Pawtucket*, with the exquisite Alexandra Carlisle.

The delectable *Miss Hook of Holland*—music by Paul Rubens, who had wanted to buy *The Merry Widow*—was packing the Prince of Wales's. Its cast included Isabel Jay, Gracie Leigh, Pope Stamper, George Barrett and G. P. Huntley. There was a popular success at Wyndham's, where James Welsh was making all London laugh in *When Knights Were Bold*. George Alexander, during 1907, staged *A Builder of Bridges* by Sutro and *The Thief*, from the French of Henri Bernstein, at the St. James's Theatre, with Irene Vanbrugh as his leading lady. And at Edwardes's other capital, the Gaiety, *The Girls of Gottenburg* glittered, with Gertie Millar, May de Sousa, Jean Alwyn, Charles Brown, Robert Hale, Edmund Payne and George Grossmith to make it sparkle, froth and shine. In this musical play, in a small part, was a lovely young girl whose name was Gladys Cooper.

There were successes and failures; but nowhere in all theatreland was there a crisis as there was at Daly's, where George Edwardes, the Guvnor, was preparing for a gamble with Fate, a gamble for which the stakes were the population of London, who swirled about the theatre all day, as playgoers. That population differed materially from the population of other capital cities. Edwardes was preparing to bid for its favours with a musical play from Vienna, a city which had not sent much to London in the way of entertainment—save waltz music and Opera—a city whose manners and tastes were very different from London's, a great city but a metropolis of a very different kind.

A picture of the Vienna which greeted *The Merry Widow* has been given. A companion picture of the London of 1907 may not be out of place. Its immense wealth and its unique position in the world have been mentioned. Its life, its manners and its customs were as different from those of Vienna as chalk is from cheese. The greatest difference was on the surface, obvious to the most casual observer. Vienna was a city of uniforms, of military uniforms of such variety and type that they bewildered the eye and made splashes of colour everywhere. In London, except for the sombre blue of the policeman, you might search in vain for a uniform, save at fixed points like The Horse Guards or Buckingham and St. James's Palaces. Now and again a private soldier or a trooper in undress uniform, out for the evening, might add a touch of scarlet to the crowd, but so rarely as to be quite an event. Officers you never saw, for the moment an officer of the British Army was off parade he would get into mufti with the greatest possible speed. Dislike of a uniform is inherent in the Englishman—at least, the dislike of wearing a uniform. Much as he may respect that for which it stands, and its tradition, he feels a fool when he wears it. No political party which insisted on its members wearing coloured shirts could hope to succeed here.

So London was a city of civilians—uniforms at a discount. It was, however, a very well-dressed city, so far as the City and the West End went. It was uniform in that respect; men dressed alike, though they dressed well. The informality which occurs today was unthought of then. Men wore the frock coat and topper, the morning coat and topper, the lounge suit and bowler—the most distinctive article of national dress—or the straw hat in summer. An increasing number of the younger ones were wearing coloured shirts, but of sober hue. The middle-aged and elderly clung to the white shirt with the starched front and cuffs. Nearly every man—and all men who had any claim to be well dressed—wore gloves and carried either a walking-stick or an umbrella. Their boots shone; few wore shoes. These boots were of black leather, glacé kid, box calf or patent leather, either complete or with cloth tops. The collars were mostly double-fold, of linen, but with frock or morning coats either the "stick up" or the butterfly collar was worn.

Ties were a matter of taste, but never flamboyant—to wear a loud tie was to be a "bounder". A man seen wearing a neat bow tie was usually a "professional". But for country wear the soft collar had arrived—though not for town. King Edward was a leader of male fashion, and he had dealt a blow at the bowler by wearing the Homburg hat—hitherto referred to as a "Trilby". But the Homburg, although much less formal than the bowler, had nothing of the ultra-bohemianism that the wider, floppier and sombre-hued Trilby proclaimed. For the Homburg made fashionable by King Edward was of green velours.

There was, of course, nothing of the café life of Vienna. London had little use for such continental nonsense—nor had it the climate. It was loyal to its public houses, and it consumed far stronger liquor than now and in greater quantities. The licensed hours were longer, much longer, then, and pubs were open all day. There was a good deal more drunkenness than we see nowadays. Few people drank coffee, except after dinner, but the tea-shops were crowded.

There was not a gay air about London, such as Vienna possessed. But there was not an air of depression, either. London, if it did not laugh and gesticulate, wore a continual smile of satisfaction and the happiness bred of wealth and security, and enjoyed a feeling of superiority to the rest of the world. The bulk of it lived in the suburbs, but it came to town at night, with the fixed determination that it was going to enjoy itself—and it always did. It could do so very cheaply because money went such a very long way.

"Society" still existed and dominated the social life of the capital. The aristocracy still claimed respect and got it. The Season was a time when London shone. Its mansions were repainted; they were gay with window-boxes of flowers; at nights the windows glowed with light. Its great

Lily Elsie and Joseph Coyne as Sonia and Danilo

Joseph Coyne as Danilo

Top: The lovers in the last act of *The Merry Widow*—at Maxim's. Joseph Coyne as Danilo and Lily Elsie as Sonia. *Bottom left*: Lily Elsie as Sonia and Joseph Coyne as Danilo, in Marsovian costume, about to perform the national dance of their country. *Bottom right*: Lily Elsie as Sonia, the Merry Widow, in Marsovian costume

houses gave wonderful receptions, and crowds would gather to watch the line of carriages, interspersed with cars, set down their loads of beautiful women, no less beautifully dressed. A-shimmer with jewels, and the very embodiment of femininity, they, with their immaculate male escorts in "faultless evening dress", would pass between the line of liveried footmen on the steps and come under the aegis of the butler as they crossed the threshold. At the top of handsome staircases stood the host and hostess to welcome the famous who came to see them, while those outside caught snatches of the strains of the Viennese or Hungarian Band, which discoursed music only half heard inside above the chatter of conversation. Vienna had got that far; it supplied a lot of waltz tunes and orchestras calling themselves Viennese to play them.

There was every conceivable luxury to eat and drink, and vintage wine was apparently laid on at the mains. The Season was the time for Opera too, and London rallied the great singers of the world, Melba, Caruso, Scotti, the De Reszkes, Calvé, Kirkby Lunn, the finest international artists of all lands. Opera was not expected to pay. It was run by a Syndicate supported by wealthy music lovers and Society people. It was a social occasion. An average night at the Opera outshone the Gala Performances of today. It was an event of the Season; but earlier in the year, as a rule, Opera in English, sung by the Royal Carl Rosa Company usually, did pretty well, too. And Covent Garden Opera House was famous for something else—the Covent Garden Balls at which Londoners —and others—of all ages revelled the nights away with a full-blooded enjoyment and lack of respectability equal to that of any other capital in the world.

Architecturally London was very different from Vienna; its vastness overshadowed it; its amazing mixtures of styles made it unique if not beautiful. Edwardian days were adding their quota to the changing face of the town, giving a lighter touch to the utilitarian heaviness of the Victorian additions and alterations. There was still enough left of Georgian London to give the city grace and manner, and many of the magnificent old mansions still stood, like great country houses surrounded by a sea of bricks and mortar. London was then, far more than now, a collection of townlets and villages, each with an atmosphere and nature of its own. Belgravia, Mayfair and Bayswater still had their houses where distinguished families lived and held court, occupying the whole house, with staffs of domestics, and spending money on which tradespeople flourished and grew rich. The descendants of those people now live in the mews and servants' quarters—and pay more rent than their grandparents paid for the mansions.

Commerce had not swallowed so much of the West End. Piccadilly

F

was still largely a residential thoroughfare; Berkeley Square, Grosvenor Square, Belgrave Square had separate houses instead of blocks of offices and flats. This was where *Debrett's* listed notabilities lived, and the people who were in *Who's Who*. Regent Street, Oxford Street and Bond Street were the fashionable shopping centres; there was even a fashionable hour in fashionable Bond Street.

These streets were mostly the domain of women; St. James's belonged to the men. That, too, was clubland, and you would see the gentlemen of England at the right hour, perfectly dressed, taking their stroll and going to their clubs. They were quiet, unassuming, well-set-up men, who, if they all looked very much like one another, owed it to the fact that they had all been to public schools and Universities, whose mould had fashioned them. If they worked at all they followed the profession of arms, either at sea or on land, the Church, or the Law. And those young men of the Royal Navy and the Army, though they did not wear their uniforms in the streets, were extremely brave and gallant soldiers, even if the backbone of the small, professional volunteer army was the highly professional non-commissioned officer. In 1907 the Army had not forgotten the lesson learned in the Boer War. But still, they had won, they had always won. It was a different tradition from that of Vienna.

The predominant note amongst the women of 1907 was femininity. Dresses were long and very full; legs were hidden from view; the sight of an ankle when a skirt was held up on a muddy day was tantalizing to the male. Women wore long hair, elaborately coiffured; but mostly they did it themselves, and they wore a minimum of make-up. To make up or to dye the hair was "fast"—and to be "fast" was to lose respectability. Women would never have dreamed of wearing trousers or of smoking in the streets. Advanced ladies, lighting a cigarette in a restaurant, were nearly always requested, most politely but most firmly, either to desist or leave. And whilst the women kept within the fashion which prevailed, they adapted it to suit their personality, so that each had her own individual note. Hats were large, and petticoats many. Underclothing was a secret; it was lacy, foamy and of a most enchanting nature, but even the shop windows forbore to display its full charm to the public eye.

These women moved with grace and knew how to walk, how to enter a room and how to sit in and rise from a chair. The evening dress was off the shoulders, but a thing of flounces and wide sleeves with puffs, womanly to a degree. Only the wealthy had fur coats. Suburban ladies got as near to their richer sisters as they could. Business girls—their numbers increasing—wore skirts and blouses. The high heels tapped on the pavement. It was a period of fur or feather necklets, scarves and stoles. The feminine attire was of bits and pieces adding up to a bewitching whole.

Yet a lady from Vienna was soon to start a new fashion which conquered the women of England—at least as regards their hats.

There were sights to be seen which have vanished. There were the Court Drawing Rooms, with their never-ending queue of carriages down the Mall, inside of which sat débutantes and Society matrons in all the glory of Court Dress, gazed at by the envious eyes of other women, and the object of ribald remarks from less reverent and proletarian males. There was the daily carriage drive round Hyde Park, the Church Parade on Sunday; there was Henley when it was a Social Function and Boulter's Lock on Ascot Sunday, with the men cool and efficient in their white flannels and the ladies most expensive, elaborate, and gloriously unsuitable in special creations for that special day. It was also the day of the parasol, for complexions had to be preserved. It was a time of plenty and prosperity.

Those who were not rich had a very good time, too. If they did not frequent the cafés as in Vienna, and did not want the very English pub, but still wanted drink, and a bit of laughter, there were plenty of places which, being in England, adopted the English habit of compromise. At the Café de l'Europe, in Leicester Square, and at scores of similar resorts, one could sit at tables, drink what one liked, and chaff the ladies of the town. The fact that all the waiters were foreign—mostly German—added to the Briton's satisfaction, and for the matter of that most of the gay ladies were foreign, too. There was the Empire Promenade and that of the Alhambra—the twin homes of ballet, if you wanted to look at it. And if you liked a truly British evening out there was the Music Hall, from which at closing-time poured crowds of laughing, happy people, whistling and singing the latest, most British hit tunes.

Ten shillings would give you a wonderful evening, and leave change for the journey home, by horse or motor bus, by Underground or tram, by hansom or taxi. Also you could get very near to a continental evening at Earl's Court. And, of course, there was the Theatre. That Theatre sold branded goods; you knew what you would get wherever you went. You knew what to expect at His Majesty's, at the Haymarket, at Drury Lane. You knew what art you would see if you visited a play in which Wyndham, Hare, Hawtrey, Lewis Waller, Martin-Harvey, Julia Neilson and Fred Terry, Alexander or Arthur Bourchier were performing, or, for the matter of that, Oscar Asche and Lily Brayton. You could rely on the musical shows of Frank Curzon and Robert Courtneidge, and if you wanted Variety which was not Music Hall there was the Palace. And above all, there was, for so many of the people of London, the Gaiety and Daly's— the domain of George Edwardes.

So, in 1907, life circled around Daly's—that very solid but very secure and very happy life of London, the world's greatest city, the world's richest city and the world's safest city, with a minimum of crime and no fear of armed burglary or beatings-up. A London which above all stood for Quality, and demanded Quality from those who sold it goods and from those who sold it amusement. It was accustomed to have it. And from nobody had it received it in fuller measure than from George Edwardes, who now in Daly's Theatre faced his greatest problem. He knew that public, and one of his sayings was that the public was never wrong. He was in a bit of bother now; he must have been wrong. It was necessary to find something new; he thought he had got the answer in his recently acquired *Dollar Princess*. But meanwhile the fort must be held. A stop-gap must go in. So Vienna must show itself to London; a lady from Vienna must take the Daly's stage; a lady who was a widow, and who had quite a new message to deliver. Would it be understood? Edwardes prayed it might be, but, in his heart of hearts, he did not think so. . . .

Outside Daly's the life of London surged through Leicester Square. That was the centre of the entertainment world, holding equal place with the Strand and Shaftesbury Avenue. It was cosmopolitan by day; but when evening fell, in the days before Daylight Saving, when a gloaming made a prelude to the night's joy, it became the hunting-ground of Londoners, native and visitors, who were out to capture pleasure. They expected to find it at Daly's, which had become an institution, its success achieved by a certain policy and largely by teamwork. But now Edwardes was going to venture on something new. He had done that before and triumphed. But always his ventures had been home-made. He did not like importations. He had adapted plays for the Gaiety, it is true, making them into something very different from their original, and wedding them to British music. But he did not like these plays from abroad, despite the success of *Véronique*. Look at what had happened to *The Little Michus* and *Les Merveilleuses*, which had come from Paris! He had refused to have anything to do with *The Belle of New York*, and when that musical play triumphed, still he did not care. He did not like it; he thought it vulgar.

Now he had turned to Vienna. He had turned to a composer new to the London Theatre, Franz Lehár, who must perforce challenge the established giants in that land, the Moncktons, the Rubenses, the Carylls, the Talbots, the Joneses, the Edward Germans. He had his doubts, grave doubts. He had done all he could with the means at his disposal. If money had been short and time just as short, he was going to give it the best he could—his own supervision, his own touch of genius and the finest cast he could rally. Maybe six weeks' grace. . . .

He called the first rehearsal. The company crowded on to the stage at

Daly's. According to his custom, he, George Edwardes, the Guvnor, sat at his table down against the footlights in front of the dropped iron curtain. Outwardly calm, inwardly torn by anxiety, he wondered what was going to happen. Would this be lucky, or would it be another defeat? Neither he nor the company foresaw that they were to be prime movers in nothing short of a revolution in musical plays as the first rehearsal of *The Merry Widow* began.

The battle was on. Would the Edwardesian Empire be restored to security? Would George Edwardes save the day? He had to fight for the favour of British playgoers, only the word used would have been "English", not "British", in those days. He had as his battleground Daly's Theatre, built for an American, bearing an American's name, which he however had made supremely British. That was one reason for his success. For the playgoers were British to the backbone in the days of Edwardian insularity. They preferred their entertainment to be in their own idiom. Despite the wide outlook of the King, despite the Homburg hat, the Edwardian days had brought a reaction against the Teutonic dominance of the early and middle periods of the Victorian age. Playgoers preferred to "buy British".

Edwardes had tried French goods at Daly's—and he had failed. Londoners preferred to go to Paris rather than have Paris brought to them. Now he was going to offer them Vienna, although the setting was Paris. Would the British people accept it, they who had such an easy contempt for foreigners and their ways, they who spoke their own language in its own accent, and followed their own fashions and scorned foreign manners? London was a very English city indeed. And that was the city and its people whom Franz Lehár, a complete newcomer to the British Theatre, had to challenge and to conquer.

The first rehearsal was the first shot of the battle.

CHAPTER EIGHT

Lehár in London

THE company which George Edwardes had got together for the production of *The Merry Widow* deserves more notice than that which is usually bestowed in histories upon the players in the plays which have made history. It is common knowledge now that Lehár's music swept London as it swept the world, that it opened up new floodgates of melodic romance, that it made *The Merry Widow* a landmark in the history of musical plays—and musical plays are important, for they are the most popular things in the world of the Theatre—that it reached a peak which has not yet been surpassed, a charm which has not yet been equalled and is not likely to be excelled, and a memory which will linger for ever. Lehár's genius did all this; but he, being Fortune's favourite, had again the astounding good luck that Edwardes, in his moment of stress, should have been able to collect a team which would give the play such a wonderful rendering, and make it come alive and pulse with excitement, both of sentiment and comedy, so as to be truly palatable to the British public, yet still remain a romance of Ruritania and—more important even than that—preserve the magical atmosphere of Vienna which Lehár had breathed into his music. For all this the company assuredly did.

Joseph Coyne and Lily Elsie, the two great ones, have been introduced already. At the first rehearsal she was wide-eyed with wonder and not quite able to make it all out, while Coyne was still in the depth of despair, quite sure of failure, for himself and the show. That curious mind, which would raise him to the heights and plunge him to the depths, was no doubt seething in confusion. Later in life he reached a stage when he would have long conversations on street corners with people quite invisible to anyone else, but most interesting and chatty to him. Joe suffered from hallucinations—and perhaps the greatest was that he could not play Prince Danilo, the part for which Edwardes had cast him in *The Merry Widow*.

To the end of his life he never understood why the chief comedy part was given to George Graves. Edwardes had, of course, well understood that the rather stilted, conventional dialogue of the original *Lustige Witwe* would never draw laughs from a London audience. The comics must be given much fuller and more unrestrained play. That was one reason why he had selected them with such care. Graves has already entered this story in speaking of *Véronique* and *The Little Michus*. He was becoming a George Edwardes "regular". He was to have played in *Les Merveilleuses*, but he did not like the part and W. H. Berry played it instead. He had made his first London success in *The School Girl*—five years before the production of *The Merry Widow*—also for George Edwardes. His line was comic old men, his speciality was gagging. He was allotted the part of Baron Popoff, Marsovian Ambassador in Paris.

Graves was born in London on the 1st January, 1876. His family had no connection with the stage at all, but from his earliest childhood George Graves had the fixed determination of becoming an actor. Indeed, he ran away from home and got employment with a Music Hall act. He was traced after a fortnight, taken home, soundly beaten and sent back to school. But the ambition had taken root. His father died when he was still only a lad, and the family fortunes were shaky. It became necessary for George to do some work. He got a job with the solicitor who had always acted for his father. He did not like the Law but he made the best of it. He received a salary of 15s. a week, a good salary for an office boy then. It is a strange coincidence that the two greatest gagsters the English stage ever knew, Arthur Roberts and George Graves, should both have made a start in a solicitor's office.

But although Master Graves applied himself fairly well to his duties, his propensity for mischief got the better of him. The managing clerk incurred his displeasure, so he substituted ink for tea in the cup which that worthy was about to drink, got the sack, but considered it worth it. So the stage claimed him. He toured the provinces; he worked hard and he lived hard, as poor young players did then. But he began to find his line and he got out of the rut in 1900, at Christmas, when he appeared as the Emperor of China in *Aladdin* at the Princes Theatre, Manchester— the town in which he first saw and admired that child, called then "Little Elsie", who now stood with him at Daly's as leading lady. In 1901 he toured South Africa, and on his return was in the provinces again.

But the eye of George Edwardes—who missed very little—was upon him. This youthful player of eccentric and humorous old men had certainly got something, it seemed to the Guvnor. No doubt that astute man knew that the gestures and manner which Graves made familiar, the right elbow cupped in the left palm, while the nails were chewed or the fingers stroked the face reflectively, the curious choky utterance and the sudden spasmodic movements, were not entirely original. They owed much to the manner of a famous Music Hall comedian named Tom E. Murray. But Graves brought his own genius to the superstructure, and having acquired the characteristics, made them peculiarly his own. Indeed, such an original mind as his and such an individual art needed no help from anyone. Although he had not the supreme individuality, nor the genial charm, nor the vivid spontaneity of his famous rival, Arthur Roberts, he was a better and more subtle actor, with a wonderful gift of character and of keeping inside a part when he seemed to be divorcing himself from it entirely. In 1903 George Edwardes gave Graves his chance in London as General Marchmont in *The School Girl* at the Prince of Wales's. He took that chance with both hands, being able to score heavily despite the presence in the cast of two comedians of individual style and of greater experience, G. P. Huntley and the well-established and popular James Blakeley.

Graves made his comparatively small part stand out and scored a very big success. He followed this with another big hit as the military-minded florist Coquenard in *Véronique* at the Apollo in 1904, and then followed Willie Edouin, that great comedian, when owing to illness he left the cast of *The Little Michus* at Daly's. How Graves scored then has been related. He went with the play to America and was a success there. His record was thus long and brilliant. His sayings and his gags had passed into everyday speech. Moreover, off-stage he continued his practical joking. Just as he had upset the managing clerk in the far-off days of his legal servitude, so he would trick visitors to his dressing-room. He served drinks in glasses which dribbled their contents down his visitors' shirt-fronts; he seated them on chairs which collapsed; they found themselves trying to turn door handles which remained immovable; they were confused by mirrors; their cigars and cigarettes exploded in their faces; they discovered foreign substances in their hats. Not all of them were amused. Sometimes Mr. Graves overdid it, in his desire to amuse himself. He offended a very important personage indeed. But nothing stopped him. It was his nature so to do. None of that prevented him from being a remarkable stage performer whose creations, despite their up-to-date gags, were a series of remarkable character sketches—often reminiscent of Hogarth.

Of Robert Evett something has already been said. This man with the pure tenor voice, and the knowledge how to use it, might not have been of romantic looks or proportions, but he knew how to create an atmosphere of romance. In *The Merry Widow* he was cast for Vicomte Camille de Jolidon, for which he was excellently fitted. He had been a Savoyard, and all that it meant. He had become an Edwardesian—a citizen of Daly's—and he had assimilated the atmosphere. Indeed, when Edwardes died, it was to be Evett who, as Manager, would carry on the Daly's tradition against truly terrible odds, and get a success in *The Maid of the Mountains* comparable in its dramatic surrounding of crisis to that of *The Merry Widow*. He would fight gallantly for Quality to the very end.

The part of the Marquis of Cascada was to be Lennox Pawle's. He had been born in London in 1872 and was a man of good education; he had been at Berkhampstead and also to a school in France. He had learnt his business at the old Theatre Royal, Margate, under Sarah Thorne, from which source had come a galaxy of stars. He had wide and varied experience as a comedian: he had played in drama at the Pavilion, Mile End Road; he had graduated to leading parts in the West End, and had joined George Edwardes for the ill-fated *Little Cherub*, in which however he was a personal success.

He had then gone to Daly's in *Les Merveilleuses*, and now here he was in *The Merry Widow*, a real tower of strength. He had formed a firm friendship with Freddy Kaye, a stalwart of the Edwardesian Empire, and the adventures of the two were so fantastic as to be almost incredible, but in their case, Truth was stranger than Fiction. Some of the stories are recounted elsewhere. They were a law unto themselves; they were always in trouble; Pawle, indeed, was suspended on one occasion, and could not make it out at all. But the Guvnor kept them—for he knew their worth.

Lennox Pawle was a very fat man with a round, innocent-looking face —until you caught the mischief which glinted in the eyes. He always made an impact on the audience, no matter how small the part. He created a character, and that character was real. He could get his laughs without any forcing; he could hold and sustain a scene. He had an impish sense of humour and a considerable feeling of his own dignity, although he could laugh at himself. If anyone offended him, their lives became a burden. He nearly drove a perfectly innocent and law-abiding citizen mad during the First World War because he, Pawle, had decided that the man was a German spy. He had not the slightest ground for such a ridiculous idea, and whatever the offence was (it was probably imaginary) the poor wretch who had occasioned it was quite ignorant of the fact that he had done so. As like as not it was something about his walk or his attire. But whatever it was, it was enough for Pawle, who followed him everywhere, kept him under constant surveillance, and would talk, very loudly, of German spies all the time.

During the First World War, Pawle appeared in the same ill-fated play

as Joe Coyne, *The Clock Goes Round*—that unlucky show of the thirteen
performances. He also played a Pierrot. That dreaded document of the
Theatre, the "Notice"—the statement that the run will terminate on a
specific date—had been posted on the notice board by the Manager on the
second night. The month was October. About half an hour afterwards
the Manager was informed that Mr. Pawle would like to see him in his
dressing-room. He knew Lennox Pawle; he scented trouble. But Pawle
received him with great courtesy. He said to the Manager, "This is a
charming dressing-room, and I like it. I fear, however, that when the
summer comes round it may be stuffy. Would you be good enough to
arrange, old man, that when May arrives I have a couple of electric fans
installed?" It was his way of letting the manager understand that he had
read the notice and knew his—and the play's—fate.

His friend and companion in mischief, Fred Kaye, was to be General
Novikovich (Military Attaché at the Marsovian Embassy) in *The Merry
Widow*, an elderly man with a young and lovely wife, of whom, not
unreasonably, he was jealous. It was just the part for Fred Kaye. He was
a small, alert man, quick, not to say explosive, in utterance, and speedy in
all he did. He had first appeared in London as far back as 1883. He had
played both in Comic Opera and straight plays, for he was an excellent
character comedian with a style of his own. He joined George Edwardes
in 1893, to appear as Major Barclay in *A Gaiety Girl* at the Prince of
Wales's Theatre. When it was transferred to Daly's, Kaye went with it,
and from that time he hardly appeared under any management but that of
Edwardes. He was really a Daly's regular. He was no star; he played small
but good parts, and he brought much to them. Part of a team, he kept
within the framework, yet retained his individuality.

Gordon Cleather was chosen for the part of M. de St. Brioche, a clear-cut,
good actor, who could sing, and who came of military stock—and looked
it. He was also an Old Edwardesian. He had been in *Ib and Little Christina*,
The Little Michus and *The Cingalee* at Daly's, in *Véronique*, and *Lady Madcap*.

The male cast of *The Merry Widow* was completed by W. H. Berry. He
has entered this story already. It remains to be said that his contribution
to what the play achieved was by no means the least. Here was a real droll.
Berry had been born a Cockney, within the sound of Big Ben, if not of
Bow Bells. The year was 1870 and the place Kennington Road. He was of
respectable, if humble, parentage, and from his earliest years he yearned
for the stage. This feeling was made all the stronger by the fact that he
got a job with Keith Prowse and Co., the famous firm of theatre ticket
agents. It was young Berry's job to take what were known as "the
returns" round to the box-office. That word does not mean returned
tickets but a list—or return—of the tickets which the agency has sold for

the particular night's performance. His wages were 10s. per week. He was in and out of all the theatres; he caught the dreadful disease of theatre fever; henceforth no other life would suit.

He became an entertainer; he sang at clubs for tiny fees, and became popular. There was something about the personality of this rather goggle-eyed youth, with the strange gait, the seeming repose of countenance but perfect mastery of timing, with the clarity of diction and the agile feet—he could dance with the neatness and lightness of a ballerina—which attracted the rough and ready audience. And if the eyes goggled they were most eloquent. He became a seaside performer—he grew very popular as such—and he was a leading light at Broadstairs in the Concert Hall there when George Grossmith Junior came across him. Grossmith, of course, told Edwardes, and Edwardes gave Berry a chance. He did more, he gave him a three years' contract; for on the strength of what "G. G." had said the Guvnor had gone down to Broadstairs, watched the show through those seemingly sleepy eyes which saw so much—and snapped up Mr. W. H. Berry.

So, under the finest management, Bill Berry—as he was to be known to all—first faced the proper footlights of a theatre. It was at the Empire, Leicester Square, which had just been overhauled and altered. The attraction was a revue called *Rogues and Vagabonds*, and the year was 1905. In the revue with Berry, and also in the contract, was Kitty Hanson, who was Mrs. Berry, and from then on, until his retirement, every contract which Bill Berry ever had included his wife. But after the very early days the Guvnor never let them appear together, or in the same show if he could help it. The revue also included an excerpt from the musical comedy *Madame Sherry*, and the Berrys were in that, too. Bill then went to the Prince of Wales's Theatre in *The Little Cherub*, in which he played Shingle, a butler, and where he first showed his genius for the singing of topical songs, at which, save for Rutland Barrington, he had had no equal. On that occasion the song was "I Wasn't Engaged for That". He had to find time to make an appearance in *Venus* at the Empire as well. *The Little Cherub*, we know, did not succeed, but it had done much for Berry, and he appeared in *See See*, another unsuccessful play of the Guvnor's, but which nevertheless enhanced the Berry reputation. So, when Graves did not play in *Les Merveilleuses*, Berry went to Daly's to play first St. Amour and subsequently Tournesol in that production. Which brought him directly into the part of Nisch (Messenger to the Marsovian Embassy) in *The Merry Widow*.

Of the ladies at that first rehearsal, Lily Elsie has been introduced already. There was Elizabeth Firth, who was to play Natalie, the wife of Popoff, a most important part. Tall, handsome and graceful, she was

an American, having been born in Phillipsburg, New Jersey. She had
made a humble beginning to her stage career in New York in 1903, when
she "walked on" in a production of Hall Caine's *The Eternal City*. She
came to London, George Edwardes saw her, realized her possibilities,
and engaged her for *The Duchess of Dantzig* at the Lyric Theatre in 1903.
She understudied Evie Greene and played for her with such success that
when *The Duchess* went to New York, she played in it. Returning to
London, she followed Kitty Gordon as Agatha in *Véronique*, and then
Edwardes put her into *Les Merveilleuses*, where again she succeeded Evie
Greene, when that wonderful woman left the cast. And so—into *The
Merry Widow*. She was not a star then, as her career shows. But she acted
and sang her way right into the front rank in that wonderful play.

The Olga—wife to Novikovich—was played by Irene Desmond, and
Kate Welch was Prascovia, a delicious satire on elderly flirtatiousness.
The Girls at Maxims were "Lo-Lo", Daisie Irving (to play the Widow
in her turn); "Do-Do", Ada Fraser; "Jou-Jou", Dolly Dombey; "Frou-
Frou", Amy Webster; "To-To", Mabel Munro; "Zo-Zo", Gertrude
Lester, also to be a Widow; "Clo-Clo", Phyllis Le Grand, making her
very first appearance on the stage, a lovely graceful blonde, shortly to
be promoted to play Olga, wife of Novikovich, to marry Robert
Michaelis, a future Daly's star, and to be a star herself; and "Fi-Fi", Mabel
Russell.

That was the cast which assembled at the first rehearsal of *The Merry
Widow*, with, of course, the Ladies and Gentlemen of the Chorus. The Stage
Director was J. A. E. Malone, the Musical Director Harold Vicars, and the
dances were arranged by that little genius, Fred Farren. The acting
manager of Daly's was G. E., Minor, the "E" standing for Edwardes.
But the whole place back and front was under the personal supervision of
George Edwardes himself, the Guvnor.

The position of things at Daly's was well known to the theatrical
profession as a whole, and the theatrical profession talks only shop and
loves to gossip. A new play—especially, in those days, a new production
by George Edwardes—was an inexhaustible supply of chatter for the
ladies and gentlemen of "the Profession"—the phrase "show business"
had not yet reached this country. So everyone was discussing *The Merry
Widow*, and to many of those whose "line" was musical comedy it was
a matter of great importance, because of the tours. It is quite impossible
for a secret to be kept in Theatreland; so everybody knew all about
everything—and what they did not know came from their inspired
imagination by process of deduction. In the bars where actors for-
gathered, in the tea-rooms in which the Ladies of the Chorus and small
parts sustained themselves whilst looking for work, on the corners of

Leicester Square, in the Strand, everywhere in the Land of Greasepaint, *The Merry Widow* was the question of the hour.

It is, of course, a recognized fact amongst actors and actresses that Managers know nothing about their business at all. There had always been a reservation in the case of the Guvnor, but this time—well, really! "What's the Guvnor up to?" they would ask. "What's the matter at Daly's? A musical play from Vienna? Whoever heard. . . ? French shows —yes—look at *Véronique* and the rest . . . *The Lady Dandies* a flop? Oh yes, but it only goes to show—cannot get a success every time even from Paris. And what about the English shows—weren't they good enough for Daly's? I should have thought so! . . . My dear, I toured in *A Country Girl*, so I know. I stopped the show twice at Huddersfield. . . . But Vienna? . . . Oh yes! *The Waltz Dream!* Hardly a success, I think, old boy? Composed by Straus, wasn't it?—not the man who wrote the Blue Danube—oh no! But he didn't write this new play—what's the name of this new chap? Lehár—how do you pronounce it? What's he ever done? Wrote a waltz called 'Gold and Silver'? What about it? Daly's wants more than that. Good waltz, oh yes, but this is *Daly's.* . . . And what a title! *The Merry Widow!* I ask you! The Guvnor always got away with 'Girls'—yes, but 'Widows', what? He may rue it; he may live to remember what that old chap in *Pickwick Papers* said—who was it? Tony Weller. Oh, you read Dickens, do you? Anyway he said, 'Beware of Widows'—Bevare of vidders. Perhaps the Guvnor doesn't read Dickens? Well, he should. . . .

"And what about the cast? I ask you, old boy, what about the cast? This fellow Joseph Coyne—an American! An American as leading man at Daly's!" (It is to be feared that the rank and file forgot or never knew that Hayden Coffin, the idol of Daly's, was of American parentage, although born in Manchester.) "What's he ever done?—a couple of shows or so. Big hit in *Nellie Neil*? Oh yes. He can dance. Well, so can others. Why should the Guvnor give him the lead at Daly's? Aren't there people who have worked for him for years who might have had a chance? I don't want to say anything but . . ." "And, my dear, Lily Elsie is to be leading lady in this new thing at Daly's. What's she ever done? . . . Oh yes, I know, I know, but why lead at *Daly's*? Some of us—I'll mention no names—have worked for the Guvnor for years and been very successful— well, we have a following you know . . . in the provinces—what about it? Don't they ever come to town? Aren't the people who have done well to get a chance ever? Oh, I know, but, my dear, I *hear* . . ."

And then, from male and female lips would come whispers of financial stress. And they were all genuinely sorry about that, for they all loved and revered the Guvnor. But acting is a very personal thing and most of them felt sore that in their own estimation—which was all that mattered to them—they had been passed over. They would usually end up, if males, by drinking the health of the Guvnor, some of them dusting down their suits, which had originated in his generosity and lack of questioning as to the whereabouts of the Wardrobe at the end of tours, and, if females, they would still wish the Guvnor good luck—but say nothing about the cast.

Rumour was rife. It was not without cause. Edwardes sent for Fred Farren to arrange the dances in *The Merry Widow*. Farren was, with Willie Warde and with Teddy Royce, one of the Edwardesian pillars of strength in this department, and was in his own right himself a magnificent dancer— about the best this country ever produced. He was the mainstay of the Empire Ballet, and there he was to electrify London with the Apache Dance, and make it weep with *The Faun*. He went to see Edwardes about *The Merry Widow*. There was a little account already outstanding, for other work done. But Freddie—as everyone called him, although his name was really Michael—was not worrying much about that. He got some vague instructions, accepted the job, and departed.

On the way out he met Charlie Cannon, one of the lieutenants of the Edwardesian staff. So, as this was an opportunity, he did mention the little overdue matter to Cannon. That worthy replied that he did not know what was wrong with the Guvnor; he had laid that account before him time and again, and it was always passed over. He would do so once more. A little while later Farren was again summoned to the presence. This time he got fuller instructions about what he had to do. It appeared there was a waltz which was something special. "Shall I go to Vienna and see it, Guvnor?" asked Freddie. No, he was not to do that. "It's easy," said Edwardes in that curious, sleepy, petulant voice of his; "first he holds her round the waist and they waltz—and then he holds her round the neck and they waltz—well, you know what to do. So go ahead! Everything all right between us?" Freddie took the opportunity of mentioning the little account. Edwardes was furious. "Why hasn't it been paid?" he thundered. "Send for Cannon!" Cannon, on arrival, temporized. "See it's paid at once," ordered the Guvnor. "I never heard of such a thing; ought to have been paid long ago. I hate things outstanding. . . ." But it remained outstanding, all the same.

Freddie Farren next met Joseph Harker, the great scenic artist. Naturally they were friends. Harker had some work to do for *The Merry Widow*. It was mostly alteration and touching up of existing scenery, and, knowing Edwardes, that had surprised him. He suggested to Farren that they should have a drink. They adjourned to the pub just opposite the Daly's offices in Lisle Street. There Harker asked Farren if he knew anything about the Guvnor's financial position. Freddie, knowing Harker, admitted that there was a little account owing. Harker told him his position was the same. So Freddie said, "I'm not worrying. I don't particularly want the money, I can get along"; and Harker said that he had his men to pay, and that it was always inconvenient for accounts to be outstanding for long—but he wasn't worrying either. "I don't mind if I work for nothing for the Guvnor," said Farren. "Neither do I," said Harker. "God bless him!" They had another drink on the strength of it. . . .

Rehearsals opened grimly. Edwardes used all his care, all his tact, although in his heart he regarded this play as a "nitter". Still, it might hold the fort and get the necessary breathing space for him. He had a difficult time. There was his leading man quite disgruntled. Coyne loathed it all. He and Freddie Farren would pop over to the Cavour bar for a drink—for Farren tried to cheer things up, being a cheery little soul himself. But Joe was past cheering. He would stand there gloomily, staring into the—to him—hopeless future. He would tuck his thumbs into the top of his trousers—he never wore a waistcoat—and say, "I'm going back to New York. I can't stand this. This is dreadful; it's no good to me nor to anybody else. It's ruin. I'm going back to New York." Then he and Farren would go back, not to New York, but to the rehearsal.

Lily Elsie was more wide-eyed than ever with wonder and fear. She was sure she could not do it. "This part wants an Opera singer," she would say, "and I'm not an Opera singer." She had seen the show in Vienna and it had frightened her. She pleaded with Edwardes to let her off. He was quite adamant. What Lily Elsie feared most was the song "Vilia". That she was sure she could not sing. It was tried out with another member of the cast, but the Guvnor would not have it. It belonged to the plot; it must be sung by Sonia. Depression reigned. And George Graves did not help. He lost his temper. He said there was no comedy at all; it was absurd to go ahead with a show like this; he was wasting his time—and the Guvnor's. He threatened to walk out, but he did not. . . . Maybe "Hetty the Hen" had slipped into his mind and laid an egg of good fortune.

It was pretty bad at Daly's just then, a change from what had been always such a happy theatre. Edwardes, however, smoothed out every row and missed no detail. He rehearsed them hard; time pressed, so they rehearsed on Sundays, and to try and keep them happy the Guvnor would take them all out to lunch. They would walk down to Rules through the almost deserted, sunlit streets of the West End on a summer Sunday afternoon, a queer procession, straggling out as they went. There was Graves watchful and alert, his curious eyes everywhere and a glint in them as he thought up a gag; Joe Coyne loafing along, hands in pockets, his round face without a smile, his eyes gazing into space, his feet kicking out as he walked; Lily Elsie moving with perfect grace, and probably walking beside the Guvnor; Fred Kaye trying to recall his part—he was a notorious bad study and a "dryer up", hence his habit of repeating his lines over and over again, which most people took for comedy, and which, it must be admitted, went very well; and beside him his friend Lennox Pawle, stout and chubby, plotting mischief all the while. Bill Berry, who always lived in a world of his own, was probably the only happy one; with Bill Berry, if he was good and liked his part, all was right with the universe, no matter what happened to the others. . . . And the Guvnor, keeping the peace, keeping the ball rolling, but torn with anxieties and worries which he never showed.

He was having the worst time of his whole career. The early rehearsals of *The Merry Widow* were a period of gloom and discontent for all and ceaseless care for him. But there were more troubles ahead. For the day came when Franz Lehár arrived.

Lehár had been to London only once before, when the Fleet from Pola had visited the Baltic. It had called at London, and he had gone ashore, as a Naval Bandmaster. He saw little of the city or its life. He sailed away with the ships and his orchestra. Now he returned, a composer famous in his own country, celebrated all over the Continent, to face the ordeal of a London production, where he was quite unknown, where his music was unknown, save for a waltz or two, and where the language in which his *Merry Widow* was to be performed was, save for a few words and phrases, as unknown to him as his own tongue was to the cast of *The Merry Widow*. He arrived with Victor Léon and Leo Stein, the librettists. They took up residence in a hotel. Then, accompanied by interpreters, they went to Daly's Theatre.

On their arrival Edwardes groaned. "Here they come," he muttered, "here comes the Troupe!"—and they were known as "The Troupe" from then on. Great politeness ruled. Welcomes were spoken, there was bowing and heel-clicking, expressions on the one side of the pleasure of seeing Lehár and his companions, on the other side, of the delight and pride of being in London, in the so wonderful Daly's Theatre, and of meeting at last the so famous George Edwardes. . . . The company looked on.

Lehár was introduced to them. He surveyed the beautiful Lily Elsie with pleasure, but he remarked that she looked more like the Merry Widow's daughter than the Merry Widow herself. He stared at Coyne, who did not seem like his idea of Danilo, and Joe Coyne stared back, his face expressionless. He greeted the comedians, then Evett, Elizabeth Firth and the rest. The rehearsal proceeded—with a piano.

Top: The kiss at last and the happy ending—Joseph Coyne as Danilo and Lily Elsie as Sonia. *Left*: Joseph Coyne as Danilo announces at the Embassy Reception that he goes off to Maxim's

Joseph Coyne as Danilo in *The Merry Widow* at Daly's Theatre

Now, Joe Coyne could not sing a note—and well George Edwardes knew it. So he explained to Lehár that Mr. Coyne had a very bad cold; he must rest the voice, he must not use it yet. The composer and his team nodded. As soon as a number approached Edwardes would shout to Coyne, "Cut the number, Joe, it's all right," and Joe was quite agreeable. That went on for some time, but Lehár was getting a little restless. Still, apparently, Coyne was in the grip of this strange vocal complaint of his, but all the rest were singing and time was getting on. They came to "There Once Were Two Princes' Children", and the position was acute. It was a "number". "Don't sing it, Joe," called the Guvnor, "recite it, please! You must save the voice." And he explained, through the interpreter, how necessary it was that Mr. Coyne should husband the vocal cords. So Joe recited the lines. He recited them remarkably well; he quite stirred the company, and he delighted the heart of George Edwardes.

Now, the Guvnor was an opportunist and saw his cue. He turned to Lehár, and beamed upon him, letting the blue eyes and the charm have full play. Lehár and his *confrères* were sitting right back in the stalls, busy taking notes. Edwardes asked Lehár to come down to him, and the composer did. The Manager asked if Lehár did not think that Mr. Coyne recited that beautifully, most feelingly and dramatically? Would it not be better to keep it that way, and not have it sung? Lehár, the position explained, seemed doubtful. Edwardes left it at that and pressed on. The big battle was yet to come and he knew it. It would be over the orchestra itself.

The orchestra pit at Daly's was not large. It had a beautiful mahogany face, but it held only twenty-eight players, and there was not much room even then. The harpist had to sit outside in a little alcove, actually on the stalls floor. Lehár demanded six more players. There were arguments, long drawn out and repetitive. Edwardes explained that there would be no room in the pit; he proved it by putting six extra people down there. The congestion was awful; the violinists could not use their arms. Still, Lehár, firmly but politely, insisted that his score and his contract called for the extra men. He was taking no chances and very rightly standing up for himself in a foreign land. He knew all about George Edwardes, but he knew all about managerial wiles as well. Edwardes then explained that if he had the extra men, a row of stalls— indeed, two rows—must be sacrificed. That would mean so much less taken at every performance, so much less in the way of royalties. He besought Lehár to hear the orchestra before forcing such a loss on both of them. To that Lehár consented. So the Daly's orchestra was called, and the Daly's orchestra played. It was magnificent. Lehár was satisfied. He agreed to the twenty-eight and no more.

G

Then he took orchestral rehearsals. Farren, and others who were there, remember the scrupulous care this man, dark, alert, and very soldier-like, took over the playing. He spent three hours getting the opening bars of "Vilia" the way he wanted it. What he required was for the melody to come across the orchestra like a wave, starting from the harp and ending with the drums, and swelling as it surged across. He got it, and the orchestra now responded to all that he did, knowing that indeed a Maestro was in the chair. He paid attention to every detail—to the few opening bars of the Maxim's scene, as if it had been a concerto. He rehearsed each man separately with each instrument. The cost was getting colossal, and poor Edwardes groaned. Although the charges then were a fraction of what they are now, still they were enormous. And where was the money to come from?

And so the dress rehearsal approached, and the gloom increased. Only Lehár, as in those crucial days at the Theater an der Wien, did not seem disturbed, but would twinkle at them out of his eyes and say nice things through the interpreter. But he watched Joe Coyne carefully. The comics he did not pretend to understand; but his Danilo was important. Joe had not sung yet—always the Guvnor had shouted, "Save your voice, Joe," and Joe, nothing loath, had saved it.

But at the dress rehearsal this could not be done. Then he had to sing —or at least speak his songs to music. When this happened Lehár was horrified. He stopped the rehearsal; he put down his baton. "What was this?" he demanded. No chance for pleas of a cold or other evasions now! Edwardes assured Lehár that Mr. Coyne was a very funny man. "But I have not written funny music," retorted Lehár. Edwardes was stung to answer. He had faith in Joe; he would show Lehár and the rest that he was right! "Herr Lehár," he said, "that man will put a fortune in your pocket, even if he does not sing your beautiful music." . . . The rehearsal dragged its weary way along. At last it was over. Lehár did not seem distressed, rather pleased than otherwise, on the whole, though still doubtful of Joe. But for everyone else, there seemed nothing ahead but disaster. They had never seen *The Merry Widow*. They knew nothing of its trials and tribulations elsewhere. But Franz Lehár knew, and there was no depression in him.

CHAPTER NINE

First Night

THE morning of the 8th June, 1907, was to the overwhelming majority of Londoners a morning just the same as yesterday's had been and just the same as tomorrow's would be. But to the little band of people who worked at Daly's Theatre it was a day of portent, on which the course of their lives might be altered. As usual, on the morning of a First Night, there was an air of false calm about the theatre. The box-office might be busy, but that was—or had been—a very usual thing at Daly's. The members of the company were conspicuous by their absence; there was no "call" for the morning, so they would not come near the theatre until it was time for them to get ready for the show. On the stage carpenters were putting final touches on the scenery, as were the scene painters; up in the Wardrobe a final overhaul was taking place and last-minute alterations being made. The "Props" was checking over his lists, the electrician his cues. The curtain was down. But in the pit was the orchestra. And to them came the man who was primarily to face the judgment of London that night, the composer of the show—Franz Lehár. He wanted just another run through of the music, a checking over of the parts, a last polish to reach the thing for which he always strove: —perfection.

He looked around the theatre, and appreciated its quiet yet opulent beauty. Here were subdued tones, no garish exuberance; here were walls of lovely wood, polished like marble; comfortable seats, shaded lights and decorations such as a theatre should have to give it atmosphere. All round him reflected that for which he himself stood—Quality and Taste. He looked at the stalls, the dress circle, the boxes, the upper circle, and the gallery, very high and very steep. Perhaps he noticed that the pit—not that of the orchestra but that of the audience—had been reduced to very small proportions, to make room for more stalls, more seats of the mighty, the smart people who came to George Edwardes's First Nights. Possibly, however, he knew nothing about pits. He might have noticed a small crowd of people in the alley outside the theatre, waiting for the seats in that pit, and, if he had come that way, a larger crowd in Lisle Street, waiting for the gallery. But in neither case was the crowd as big as usual. This play from Vienna, the work of an unknown man, had caused little preliminary excitement. So far, the General Public were taking it very calmly. Had Lehár observed those queues—for they were queues, the theatre being then the only place for which anyone queued—he would have seen quite a high proportion of foreigners, and of his own countrymen, coming from neighbouring Soho.

Lehár stood there, his back to the orchestra rails, and appreciated that theatre, so well designed, so well decorated, so spotlessly clean, so well run and disciplined—different from many to which he had been accustomed. And he, the artist, was aware of its atmosphere.

He was still a young man, as years go. He was a successful man. He held himself erect, and the soldierly bearing was most marked. He glanced around with head in air, he surveyed the ground, for indeed he was a soldier preparing for battle. In a few hours' time he had to fight London, and he hoped that his would be the victory. He was calm outwardly. For he knew *The Merry Widow*, he had led it time and again to victory, sometimes when disaster seemed certain. He had never lost faith in this work of his. And this time the battlefield seemed favourable to him. London, greatest city in the world, was his friendly antagonist, was to pass a judgment upon him which must, either way, greatly affect his future. He accepted the challenge. He had confidence in his work—his only lingering doubt was Joseph Coyne. He turned to the orchestra, and the rehearsal that was to give the very last finishing touch started; the melodies of *The Merry Widow* swelled into the empty auditorium, heard only by cleaners, who stopped their work to listen, by the housekeeper, who failed to reprove them, and by the people working in the bars, who, as the music reached them, forbore to make their usual clatter and noise. Everywhere, it seemed, the theatre and the people of the theatre held their breath. . . .

Upstairs in the Guvnor's office things were not so calm. For Edwardes these last few hours of tension, of hope, of calculation, were almost unbearable. The Libraries—the ticket-selling agencies—had not bought blocks of seats, as they were wont to do for his shows. They had held aloof; they would, if you please—wait and see. They would be in the First Night audience, of course, and would talk afterwards.

There were messages from people anxiously asking for First Night seats, although the Guvnor had his own careful method about such things, and saw to the allotment of stalls, boxes and dress circle personally. He knew where they should all sit, and he knew their claims to precedence. But there were always last-minute enquiries, people who simply *must* bring a friend, people difficult to refuse. Edwardes was worried and very nervy. With him was his right-hand man, J. A. E. (Pat) Malone, tall, strong, resolute of face, with determination in every line of it, the man who put the shows on the stage under the Guvnor's supervision, the man who did the donkey work, who did the sacking, the nasty bits, who knew the secrets, and who knew all about production of plays and how to choose artists. Hard he might be, stern he might be, but that was perforce. He knew his business backwards—and he knew the Guvnor. Today he was worried far more about his Chief than the show. He knew the true conditions, and he was worried about Edwardes.

There was nothing more he could do downstairs, in his stage domain; there his lieutenants could cope with any small matters which might arise. So far as he was concerned the curtain was up. But there was something he could do about the Guvnor—get him out of the theatre for a bit. He did it. He took him down to Richmond to lunch; he never left his side all day. And as they left the theatre, through an open door came the strains of *The Merry Widow*, as Lehár rehearsed that orchestra. They glanced at each other. Yes—there it was! *The Merry Widow*—which way would it go? . . . Nothing they could do about it now. Taking the Guvnor by the arm, Malone led him off to the carriage which drove them to Richmond. . . .

Across Leicester Square the lights twinkled and shone. As far as the eye could see, right along Coventry Street, right across Piccadilly Circus, and up Regent Street and along Piccadilly, was a line of cars and carriages converging on one spot—Daly's Theatre. Crowds of hurrying people, gazing at them, knew the reason. Larger crowds of leisurely pleasure-seekers stopped to watch them, as they went by with their load of smartly dressed occupants, dainty, elegant women shimmering in silk and satin, and twinkling with jewels, men in correct and full evening dress—silk hats shining, white ties and shirtfronts agleam, and, often, diamond studs glittering in the midst of the starched plastron.

And there were people, also in evening dress, rather more flashy and less tasteful, but often with a greater display of jewels and furs on the part of the women, and higher collars and considerably more cuff on the part of the men, many of whose fingers were bejewelled, as they showed when they used them to gesticulate, who were going through the door marked "Upper Circle". Here was where the lesser lights sat on Daly's First Nights, those whose social eminence, sporting fame or artistic capability did not qualify them for the seats of the élite. But they represented Money, all the same.

Upstairs in the gallery and downstairs, at the very back, in the pit, sat the General Public, or such of them as had gained admittance. But on this First Night, although the reserved seats were packed as usual, there was no great crowding in the unreserved portions. And there was not quite the same air; there was an impalpable question mark everywhere; there was not quite the same expectation, the same confident expectation of certain and unalloyed pleasure. The old favourites were missing; here were new names, and the most important and least known of the new names was that of the composer of this piece they had come to see—the name of Franz Lehár.

The Guvnor sat in his usual box, looking at the house. His fresh-complexioned face was perhaps a trifle paler than usual, but the eyes, beneath their lids, showed glints of blue as he gazed at that audience which held Fate in their hands. No need to worry now—in a few minutes the flag would fall and they would be Off! He was a gambler. He had made his bet, placed his stake; it was up to Fortune now.

Behind the curtain there was nervous tension in the highest degree, either the calm of despair, disturbed by a feeling of physical sickness, or the flame of temperament, the temper of overtaut nerves. Lily Elsie just waited. Joe Coyne said afterwards that he felt like a criminal waiting the fatal drop or like Sydney Carton ascending the steps of the guillotine. He knew it was Death; he was certain. . . .

The audience buzzed and chattered. There was a tapping of bows on violins. A shortish, square, erect figure climbed into the conductor's seat and a spatter of applause arose. Franz Lehár faced his judges and gave his sharp, mechanical, military bow. Then he turned and bowed to his orchestra. Baton raised, he waited. The lights dimmed and the stick descended. The first strains of *The Merry Widow* went out to that audience at Daly's Theatre. . . .

There is no overture to the original operette (though Lehár many years later composed one for it). At Daly's on that June evening of 1907 there were only those few exhilarating bars of introduction before the curtain rose on a ball at the "Marsovian" Embassy in Paris. The native land of the Widow had not always been "Marsovia". In Vienna (we are reminded by Adrian Ross in his rhyming story of the play for the anniversary souvenir at Daly's)

> In Vienna the name
> Of the place whence she came
> Is called Pontevedro, a term you can see grow
> By twisting the very well-known Montenegro

—and indeed the original authors say bluntly in the foreword to the published play, "By 'Pontevedro' is meant 'Montenegro'." This ruffled some susceptibilities . . . and by an odd coincidence the name "Ponte-vedro" had an unlucky association for Lehár. *Rose of Pontedevedro* had been the name of the rival Opera which had defeated him in his attempt early in life to win the Grand Duke of Coburg-Gotha's prize. Anyhow the name had vanished from the London version of the *Widow* as it would later from the Paris one, and so there was no offence to anybody. . . .

To the audience at Daly's it was all one, "Pontevedro" or "Marsovia". They had been to many such balls before; there was nothing specially interesting in the scene before them. But *had* they been to such a ball before? For, as they listened, they found a much better story than usual unfolding itself before them. Here was a mixture of the Balkans and the French, and things were happening in much more logical sequence than was usual in musical comedy or operette. Not only was the story being well and clearly told, but the characters who were telling it had a reality curiously rare in such entertainments. One could believe in them.

It appeared that Marsovia, like most of these petty Balkan states, for which the audience had a hearty contempt, was bankrupt. Practically all its wealth had been in the hands of a banker, who, when he died, had left it to his wife, a young and lovely girl, now a widow. She might marry again. If so the money was lost to Marsovia. So Baron Popoff, the Ambassador in Paris, had been instructed from headquarters that he was to see that this widow, who was arriving in the French capital, on no account married anyone but a Marsovian.

The Ambassador was in difficulties. All the Marsovians in Paris were married—including himself. But stay, there was one bachelor! That was Prince Danilo, Secretary to the Embassy. A young man who took his job very lightly, he had been sent there because he had become entangled with a Marsovian girl, a real beauty but a plebeian. His aristocratic old Uncle could not stand that, so Danilo was bustled off to Paris to break the love affair—and the girl, who loved him, was left lamenting. But not for long. She had her pride. She had thought little of a lover who yielded to avuncular demands when Love called the other way. She had taken her revenge. She had married—and, of course, married that banker above-mentioned, and was now extremely rich, as well as lovelier and more desirable than ever. Moreover, she held the future of her country in those tiny and delightful hands. . . . Here was really something! . . . And the intriguing thing was the fact that the man who could save the situation was the lover who had left her!

There were lots of other interesting things going on, too, it appeared;

there were faithless wives and wives for the moment resisting temptation. They saw the wife of the Ambassador, Natalie, informing her would-be lover, Viscount Camille de Jolidon, that she was a dutiful wife—and doing so in a very beautiful and compelling melody. And since the lover was Robert Evett, who had a fine tenor voice, who could wear his clothes and act, and who was by now a Daly's favourite, they liked that. They liked Natalie in the person of Elizabeth Firth, too. She could sing really well, and British audiences will always react to good singing.

The two principal characters had not yet appeared, but the audience had had no excuse for yawning. They had seen their old favourite, Freddy Kaye, in the character of the elderly fire-eater, General Novikovich, running round, repetitive and muddled as ever, with threats against his wife for flirting. It appeared to them, and to the sardonic Councillor of the Embassy, M. Khadja, that it was not the General's wife who wanted looking after so much as the Ambassador's. The Ambassador himself, however, had not, apparently, realized this, and as His Excellency was George Graves, they already scented lots of fun.

It was not long delayed. A flunkey opened folding-doors and admitted Nisch, Messenger to the Embassy, carrying hat and coat and removing his white cotton gloves with an anxious care that held every eye in the house spell-bound. W. H. Berry infused genius into the part of Nisch. He made him a pompous, self-satisfied man with a tremendous sense of his own importance. His whole air and even his gait showed that. For an instant it almost seemed that it was the Ambassador who had arrived! For Nisch might be only a messenger, but he was messenger to an Embassy, and therefore each of his errands, even if it were only to fetch a cab, was, in his estimation, of international importance. He was every official in the world dressed in a little brief authority. It was not only excellent comedy but a little masterpiece of character acting.

For a moment he stood waiting, and then, like a bomb, like a cataract, Baron Popoff, the Marsovian Ambassador, burst upon him, to cross-examine him upon his mission. To say that Graves entered upon a scene is an under-statement—he erupted on to the stage. You heard him "off", demanding the whereabouts of Prince Danilo, long before you saw him; then, as he shot in with a weird, scrambling rush, shouting in his peculiar voice, "*Where* is he? . . . *Where* is he?", the character of Popoff was at once implanted. Surely never before had such an Ambassador as this stormed through even a stage Chancellery! The consequential Nisch could hardly get a word in as the flood of rebuke poured out in that queer, throaty voice, with a baleful intensity, as if the fate of the world were at stake. Nisch, it appeared, had been sent to find the Prince, and bring him back to the ball that he might woo the Widow for his country's good. . . . And now here was the Messenger without the Prince! What did he mean by it?

Graves had a wonderful way of preparing his audience for an attack. He would stand quite still and gaze at the person playing opposite him; he would then place his right hand on his cheek, the right elbow supported by the left hand, and, with legs apart, listen to what was being said. You knew he was cogitating, that he would deal with the situation swiftly and efficiently. Then he would shut one eye, and focus the other upon his opponent until it appeared to protrude, while the audience waited, spell-bound, for the utterly unexpected but perfectly apposite remark which demolished all defences. . . .

Add to this the explosive interjections, the shattering "asides", the fearful innuendo in the roving eye, the leaps from Marsovia with its *haute politique* to reminiscences of London boarding-houses and fish-mongers . . . and back again . . . it was all a bewildering phantasmagoria, in which George Graves, without realizing it, was carrying on the best traditions of the classical *commedia dell' arte*. Such, in the plays of Carlo Gozzi, is Pantalone, who may be Vizier at an Oriental Court without ceasing to be also a doddering Venetian grandfather; such is Tartaglia, who knows how to be at once Grand Chamberlain and a waterside ruffian of the back canals. The gagging "comic", who breezily defies anachronism and inconsistency in historical parts, is familiar to us in England from our pantomimes; but this amazing creation of Graves's fantasy, who, despite all his wild loops through the land of Leicester Square, yet somehow contrived to remain all the time "His Excellency", in full and authoritative control of the situation, was something unique.

And no finer foil could be imagined than Berry. With his immobility, his face that could be as blank one instant as it was expressive the next, he held his own. He was playing opposite a comedian of lightning gags and devastating impromptu descriptions of the actors on the stage with him. Yet when Graves told Berry that, so far from being the diplomatic eagle he fancied himself, he looked "more like a horn-billed duck", Berry in a flash contrived to do so, and shared the laugh. . . . When the Ambassador shambled off again, still oppressed by the threat to Marsovia's solvency, after allowing Nisch at last to inform him that the Prince would come as soon as he could disentangle himself from certain lovely ladies at Maxim's . . . . well, one wonders what Lehár can possibly have made of him.

Edwardes, meanwhile, sat looking at the audience, which was strangely quiet for a First Night. There had been some laughter, there had been some applause, but it had not had the warmth and excitement usual at a Daly's First Night. But they were quite quiet, there was no rustling, no inattentive coughing—and the leading people had yet to come. How would Elsie and Joe hit them? He had banked on his judgment in giving those two the big chance—well, he would soon know. . . .

And Lily Elsie entered; Sonia, the Merry Widow, had arrived at the ball. This slight, lovely creature, slim and graceful, stepped on the stage to fight not only her own battle but that of Daly's, the Guvnor and Lehár. Here was the title rôle, here was the Merry Widow. She got her welcoming applause, not so full-throated maybe as that which used to greet Marie Tempest, Evie Greene, or Isobel Jay—but she got it. And there was a flutter in the house, too, which to experienced ears meant much; there was a little whisper of indrawn breath at this picture of English loveliness.

There was nothing of the Balkans about this Widow; she was not the stately and mature figure that "Hanna Glawari" had presented at the Theater an der Wien; but who cared for that? This was an English Rose, catching the dew of dawn on a June morning—and that was just what they wanted! The men on the stage thronged round her—and the men in the auditorium would have loved to have done the same. Edwardes was watching, and maybe gave a little sigh of satisfaction and relief. Every woman had her opera glasses or her lorgnette on this figure too, as had the men. The women wanted to see her dress, that creation of pastel shades in pink and blue, with the blue ribbon through the blonde hair, matching the eyes beneath it, and the men wanted to see the girl in the dress. Yes; she looked lovely! But could she sing it, could she play it? Every eye was upon her.

The eyes of Lehár, too, never left her. Here was the first real attack in his battle with London; here was the first advance of the picked troops. She was certainly not the sort of Merry Widow to whom he was accustomed; but he had felt the response of the house, and his hopes were high. He was not worrying overmuch about this first, introductory Act —his plums were in the second and third—but this Act must go well, too, and he sensed that Lily Elsie had made a good impression. But what about Danilo? . . . The Widow in song invited all the guests to her mansion, for a Marsovian fête. Would they come? . . . Would they not! And so she walked off on the arm of the Ambassador, the men flocking round her. . . .

The moment of crisis was approaching. Both Edwardes and Lehár felt the tension. Danilo—Joe Coyne—was due. Edwardes believed; Lehár was doubtful—very, very doubtful. He had not been able to do anything about this very odd bit of casting—this leading man in a romantic Viennese operette who was not handsome, dashing or carelessly debonair, and who could not sing. . . and now the moment had come. Nisch, the faithful messenger of the Embassy or Legation—they called it both on the programme, by the way—had after all prevailed with the errant Prince and made him come to the Embassy. No Cinderella was ever more eager to go to a ball than Danilo was loath to do so. And so he arrived; Joseph Coyne made his entrance.

Many of that audience had never seen him before, but, by long custom, expected the usual hero of operette, of musical comedy. They had seen, for so many years, the handsome face of Hayden Coffin, heard his resonant baritone voice, noted his confident bearing, which had "Hero" written all over it. And here came a figure in evening dress, making an entrance without dash, with absolute reluctance, with an odd walk, and a face not handsome, not even good looking, but round, a bit blank and above all worried. Indeed, Danilo did not want to come to the ball. He had been at Maxim's—amongst his girl friends—doing his best to make things gay with champagne. He was very, very tired, he was annoyed at being fetched along; he was perhaps not altogether quite sober.

It was so different from the usual entrance of the hero that the audience sat amazed. What did this mean? Lehár watched Coyne as a cat watches a mouse. If his Widow tonight was strange to him, his Danilo was even stranger. He seemed to have nothing in common with that of the dark and passionate Louis Treumann, half Parisian fop and half Balkan savage, speaking in a curious South European accent, partly Hungarian and partly Croatian. . . . And what about the singing?

Lehár's baton rose—and Coyne had his first number. He told of the joys of Maxim's, and of the girls there. Literally he *told* it, speaking the words, but speaking them so clearly, with such quiet meaning, and in such perfect time, that the melody behind them, with all the lilt of Maxim's and ladies in its dancing notes, was brilliantly enhanced by it. Then, overcome with fatigue, boredom and wine, Danilo fell fast asleep on a sofa. Not the behaviour of a hero. The audience looked at each other—this was strange, but it was rather nice, rather a pleasant change.

Before they could think about it, the Merry Widow was back. She saw Danilo, her former lover, fast asleep. She wakened him. They met. And there was a thrill for everyone in that meeting. They played their scene and played it for all it was worth. Danilo covered his embarrassment—and the Widow took the initiative. This was where the point of Widowhood came in. Here was no ordinary heroine, shrinking in maidenly modesty before the man she loved; here was a rich woman of the world, coming face to face with a man whom she considered had slighted her. She taunted him; she said that probably, now she was rich, he would like to resume that romance of theirs?

But Danilo was not a fool. He was stung by his position, and still worse by his knowledge that he not only loved this girl still, but loved her all the more. And not on account of her money. He repelled her suggestion. He informed her in good set terms that on his oath he would never tell her again that he loved her. The Widow laughed. She would make him propose. He was firm in his refusal. They parted on bad terms; but it was now evident that something new in musical plays (if not in Shaw's) had arrived. In this one the Woman was to be the Pursuer.

The Ambassador now explained the situation to Danilo. The Prince was sorry, but he could not wed this Sonia. "So, you'd *thwart* me, would you?" screamed Graves, imparting to the word a fearful resonance like the ripping of tough canvas, but Danilo was smilingly obdurate. He had an oath in Heaven! All he could do for his country was to promise that he would upset the apple cart of other suitors of non-Marsovian race. And with that Popoff had to be content. He was himself involved in some trouble, for old General Novikovich had found a fan with the words "I love you" written on it, and was proclaiming with lachrymose howls that it could belong to nobody but his wife. Popoff had to exercise all his diplomacy to make the General believe that the fan belonged to his own wife, Natalie . . . which was the unfortunate truth, though Popoff did not know it.

To see Graves holding the General in his arms, contemptuous of the old fool, yet sorry for him, and slightly ashamed of such a scene in public, was to watch superb comic acting. Now he would try to shut the General's mouth, now to staunch his tears, kicking them away from him on the floor, and ejaculating, as he held the weeper off from his chest, "Damme, sir, you're sopping me through!" It is pale in print, but, with George Graves's agonized intensity, it was convulsing to watch.

And the ball went on, Danilo a lonely figure in evening dress against a swirling background of colour, while the music began to mount to the heights of Lehár's power with the defiant invitation to the dance,[1] and the tender melancholy of "The Night of the Ball Will Go By", bringing with it the forgotten fragrance of a hundred summer ballrooms and all the impulsive despairs of youth. The cotillion was announced; the ladies had the choice of partners. All the men pushed forward, hoping to be the Widow's choice. She flung her challenge—she chose Danilo. There, in front of them all, he refused. But he claimed the right as chosen partner to do what he liked with her choice. He put the dance up for auction—10,000 francs to dance with the Widow, the money to go to charity!

That stopped the impecunious suitors. But Natalie had urged her persistent lover Jolidon to marry the Widow. He stepped forward; he would pay the price; he would dance with the Widow—but he had his eye

---

[1] "O *kommet doch, o kommt, Ihr Ballsirenen!*" in its better-known German title.

on Natalie all the time. She may have been a dutiful wife, but she was also a jealous woman. She could not bear to see her lover, when it came to the point, dancing with anyone so entirely desirable as Sonia. She bore Jolidon off . . . the dance began.

Sonia and Danilo were left face to face. He challenged her. "You see how mean men can be," he told her—"now, left alone, will you dance with me?" But she, angered by his trick, refused. So Danilo danced alone. The orchestra, under Lehár's inspired baton, swung into a waltz, and Danilo danced it; he danced by himself, round and round Sonia, weaving a spell of rhythm and music, it seemed, and leaving her in no doubt as to his love. She resisted—but who could resist this man with the sad, eager expression, the wondering eyes, the easy, unassumed, natural charm, the man whom she loved and who, she knew in her heart, loved her? She was in his arms; they waltzed together, she protesting that he was bad, but that he danced like an angel; and as they danced, pursuer and pursued, two lovers at arms' length yet clasped together, the curtain fell. . . . Such a conclusion to the act of an operette was as new to an English audience as it had been to the Viennese. They were used to a massed chorus pealing out a thunderous finale, and they had been given instead the lonely figure of a woman lured unwillingly into the waltz by the eyes and hands of a man who seemed at once to woo and to disdain her.

There was applause, but not a full-throated yell of approval. This was all so unconventional. The spell broke, the audience stirred, the men went to the bar, the whole place chattered. Lehár slipped out of his seat and went out of sight. He was as amazed as anyone. This Danilo who could not sing had unquestionably got his audience—Lehár knew that. He had watched every move; he had sensed every reaction; he had even not worried about the singing. There was something about this Danilo that was different; of course the British were a mad race, maybe this was their idea of romance. But even he, Lehár of Vienna, felt the power this odd man Coyne was putting over the footlights—well, we should see. . . .

Edwardes was talking to friends, regular First Nighters, sportsmen, his audience. He was listening to what was being said; he was watching them as they said it; always, he watched. Panic had gone—but early yet to judge—much less enthusiasm than usual—but . . . the best was to come. Maybe this was not a "nitter" after all. And underlying it all was his growing satisfaction that he had been right about Lily Elsie and Joe Coyne; of course he had been right! What fools these actors, these actresses, all were! They never knew what they could do, only what they would like to do! . . .

The audience itself talked. It expressed surprise. This was a bit different, eh? Not quite what one expected? But what pretty music—and Lily

Elsie, eh? By Jove, yes! And this fellow Coyne? Good, don't you think? None of that high-falutin' hero stuff, of which one was getting a bit tired. Sympathize with him, a good chap, behaving like a gentleman, what? And they all admitted that this seemed a real show with a good story. The women were in no doubt at all about Joe Coyne. He had charmed them; they were all for him. . . . Oh yes, quite amusin', quite fresh—nice tunes —and that girl Elsie—by gad, she's lovely! . . .

The bar bells shrilled; the best people returned to their seats. The pit and gallery rushed back to theirs. The foreign element, so strong that night, had already surrendered to this show; but the rest, admitting that they liked it, were not yet carried away. Lehár was back in the conductor's chair again, and the Second Act started. . . .

Now it was the Marsovian fête. There were the exotic, the colourful costumes of the Balkans; there were gypsy melodies and virile Tzigane dancing; the whole thing gathered speed and tempo without losing for one instant the inherent romance—just as Lehár intended. An awkward moment arrived, although the audience knew nothing about it. For Lily Elsie had to sing the song she feared, "Vilia". But tonight something inspired her. She sangt hat song with such romantic magic; she looked so lovely in that Marsovian costume, its black and gold throwing up her delicate beauty; she sang the alluring, slightly sad melody with such yearning, haunting charm—that the audience surrendered. She had been afraid of it, had she? She had not a prima donna's voice, had she not? Well, maybe she was right; but she had something better. She had appeal, sensitivity, glamour, and she understood just what that song of pure romance needed. . . .

The audience was sitting forward by this time. What they wanted now was more of the clash between the lovers, and they got it. They got it in the Cavalier song, with Lily Elsie's fresh April-like voice, in the expression on Joe Coyne's face, now mobile and at work, and in his wonderful dancing—you almost saw the horse this silly Cavalier rode. Yes, they were leaning forward now, their chins exposed to the perfect timing of the composer.

For now came the first really smash hit, a number which, nevertheless, everyone had feared beforehand. It was a sextet which in the Vienna production had proved one of the great moments of the evening and been accepted as the successor to Lehár's already famous comedy march song *"Nechledil, du schöner Mann!"* But in London the rehearsing of it had given great trouble to Freddie Farren, the ballet master. For in this song, called "Women! Women!", he had had to take the six principal comedians and make them work like chorus men. They must keep in line; they must each do exactly what all the others did; it must be drill, drill, drill, and unanimous effort . . . no playing for separate hands, no sneaking of the best positions, no scoring individual laughs. The line-up was Graves, Berry, Pawle, Kaye, Cleather and O'Connor. What a team to drive!

Farren had a dreadful time. They would break line . . . they would get in front of one another . . . each would try to be the last to turn . . . every one of them wanted to stand out on his own. Berry was the adept at this; he had been in a troupe; he knew all about "concerted". Edwardes laughingly called the sextet the "Pierrots", but he was determined that they should do it properly. He urged Farren to get them right, and Farren fought with them, and rehearsed them over and over and over again. With real chorus men it would have been child's play. But six "comics"—that was a different matter.

But now, on the night, the six sang that number as it should be sung, with all the gusto and force at their command, with all they could give it. Its strength, its swing, its power, its march-*cum*-waltz-*cum*-galop rhythm hit that audience right on the point of the jaw. They roared approval. They wanted it time and again. This was their meat; this was the food for that strong, full-blooded generation, and they responded in the true style of a Daly's First Night. Lehár had known what he was doing when he placed that number where he did. Here was the law of contrast, the first law of the drama, in superb example. That number "Women! Women!" sent *The Merry Widow* scudding forward on the full flood-tide of success. After that, it was roses all the way.

But "Women! Women!" was not all. Before its excitement had quite worn away, the audience were faced with the clash of the lovers again. Here was the man still refusing to say those words which meant so much to both, and here was the woman trying to make him. They had completely captured the audience by now, this couple. The public on this First Night were heart and soul in the battle; those two young people had won them. . . . And then came the great moment, came the strains of a waltz, and it happened to be *the* Waltz—and the two young people were dancing, poised yet seeming to improvise, he holding her round the waist, round the neck, whilst she swayed like a willow in the wind, a flower giving to the breeze.

Yet the Waltz, too, had been a source of trouble at rehearsal. Lily Elsie and Joe Coyne had not liked it any more than they liked their parts. For it had to be done Viennese fashion—the man moving to his right and the woman to her left without changing, for the Viennese never reversed. But Farren (with whom nobody could quarrel) had smoothed this out, too, and now that Waltz was sheer entrancement. It crept over the senses, it caught the fancy, it was compelling. Slow, quiet, sensuous, yet simple, it was quite different from the Viennese waltzes the English Public knew already; it was as different from any they had heard as *The Merry Widow* was, say, from *The Country Girl*. But it was electric. The audience, men and women, swayed in unison with that melody, in unison with that couple who waltzed. They were carried away by Romance, by super-magic, such as comes only in a theatre, and comes there very rarely. . . . The men all wished to be Danilo, to hold that adorable piece of girlhood in their grasp; the women yearned for Danilo's arms to be about them. They almost wanted to cry out and tell him to say "I Love You"—the emotional strain was amazing.

At last it was over and the applause broke out. The men in evening dress cheered and beat their hands together until they were sore; the women quivered and cheered shrilly, and as for the pit and gallery they went quite mad. Danilo and Sonia had to dance it again and again . . . and at length, when they were worn out, the show went on.

Drama followed, spiced with comedy. Natalie, the Ambassador's wife, was in the little pavilion with her lover. But the Ambassador had his own reasons for wanting to use that pavilion. He had just received a pressing dispatch from his home government bidding him in peremptory words to secure the Widow's millions without further delay. The terms of this document of State had led him, by some mental process peculiar to himself and his creator, to dwell awhile—a good while—on his early experiences as a poultry fancier, and to relate the immortal saga of "Hetty the Hen" and her remarkable habits. That barnyard lady became so famous in time that people would drop into the theatre just to hear her latest feats; yet she seemed to be, quite naturally, part and parcel of the Marsovian Embassy. But at last he got busy upon his task.

Natalie had decided to part from her lover. He had written on her fan, "I love you": she had written, "I am a dutiful wife". Be that as it may, they were in that summer house when Popoff, with quite other views, looked through the keyhole. Nobody who saw Graves play that scene will forget how he handled it; how he removed the piece of fluff which impeded his vision—and then—saw his wife with Jolidon! . . . Nobody will forget his fury, his roarings, his splutterings, his drawing of his dagger and sharpening it, his renewed yells that nobody must *"thwa-art"* him! . . . He had expected to see Jolidon with Novikovich's wife. Instead, he had seen his own!

But in the confusion the Widow came to the rescue. Through the good offices of Nisch she slipped into the back door as Natalie slipped out, and when that door was open, and Popoff, not to be *thwa-a-arted* any longer, was about to take revenge, behold! there was Jolidon with—the Merry Widow! And a witness to the scene was Danilo. There was the woman he loved in the most compromising position possible! But Sonia

Lily Elsie as Sonia in *The Merry Widow* at Daly's Theatre

The Merry Widow Hat—as worn by Lily Elsie at Daly's—which became the rage of its time

was mistress of the situation. She sang the news of her approaching wedding with the Vicomte, ostensibly to crush but really to sting Danilo into speech. He did not rise to the bait. Instead, he recited that poem about the Prince and the Princess, the two children of Kings, who had parted because the Princess was faithless and the Prince went away. And Danilo proposed to do the same. Said Sonia, "Where are you going?"; and, with a quiver of violins, flashed the reply, "I go back to Maxim's!" . . . and the curtain fell.

In the interval the excitement was tremendous; the audience needed no special summons to get back to their seats for Act Three. On all sides one heard Lily Elsie, Coyne, Graves, Berry, Evett, and . . . Lehár! On all sides they were whistling, humming and beating time to that Waltz which still danced before their eyes. So the curtain rose on Act Three to an electrified house. It was Maxim's and it was all of Maxim's.[1] There were the lovely, lively and not respectable ladies; there was the chatter, the laughter, the music, the popping of champagne corks.

Moreover Edwardes had, with the sure instinct of showmanship, kept a superb bit of comedy back until now. In the cast was an actor named Ralph Roberts, a small man playing a small part. It was described on the programme simply as "Waiter at Maxim's", but what the fantastic little fellow made of it was prodigious. Into the smart setting of Maxim's he introduced, with delightful incongruity, a mid-Victorian waiter, who yet still contrived to be French, with long side-whiskers. He was always in a hurry, seldom out of trouble, and usually involved in complications with the champagne coolers. In less artistic hands, and under any other producer than Edwardes, the character would have developed into mere clowning. But it was held to its place in the picture, and nobody who saw *The Merry Widow* at Daly's ever forgot the Waiter at Maxim's.

No, the last Act assuredly did not tail off; the suspense was still taut. Everybody seemed to have reached Maxim's. There was Nisch, watching Frou-Frou dance upon the table at which he sat. What an expression he had, inwardly racked by the responsibility of his messengerial position, by his innate respectability, and by the disgrace of being in such a place as Maxim's at all! But the dainty ankles and flashing limbs were too much for him. He would gradually surrender to the charm, examine the ankles—a few inches from him—through opera glasses, and then throw everything to the winds and join in the dance.

Frou-Frou on the table was Mabel Russell. She was to become a star both of musical comedies and straight plays, making a tremendous hit

[1] English readers will be surprised to know that in the Viennese original of *The Merry Widow* there is no scene at Maxim's at all. The Third Act represents simply a cabaret in the Parisian style organized by the Widow (with real *grisettes*) at her fête, in order to tease Danilo by the suggestion of his favourite haunt.

H

as the girl crook in the melodrama *Within the Law*, at the Haymarket in 1913. This dainty, dark, talented girl—an exquisite dancer—had the stuff of a real star. She married twice, first in 1912 Stanley Rhodes, who died so tragically the same year, and then, in 1917, Hilton Phillipson. One thing it is safe to bet is that neither she nor Bill Berry, when she was dancing on the table-top, dreamed that in 1923 she would become a Member of Parliament, sitting for Berwick-on-Tweed!

She did not stay long in the part of Frou-Frou. She was wanted at the Gaiety in *The Girls of Gottenburg*. It was well that she went there, for, on the second night, Gertie Millar sprained her ankle on the stage during the show, and Mabel Russell, without rehearsal, took over the part and played it until she returned. Her place on the table top at Maxim's was taken by Gabrielle Ray, that amazingly pretty piece of blonde girlhood, as light and graceful as thistledown. She had a reedy little pipe of a voice; but nobody complained of that when they were watching her long legs and thrilling to the joy of her dancing. Berry had to throw Gabs Ray all over the stage—and catch her. Sometimes he failed to catch her, and down she would come with as big a bang as such a tiny person could make. "How's your . . . where I dropped you last night?" Berry gagged, and Gabs admitted it was sore.

Yes, they all arrived at Maxim's for this last Act, even the Ambassador himself—and what an arrival his was! With cloak, cigar, and shiny top-hat, under the brim of which that roving eye gleamed more wickedly than ever, George Graves looked the epitome of dignified guiltiness.

Last of all, the Widow came too. And what a gasp when she appeared. For she was wearing a hat . . . a hat? no, a HAT—the sight of which sent every woman into ecstasy and the quick resolve to have one just like that at the earliest possible moment. But still the battle raged; still Danilo would not say those three words which meant so much; still Popoff feared for Marsovia and its money; and then, at last, after about the best constructed last Act of any musical show, Sonia admitted to Danilo that she was not going to marry Jolidon, and the forbidden words trembled on his lips.

Coyne was just as amazing as Lily Elsie. The eyes of both were saying what their lips must not utter; and then came the strains of that Waltz again—the audience applauded at the mere sound of it—and again that wonderful pair were dancing, and hovering on the brink of surrender. Yet even now Danilo still held back. The Ambassador then said he would divorce his faithless wife and marry Sonia, to make the money safe. He was, however, placated by the production of the supposedly incriminating fan, with, however, Natalie's inscription, "I am a dutiful wife" . . . And Nisch kept his secrets to himself.

But the time had come for Sonia to throw her bombshell. She declared, "Oh, if I marry again, I lose all my money." This staggered Popoff, but it brought Danilo to his feet. This altered everything; this made her again the penniless girl he had first loved; this removed any stigma of fortune-hunting! He could now say, with all his heart, what his eyes, his hands, all of him but his voice, had been saying all the time. He said them to Sonia, the words he had sworn he would not say—"I love you". And she, now triumphant, told him that according to the will, although she lost everything, it all went to her husband! Truly the words of that sextet which had stopped the show and quickened the pace, both at the same time, had been right—it had said about women "You may study their ways all you can, but a woman's too much for a man". Indeed the Merry Widow, soon to be a widow no longer, had lived up to that. She had got her man.

She had got more than that; she had got every man, woman or child in the theatre. The curtain fell on scenes resembling pandemonium. The audience, from stalls and boxes to the back of the gallery, were mad with delight. This was Success—success of the biggest and brightest kind—success of the sort one seldom sees in a theatre. It was a triumph; it was more, it was the birth of a new era in musical plays. It placed Graves, Berry, Evett, and the rest on the heights; it made new names, it consolidated reputations. And at the topmost, dizziest peak of this mountain of success stood two people—Lily Elsie and Joseph Coyne, almost unknown in London prior to that night, so far as fame went, but now taken to the hearts of the British playgoing public and enshrined there for life—with memories to endure as long as anyone lived who saw them. Joseph Coyne was always "Joe" until he passed on, and today people love his memory. Lily Elsie, happily, still graces this world with her beauty.

That night was indeed remarkable. The applause went across the foot-lights like a prairie fire, accompanied by roars of cheers, warm and glowing with pleasure and affection, such cheers as are seldom heard by players, such cheers, such feeling as a few only encounter once in a life-time—and the majority never know at all. Such applause is the most intoxicating drink, the headiest stuff of all acclamation, and it can only be heard in a theatre. Public heroes, great statesmen, savour some of it, but there is never the same affectionate warmth about that, because they have been themselves, while the others have been Illusion and reaped a double meed thereby. It is what makes the frustrating, heartbreaking, uncertain life of Theatreland worth while . . . and it comes so seldom! The particular triumph of these two, Lily Elsie and Joseph Coyne, had not been gained by boosting or publicity; it had been gained by themselves and their talent, and by the understanding of George Edwardes. They had won, despite themselves. Neither had wanted to play their parts; they had done so against their will. But the Guvnor had known best. . . .

It seemed the applause would never stop; shouts for the players filled the air. "Coyne!" . . . "Elsie!", came the yell time and again; "Graves!", "Berry!", "Evett!", "Firth!"—all of them! They took calls in a row, with the chorus, bowing to that tempest which came to them. They took calls in groups, by twos and threes, and by themselves. Everybody took calls —Captain Basil Hood for his excellent book, a model of its kind, Adrian Ross for his almost perfect lyrics, and, of course, there were howls for the Guvnor. He took his call, upright and erect, his blue eyes gazing at his audience, his mouth smiling under his moustache. The cares had fallen away; this "stop-gap" had done the trick. No more worries now! . . . And then they began calling again for Lily Elsie and Joseph Coyne, and those two responded, she a little dazed and wondering, Coyne cool and a bit saturnine.

But there was somebody else they yelled for too—another name which resounded through those quivering walls, that of Franz Lehár, whose magic had been the real reason for this wonderful, unforgettable evening of real theatre. And Lehár took his bow, his first one in London. He had come, he had seen, he had conquered. London lay joyfully at his feet, the willing captive of his dancing notes. He seemed calm, and he bowed with his usual military precision, but his eyes glistened with gratitude that this should happen to him. He, who had heard so many plaudits, knew that the true, deep ring was here, knew that he was now throned in London's affections . . . and indeed London went Lehár mad.

He had done more than merely score a success. His Waltz was to be whistled, sung, hummed, ground out on piano organs (the broadcasts of those days), played in restaurants by orchestras, at the seaside, in parks, at exhibitions, on parade by brass and military bands, tinkled on pianos in innumerable homes, churned on records on the new popular gramophones, danced by couples who would imagine themselves Sonia and Danilo at parties everywhere—there were no public *Palais de Danse* then. He bowed in thanks. He had indeed started a new epoch. His music would enrich still further the bright gold of the Edwardian Empire, and it had saved the Edwardesian Empire. Indeed, he was Fortune's Favourite, but by talent, not favouritism, on that night of nights. . . .

The audience poured out, an excited, noisy, gay mob, whistling and singing, to spread the news. The critics went off to write their eulogies, the members of the company to celebrate in their own way, treading on the inflated, sunny air of happiness and success. Before George Edwardes left the theatre he gave instructions that a new production was to be prepared right away—no need for economy now. Everybody in that theatre, from principals down to stage hands, from box-holders up to the "gods", was immensely happy—except for two people. One was the man who had written the original English version, and never seen or heard a word of it; the other, a man whose name had been called until throats were hoarse with the calling—Joseph Coyne. Joe could not see what the fuss was about; he still did not like the part; he still thought he was rotten; and he thought so to the end.

CHAPTER TEN

Waltz Time

THE day after the production of *The Merry Widow* Daly's was besieged. Edwardes had his call in the morning, and told them they were all good boys and girls; Lehár beamed upon them, bowed, shook hands and paid compliments through the interpreter. A few cuts were made, some tightening up took place, and *The Merry Widow* was in full sail.

What had happened overnight was a revolution in musical plays. The focal point was now Vienna, the master musician, Franz Lehár. His name was heard everywhere; music shops were crowded by people demanding copies of the Waltz, copies of the Selection; and the publishers worked hard to cope with the demand. The days of Monckton and Rubens were ended so far as Daly's was concerned, although they were as strong as ever in their other theatrical homes, at the Gaiety, which never came under the Viennese spell in the days of Edwardes; at the Prince of Wales's, the Shaftesbury and elsewhere. But Daly's was now Viennese. It did not matter that not a scene of *The Merry Widow* took place in Vienna, that not a character was Viennese. The soul of it was that city of light and laughter, expressed through the music of its son, Lehár.

There was no worry now, at Daly's, about finance, no hurry for the successor—that was due for a long wait. A new type of music, music which pulsed with passion, which was lit by romance, had arrived. Those were the days when the world moved to waltz time, and the King of the Waltz was Franz Lehár. It was Waltz Time everywhere, and the Waltz of Waltzes was *The Merry Widow*. Lehár could go home, satisfied, and not a little proud. There was no conceit, no loftiness, no display of self-confidence over this tremendous success. He was just the same, gratified but grateful; *The Merry Widow* had conquered again. Its London success had eclipsed its success everywhere else. The original Viennese First Night had been a mere shadow of the London one.

Lehár was never above learning, and he had learned something at Daly's. He had received a most unexpected lesson; he had seen something he did not believe possible. His objection to and doubt of Joseph Coyne as Danilo have been recorded; but he had watched that man's success take place before his very eyes. He had seen a Danilo who could not sing give an entirely new rendering of the part—and he knew that this was the way in which Danilo should really be played. At all subsequent productions in other parts of the world he insisted that Coyne's method of reciting instead of singing the legend of the Prince's children should be followed. Seldom has an actor received such a tribute.

Coyne had awakened that morning to real fame. So had Lily Elsie. Her triumph had left that lovely lady very dazed and a little mystified. She was not conscious that she had done anything out of the way—only her best. But Lehár had seen in her, too, a new type of Merry Widow. He did not insist that all the Widows should be played that way in future, because he knew that it was Miss Elsie's own personality which had supplied the new touch. You could not find anywhere else that calm, serene beauty, unruffled and peaceful as the moment of dawn on a spring day, that perfect example of English womanhood, with such lissom grace, such elegance, such a fresh voice and so much understanding of acting to go with it. No, that must remain with Lily Elsie. But Lehár no longer saw Danilo as the hero of operette; he saw him as the real live character which Coyne had created. Lehár would never compose a score to a book which did not inspire him, and what he looked for in the book was Life. He had found it in the *Widow*; he had given it a soul with his music; that was a great part of the secret of his success. But he now knew that the characters, always real, could be played in other ways than those he had known on the Continent.

Graves was another case in point. He was an entirely different Ambassador from any of the others. That was the art of being George Graves, who brought the puppets of musical plays to life in his own way. If Lehár, with his scanty command of English, can have understood very little of what Graves was saying, he was far too subtle a man of the Theatre not to have appreciated the expression and the pantomime, and to have realized that a great master of humour stood before him. As for Graves's fellow-countrymen, they took him from that night to their hearts. They could never tire of him—he was new at each performance. It was of course a bit of a trial to play with him, but he never shook Bill Berry. He too had full scope in *The Merry Widow* and he had taken it. From now on Berry ranked among the comic stars of London.

In private life this fine actor of the old school had a great deal of dignity and always kept up his position of leading comedian. He was very consciously a celebrity. He held court in his "local" on a Sunday evening, during set hours, and he had a certain number of drinks. It was never exceeded. Berry was always a very careful man and saved his money. As life crept on he became more and more a creature of habit. He had so many pipes a day, each lit at a certain time—right on the dot. He did the same things at the same time daily. He had what he called a "shut-eye" every afternoon at four; nothing must disturb that. Even when a friend told him he was going to eulogize him over the air he could not listen, much as he wanted to, because it would happen during the precious nap. He did not listen either. He went to bed at the same hour every night, come what may. Air raids and bombardments never altered that.

In his retirement he lived in a charming bungalow which he had bought, perched on the Kentish cliffs. There he cultivated his garden, and there he tended his fuchsias. There were only about a dozen, and truly they were not remarkable; but to Bill they were the best in the world, so everybody praised them. He went down into the village at certain fixed times; he spoke to the same people; but he loved to be recognized and pointed out. He was always a bit hurt when young people were not familiar with his face or name, even after twenty years of retirement. He had a toy theatre, modelled on Daly's, upon which he set scenes he had himself designed and painted. He had a collection of Toby jugs and of little figures from Dickens—he adored Dickens. He always wanted to play Mr. Micawber, and wonderful he would have been.

It was a very small, a very narrow, world after his triumphs at Daly's and his ten consecutive years of glittering successes at the Adelphi after that, but he did not notice it. It was his world, and he was content. Even in his days of stardom he was a self-contained entity in all his plays. He knew the rest were there; he played with them, and was a most unselfish comedian—but to him they were shadows. He was the substance. Naturally in his later years he lost touch; he had few who made the journey to see him. But those who did got a royal welcome, had the flag run up the flagpole in their honour, and were regaled with sherry, biscuits and gags.

The gags it is true were a bit old-fashioned, and Bill would insert humorous asides to draw attention to them; but he still had that amazing, mobile face, that glint in the eye and that air of complacency which had been so great a part of his stock-in-trade. And so long as they did not overstay their welcome—by which is meant so long as they did not interrupt his unalterable daily time-table—he rejoiced in them and made them at home. He was a most regular and voluminous correspondent. He prefaced each letter by saying it did not need an answer, proceeded to ask about a dozen questions, besought you not to hurry to reply—any time would do—and if he did not get an answer by return a post-card would come asking if you were ill or if his letter had gone astray.

But old Bill Berry was a great comedian of the great days, a star who deserved his stardom, who really lived up to his billing; and if he remained true to his epoch and his jokes, well, they were good jokes, and at least he took them into retirement with him. He loved to talk about old times—and the talk always got round to *The Merry Widow*. He lived to be eighty-one, and died as he had lived, a simple, honest, clean-living man who never sullied his conversation with coarseness and never cracked a vulgar gag on the stage. He did not need to; he was a really funny man without such aids. And it was his performance of Nisch in Lehár's *Merry Widow* which had put him in the front rank. . . .

Everybody wanted to see the piece. The agencies could not buy fast enough; the public rushed for seats; the queues stretched for amazing distances. The Merry Widow was the toast of the town, was on everyone's lips—and, at least part of her, on every woman's head. For London burst out into a perfect rash of "Merry Widow hats". It became more than a fashion, it became a rage. No woman with any claim to being "in the swim", as the phrase then went—and naturally that meant every woman —was without her Merry Widow hat, indeed, without as many as she could afford, of different colours. The fashion swept from Mayfair to Mile End, from Bayswater to Bow. The ladies in the suburbs and the *grande dames* of Park Lane (then in its zenith) were all Sonias so far as their headgear went. And if they did not all quite succeed in looking like Lily Elsie, still they were very, very charming hats indeed.

It seemed that nothing could stop *The Merry Widow* from running. All previous plans went by the board. *The Dollar Princess*, as we have said, was postponed *sine die*. The Guvnor had another play, too, designed for Daly's, which was only in course of preparation, composing and writing when *The Merry Widow* was produced. It could not get into the theatre for which it was designed. So Edwardes sent it to the Gaiety, which had been the official destination for the *Widow*. That evened matters out, he thought. The play was *Havana*, with Evie Greene in the lead, and with music composed by Leslie Stuart. Alfred Lester had a fine comedy part, suited to his melancholy style, but a foil was needed. The Guvnor told Bill Berry he must leave Daly's and go to the Gaiety. Berry did not want to go; much as he adored and revered Edwardes, he was in revolt, polite but firm. Edwardes told him then that there was to be a special scene which he was to play with his wife Kitty Hanson, who was always engaged jointly with him, but seldom allowed to appear in the play, and that broke Berry down. He went. He succeeded personally, but *Havana*, which was wrong for the Gaiety, did not have a very long run, and Berry came back to join *The Merry Widow*, getting a tumultuous welcome. . . .

He and Kitty were married a long time; he had been in humble circumstances when they wedded, and she rose with him to share his prosperity. Her later years were sad for both of them, by reason of her health and infirmity. Then his Kitty died, and Berry announced that his heart was broken. A few months later he married an old friend of his and his wife's. He was ageing and lonely, and she understood him well. She made him happy; he would introduce her as "his darling". If you wanted really to please the old man, who lived on the memories of past glories, you would enlarge on his talents and his superb performances. He would sit very quiet, listen attentively, and swell with pride. Then he would nudge the second Mrs. Berry and say, "Do you hear? That's me he is talking about." He meant no disrespect to his first wife's memory by his second marriage; he was used to being married and he was a slave to habit. In all things he disliked change. The cook, who did a lot else beside cooking but who was a very good cook indeed, and whose name was Daisy, had been in his service for forty years. . . .

There were frequent comings and goings in the cast of *The Merry Widow* during its long, long run. It ran past two anniversaries, and played for 778 performances. Lily Elsie would take holidays, and when the play was first given in Manchester, in 1908, the Guvnor sent her there in answer to a clamorous demand. The people of Manchester had, many of them, known her as a child, and they loved her quite as much as the Londoners did. They welcomed her as a star with true North-country loyalty. During these absences of hers from Daly's the other Merry Widows who played there were Emmy Wehlen, a German actress of great charm, Constance Drever, Gertrude Glyn, Daisie Irving and Clara Evelyn.

There were many Widows on tour, for the play swept the provinces as it had swept London. Amongst them were Gertrude Lester, Deborah Volar, Norah Barry, Phyllis Le Grand—who had made her first appearance on the stage on *The Merry Widow's* First Night as a girl from Maxim's —Adrienne Brune, Helen Gilliland, Louie Pounds, and nearly all the girls who had played it at Daly's in Lily Elsie's absence. To say that her absence from the cast made no difference would not be true, for she was unique; but the impetus of the play carried it along, even without her. It went all over the country by means of its tours; it visited every city and town where it could be played. Two of the touring Danilos who were specially pre-eminent were W. Louis Bradfield, a West End star in his own right, and in the opinion of some of his admirers the most fascinating of all the Danilos, and Leonard Mackay, a big, strong type of man, who played the part with a touch of hardness, but was undeniably effective.

Mackay played lead, also, opposite to Evie Greene in *Havana*, and was in *Autumn Manœuvres* at the Adelphi. Later he was to have an important part in *Desert Song* at Drury Lane. Among the actors who played Popoff on tour were Lionel Victor, a clever little comedian, who was afterwards at Daly's in *The Waltz Dream*, and later in life became almost a fixture in the never-ceasing *Lilac Time*; Eric Thorne, already bearing the laurels of provincial fame in Gilbert and Sullivan; and that ripe, sound and resourceful comedian, still as fresh as ever, James Godden.

The Widow even went into the very small places, with what are known as "Fit-Up Companies", playing in Corn Exchanges, Town Halls and the like, where the platforms had to be made into stages by "fitting up" a proscenium arch; and with all its visits, for it kept on going back, it never reached saturation point. The public could never have enough of it. The dates of its run at Daly's were from the 8th June, 1907, until the 31st July, 1909, and well over a million people saw it there. It received many Royal Visits, and King Edward VII became a real *Merry Widow* fan. He saw it four times. At Daly's alone it grossed over a million pounds at the box-office—this play which was not expected to succeed. . . .

It gave its name to dishes in restaurants, as well as to hats and all sorts of other things. It was the cause of an outbreak of Sonias in this land; clergymen officiating at the font grew quite accustomed when christening a baby girl to hearing that her name was to be Sonia. Changes in cast could not affect it, for, under the care of Edwardes, those changes or temporary substitutions never let down the quality. Mary Grey played Natalie after Elizabeth Firth, and sang delightfully. For a time Tailleur Andrews was the Jolidon instead of Robert Evett, and he had a fine voice. Basil Foster, of the famous cricketing family, became M. de St. Brioche. The Maxim's Girls often altered; but always retained their beauty and charm, for newcomers included May Hobson, Alma Griffiths and G. Carrington.

When Fred Kaye was away for a time General Novikovich was admirably played by Robert Nainby, one of the famous Gaiety Theatre team, who specialized in peppery foreigners, mostly French. His Commissaire of Police in *The Circus Girl* remained a hilarious memory, and his Novikovich was as good. Even George Graves went away at last, and that sound comedian J. F. McArdle replaced him, closely following his style. W. H. Berry, as stated, went to the Gaiety for a while and his part was played by Penderell Price, and probably by others too. When Lennox Pawle took a holiday, Arthur Longley played Cascada. Joe Coyne did indeed go back to America, but not for the reason he used to tell Freddie Farren in the Cavour—he just went for a holiday. He and Berry rejoined the cast on the same night—and received tremendous ovations.

Lily Elsie stepped not only into stage fame but into picture-postcard fame, which was the fashion at that time. Frank Foulsham, the great stage photographer of the period, although he seldom took a picture himself, was in many ways the creator of the picture-postcard craze, and he admits doing very well out of *The Merry Widow*. His firm, Foulsham and Banfield, made at least £600 out of pictures of it published in the Press.

The First Anniversary on Whit Monday, the 8th June, 1908, was a tremendous occasion. Edwardes presented every member of the audience with a souvenir, a beautifully bound book, with truly delightful coloured illustrations by Talbot Hughes, and the story of the play told in rhyme with grace, wit and clarity by that master of the art of lyric-writing Adrian Ross (who was in private life Arthur Reed Ropes, M.A., an historian and a most learned man). Those were the days when Managers made these souvenir gestures to their public, and the souvenirs were things of beauty. Sir Herbert Tree excelled in producing them, and that of *The Arcadians*, too, was a notable work. But the *The Merry Widow* souvenir books caught exactly the spirit of the play, and those lucky enough to get them treasure them yet. It was worth noting that the description applied to the production was "the Universally Popular Play with Music".

There was a *Merry Widow* dinner in 1909, at the Hotel Cecil. It was given by the O.P. Club, a famous club of playgoers, who desired to honour all connected with this memorable production. The Guests of Honour were George Edwardes, Joe Coyne, Lily Elsie, Robert Evett, Elizabeth Firth, George Graves, W. H. Berry and, of course, his wife Kitty Hanson. Sir Max Pemberton was in the chair and in support was Carl Hentschel. Everyone made speeches. Lily Elsie was scared to death, but scored just as she did on the First Night at Daly's. Sir Max Pemberton gave the toast, and George Edwardes replied. He rose to his feet. "My Lords, Ladies and Gentlemen," he said—and paused. His secretary sitting nearby, with a script of the speech, prompted him. "Go on, Guvnor," he urged in a loud whisper, "thank 'em, thank 'em!" And whenever Edwardes paused for effect he received a very loud prompt. But it got laughs. Sir Max Pemberton, too, drew laughter by describing Daly's as "a secondary school for Peers".

The second anniversary was another great occasion, bringing another souvenir, with grateful thanks for the public's support in a Foreword by Edwardes. But perhaps the last night of that remarkable run—for runs were not as a rule so long then as they are now—transcended everything else. The whole of the interior of the theatre was a mass of real flowers, with a main *motif* of rambler roses. People waited many hours for admission, and there were members of that audience who had seen the piece ten, twenty, thirty, forty, fifty times.

Amongst these regular frequenters was a dark young man of extreme handsomeness, with a profile which caused people to turn and look at him. He could not keep away from Daly's in the days of *The Merry Widow*. He sat in the pit; he sat in the gallery; and he drank it all in. He watched the beauty of complete artistry in stagecraft; he watched every detail; he forgot none of it, and he stored it up for what he hoped would be future use. Especially he noted the Quality of everything he saw. He had laid his heart at the feet of Lily Elsie. He would sit entranced when she was on; he would rush round to the stage door to see her come out, and shyly beg her autograph. But, above all, he listened to the music. This was what he considered music—this was near his ideal. And he had music born in him, for he drew his first breath in an atmosphere of song, in that land of song which is Wales. This music of Lehár was to him inspiration. The man from Vienna was his Master.

Years afterwards, when he became an idol of the Theatre himself, when his music swept audiences off their feet, when his melodies drew immense crowds to the plays which he not only composed but wrote and played in, when armies, indeed nations, sang his songs, he would state proudly that Lehár had been his guide, that he had founded his style upon him, that to the music of Lehár he owed more than he could tell. His name was Ivor Novello. And in time he had the immense joy of playing with his idol, Lily Elsie, in one of his own plays. She stood by him at a time of crisis, a thing she would always do; and between them they added an early success to Ivor Novello and another jewel to the crown of Lily Elsie. Their friendship endured to the end of Ivor's life, and it really began, although they did not then know each other, in *The Merry Widow*.

Fantastic prices were offered for seats that last night. Everybody wanted to see the play and the people they loved for the last time—in those characters at any rate. There was, however, an air of sadness engendered by the fact that they were saying good-bye to something they had loved so much. As every member of the cast made his or her entrance there was a roar of cheers. Every tune got its applause when it started, its encore at the end. That audience, embowered in flowers, was loath to let *The Merry Widow* go. It tried to steal minutes to keep it from the end. The Waltz was danced until both Coyne and Lily Elsie were exhausted; Joe said he believed they did it forty-eight times—or perhaps forty-nine. He didn't know. It is certain that they did it more than half a dozen times.

Every number, every dance, every joke, every situation, "stopped the show". The audience had decided that if it must say good-bye, it should be a lingering farewell. But at last the curtain fell and remarkable scenes of applause and emotion took place. The First Night, exciting as that had been, was as nothing to this. The audience climbed over boxes, up walls and took toll of the flowers for trophies of remembrance. The company stood on the stage, behind an embattled array of bouquets and baskets of flowers. The audience hurled further blooms at them. Berry kept one spray of roses, which fell at his feet, thrown from the gallery, until his dying day.

The Guvnor made a short speech of thanks and farewell; he ended by saying, "We love *The Merry Widow* . . ." and he got no further, for a bit, although he had more to say. There were yells of agreement. People shouted, "Who loves Lily Elsie?", "Who loves Joe Coyne?" and there was a roar of "We all do!" from every part of the house. But Edwardes stood, quiet and watchful, savouring his moment of triumph, all the sweeter because so unexpected. At last he got in his final remark, which announced the production of *The Dollar Princess*. And so the curtain fell; the first run of *The Merry Widow* was over. But the audience cheered on, and when it finally dispersed, many were in tears that this magical thing was taken from them.

But as Joe Coyne took off his costume of Danilo for the last time he said he did so with pleasure. Despite that cheering, despite that wonderful display of affection, he still thought he was rotten. . . .

CHAPTER ELEVEN

"*The Count of Luxembourg*"

THE two years following the first production of *The Merry Widow* were not particularly fruitful in Lehár's development. He may have been a trifle distracted by this sudden, amazing success. He may have already realized dimly that there could be no repetition of *The Merry Widow* in its own kind, and that he must strike out new paths. To the lay mind it might well seem that the achievement of such a dazzling score as that of *The Merry Widow*, in which, it may be truly said, there is not a single dull moment,[1] was a feat that might exhaust any composer for a short space. But, on the whole, it appears most likely that what was preoccupying Franz Lehár at this time was the inner necessity of his own nature to rise continually to something higher.

In a document published many years later under the title *Bekenntis* ("Confession") he set forth the convictions that had guided his musical career. He had, he says, always had it in mind to "enlarge the framework of operette". He had come to perceive more and more that "people did not regard it as an art-form, but simply as a means of entertainment, something to be diverted by and then forgotten". The phrase "nonsensical as an operette" had passed into the language.

I searched for the reason, and found that it lay at bottom in the many improbabilities and stupidities of the plot. The characters on the stage were agreeable and pretty, but they lacked heart and soul. I formed the resolve to create real people, and to depict them in such colours that they might actually have lived among us. They were to experience love and suffering as we do. Naturally I had to express this deeper intimacy in the music. I had, without realizing it, to employ operatic means whenever the plot demanded it.

[1] Even the few bars of "background music" played behind the scenes during the dialogue at the beginning of the Ballroom Act have an enchanting quality of their own.

And he goes on to say that while the artists were delighted to have these greater opportunities, and even Opera singers offered themselves for the rôles, the managers were horrified at the demands made on them for larger orchestras and so on, and even a part of the critical world regarded such "flirtation with Grand Opera" as illegitimate.

These passages from the "Confession" indicate the goal that Lehár set himself; but at present he could only feel his way towards it. In 1906 and 1907 a couple of one-act trifles were thrown off—a piece for children entitled *Peter and Paul Travel in Lazyland* and *Mitislaw the Modern*, a cabaret sketch for Louis Treumann—and, in the year after, *The Man with Three Wives*, a musical comedy in the vein of *Die Juxheirat*, in which the acute music critic of the greatest of the Vienna daily papers, the *Neue Freie Presse*, detected the composer's "struggle with himself" and the "almost puritan rigour" of his endeavour to conquer his own failings. "He avoids cheap effects and surprises by his wealth of ideas"; but, adds the critic significantly, "a Vilya song would be sought in vain in the new operette". It was as has been hinted. There could not be two *Merry Widows*.

Something a little nearer to his new ideal Lehár might seem to have found when in 1909 he composed for the Johann-Strauss Theatre *Das Fürstenkind* ("The Prince's Child") to a libretto by his luck-bringer, Victor Léon, based on a French novel by Edmond About. This is a romantic tale of a disguised nobleman who leads a band of brigands in the mountains of Greece, of his innocent daughter, beloved by an American naval officer, and of a lovely English girl traveller held to ransom by the brigand. There are moments when the treatment seems to tremble on the verge of grand passion, and indeed Grand Opera, but in the end all resolves itself into gaiety and the eternal waltz. In Vienna *Das Fürstenkind* was a success; but not quite the kind of success Lehár was now seeking.

But it seemed to him possible that he had found what he wanted when the libretto of a romantic Hungarian operette, entitled *Zigeunerliebe* (*Gipsy Love*), was offered to him by its authors Dr. A. M. Willner and Robert Bodanzky, who were working for the Carl Theater. A Hungarian gypsy tale! In setting this Lehár could surely draw upon elemental depths in his own nature, and escape for a while from scented ballrooms and French fun. He set eagerly to work; but, as once before in a crisis of his life, was pulled up sharp by a disagreeable reminder from Messrs. Wallner and Karczag, the Directors of the Theater an der Wien. *Zigeunerliebe* might be destined for the Carl Theater; they had no grounds for protest there. But Lehár was under contract to them to supply a new operette for the Theater an der Wien by the end of 1909. Had he forgotten that? They were in a sour mood, for Lehár's last work for them, *The Man with Three*

Two views of Lehár's Villa
at Bad Ischl, where so much
of his work was done

Bertram Wallis, here seen in *The King of Cadonia*, who scored a big success at Daly's, co-starring with Lily Elsie in Lehár's operette *The Count of Luxembourg* in 1911. King George V and Queen Mary attended the First Night

Wives, had not been a great success, whereas *Das Fürstenkind* at the Johann-Strauss was proving a big winner.

Lehár was exasperated. His head was full of the rhythm and melodies of *Zigeunerliebe*; spiritually he was living in the wilds of his native Hungary; and now he was abruptly required to wrench himself away from all that, and to compose, within the very short time remaining if he was not to be guilty of breach of contract, a whole new operette on some quite different subject.

And where was such a subject to be found? His new librettists, Willner and Bodanzky, a resourceful pair, immediately slipped into his hands the book of an operette with a wholly Parisian setting, *The Count of Luxembourg*. It was on a well-worn theme—the marriage of convenience; but it would do as well as another. Lehár, however, did not intend to waste much time or creative endeavour on such *clichés*. Karczag urged him on. "You must have something up your sleeve!" he pleaded. Lehár had. He produced it in three weeks . . . three weeks to complete the whole score! The job was done, but, "Slovenly stuff!" Lehár murmured shamefacedly to his friends. "Nothing in it!"

There is, however, a fundamental law of psychology that is always being ignored, and yet is always asserting itself—the "law of reversed effort". The moralists are unfortunately not right when they assert that a man's most conscientious work is his best, that genius is an infinite capacity for taking pains, and so on. On the contrary. That which a man throws off in a hurry, which he allows to stream from his unconsciousness just as it comes, without checking the flow by worry and second thoughts, that often exceeds the best he can produce by conscious struggle.

Of this law *The Count of Luxembourg* was to prove an example. It could not mark a step in the progress of Lehár's art; it could not be another *Merry Widow*; but, written with fine carelessness, and suffused with the memories of Lehár's own brief days of Bohemian striving and shifts to keep alive, it sang its light-hearted way to the hearts of his public. Produced on the 12th November, 1909, at the Theater an der Wien, with Otto Storm in the name-part, Fräulein von Ligety, a beginner who soon left the stage to marry, as the heroine, Louise Kartousch as the soubrette, and Max Pallenberg (who was shortly to grip the London public with the macabre humour of his *Spielmann* in Cochran's great spectacle, *The Miracle*) in the leading comic rôle, it was received with tumultuous applause. Its waltz seemed for the moment to eclipse even the *Merry Widow* waltz. . . .

It was not until the 20th May, 1911, that London heard it. On that date Edwardes produced *The Count of Luxembourg* at Daly's. It might be true that Lehár considered this piece a mere trifle; Londoners could not

I

look upon the production of a new play by their favourite composer in this light, and competition for First Night seats was very keen. Crowds for the unreserved parts waited practically from dawn; the management gave them refreshments during the day. The First Night atmosphere was really electric. There was a special reason, as will appear.

Lehár renewed his acquaintance with Lily Elsie, who played Angèle Didier—and who was now, of course, a star of the very first magnitude —very different from the scared girl who had been Sonia at the beginning of the *Widow*. She was now the beloved of all Daly's audiences— the beloved of the country. He met again some of the people he had known before, Fred Kaye, Gertrude Glyn, and a few others. Important among those few others was W. H. Berry. Huntley Wright returned again to the scene of his former triumphs. But Lehár also met a new leading man. Joseph Coyne was not in *The Count of Luxembourg*; instead was a figure of a very different kind, a man of stature and commanding presence, a man of handsome masculinity, with a fine voice, and also an excellent actor, who was the idol of the ladies in a very different way from Joseph Coyne. His name was Bertram Wallis, and he played Count René of Luxembourg.

Bertram Wallis, then at the height of his popularity, had been born in 1874; so he was thirty-five when he played in *The Count of Luxembourg*. He had been trained for the stage by John Millard and Charles Fry, two experienced Shakespearean performers; he had studied music at the Royal Academy, where he won many high awards. Then he joined Ben Greet's company, and could have had no finer start. His first appearance was at the Pavilion, Folkestone, in *Masks and Faces*. His first London job was at St. James's Theatre, in George Alexander's production of *As You Like It*, in which he played Amiens and had a song. He stayed with Alexander for several plays, and then went into musical comedy under Edwardes, touring in *A Greek Slave* and *San Toy*, in which he played Hayden Coffin's rôles. He went to America in 1904, and was with Charles Frohman from 1906 to 1908, playing leading parts in musical plays.

He came back here in 1908, and at the Prince of Wales's Theatre in *The King of Cadonia*, a musical play by Paul Rubens, he created a tremendous sensation. This fine specimen of manhood, with the spreading chest, the rather heavy eyes, the regal carriage and the resonant voice, who could act as well as he could sing, stepped at once, not only into the rank of leading players but into the front rank of matinée idols. Women flocked to the Prince of Wales's. They stood outside the stage door, those who could not get in, just to catch a glimpse of him through a window as he passed by. It was the greatest conquest since the Danilo of Joe Coyne, and by an entirely different type of man with an entirely different manner. Bertram Wallis was essentially British, and there was the hint of the bulldog always about that rather full but fine countenance. Men liked him, too. His manliness had a dash of the open air about it which appealed to sportsmen. This was, again, not the typical stage hero, but a man. And when he sang as he did in that show, dressed in a glittering uniform, "There's a King in the Land Today"—well, there was no question about it at all. He followed this triumph with successes in *Dear Little Denmark* and *The Balkan Princess*, both at the Prince of Wales's. He toured and conquered the country. He went into management at the Globe Theatre in a straight costume play *Beau Brocade*, but it was not a good play, and not even he could make it a success. Then came the call to Daly's, and he became the Count of Luxembourg.

It was a trite story; but Basil Hood, who wrote the English book, and now had his name on the programme, which he had never had during the run of *The Merry Widow*, had greatly improved the original version. He had fitted it to this country's needs. Hood was a first-rate craftsman, who understood the Theatre. He could write original libretti with as much skill as he showed in adapting continental originals. He never tried to pass off a translation, just slightly altered. He took the story and told it in the way in which he knew it would appeal to British audiences. He claimed that in *The Count of Luxembourg* there were not more than thirty lines which had been spoken in the Viennese production; the rest was his own. He put in new scenes, new sequences; he put in new characters; he made it almost a new play. He went to Vienna to discuss the question with Lehár and with A. M. Willner and Robert Bodanzky, who wrote the Viennese book. He received the heartiest co-operation from all. Lehár knew what Hood had done to *The Merry Widow*, and had great confidence in him.

Hood knew one great thing about adaptation. He knew the important fact that continental ideas of comedy differed very much, both as regards character and dialogue, from the British idea. It was to that department that he paid the greatest attention. He knew, too, that construction was never the strong point abroad, but that British audiences disliked clumsiness and gappy, incredible happenings. He saw to it that there were none. The original story of *The Count of Luxembourg* was not perhaps of the best, and Hood's alterations helped a lot.

A Grand Duke, of middle age, wants to marry a lovely Opera singer, but he cannot do so because Court etiquette—so strong in Middle Europe —forbids him to marry anyone below the rank of a Countess. So Angèle Didier, the Opera singer, must become a Countess. There is in Paris a poverty-stricken Count, René of Luxembourg, who strives to make a living as an artist. He has a close but lowly friend named Brissard (a character invented by Hood). Hard up, he listens to the temptation of the Grand Duke, who offers him £20,000 if he will marry this girl—and then divorce her. A condition is that he must never see his bride; she must be not only purely titular but invisible too. The Count accepts. He marries his unseen bride with a picture on an easel between them and her hand thrust through to receive the ring. The simple ceremony over, she departs, and the Count proceeds to have a good time on the money he has earned as husband in name but not fact.

The Grand Duke gives a reception worthy of his rank in his Paris mansion. His Angèle is there, and he makes the mistake of inviting the Count as well. The two meet—it was a novelty to keep the leading characters apart for a whole Act—and they fall in love. There are complications, but in the end, of course, they marry, and presumably live happily ever after. The scene of the meeting was beautifully played by Lily Elsie and Bertram Wallis; they were both such attractive people that the sudden falling in love was more than understandable.

The great feature of the score was again a waltz—of course, a waltz. Once again the lovers waltzed, not this time in conflict as in *The Merry Widow*, but because of the magnetism of love. It was a beautiful waltz, because Lehár could not write anything else, but it was not quite the *Merry Widow* waltz. However, it was a sensation, for that couple waltzed up and down a great staircase, doing it with ease, grace and perfect timing. Like all Lehár's waltzes the tune was simple yet had passion beneath it— always the tempo of his waltzes was the beating of lovers' hearts. That waltz was acclaimed and had to be repeated time and again. It swept London, like its predecessor, but it had not quite the same allure, being hampered probably by the fact that this was not the first Lehár operette which the public had seen. But *The Count of Luxembourg* waltzed up the staircase of success with Lily Elsie and Bertram Wallis.

The rest of the cast was excellent, too. There was Huntley Wright, a firm Daly's favourite, as the Duke, Gladys Guy as Juliette, Fred Kaye, Willie Warde, Gladys Homfrey, May Marton, Kitty Hanson (getting into the same show as her husband W. H. Berry again), Alec Fraser, Paul Plunkett, Ridgwell Cullum, Charles Coleman, Gervase Whitehead, Garnet Wilson, Lena Liebrandt, May Hobson, Gertrude Glyn, Madeline Seymour, Clarina Cliffe, Margot Erskine, Gladys Desmond, Doris Stocker, Doris Keppel, Mai Leslie Stuart (daughter of the great composer), Beatrice von Brunner, May de Sousa, a very pretty American girl, with considerable talent, who came to a tragic end years later, and, of course, W. H. Berry.

A special dance was done by Jan Oy-Ra with Beatrice Collier, who had partnered Fred Farren in the famous Apache Dance in *A Day in Paris* at the Empire a few years before. This brilliant young girl had remarkable gifts both as a mime and a dancer. English ballet has never had an artist to surpass her in wordless character acting. Her face and body were transfigured by the emotions of her rôles; and it was almost impossible to believe that the starved and sinister haunter of the Paris underworld was the same person as the lovely, impertinent ballerina of *The Dancing Master*. Miss Collier's career was checked by an injury to her foot, and soon after her return to the Theatre she retired again, to marry, leaving a gap in our native ballet that was never filled. Her appearance in Lehár's *Count of Luxembourg* must have been her last, or almost her last, in public.

Oy-Ra also arranged the dances for the show, and Edward Royce produced for George Edwardes. The first scene was Brissard's studio in Paris and the second the Reception Hall of the Grand Duke, also in Paris. So once again Paris was the locale for the truly Viennese music of Lehár. London clung to the notion of Paris as home of romance; but it placed the music of Vienna before that of the French capital.

There were none of the anxieties of the First Night of the *Widow*. Nobody feared failure, nobody disliked his part. Lily Elsie was an established Queen at Daly's. Indeed, she stood in the same relation to that house as Gertie Millar had to the Gaiety; each of them was the embodiment of her own particular theatre. Now, however, Gertie Millar had left the Gaiety and gone to the Adelphi—or would be going in November of that year—to be partnered there by Joseph Coyne in *The Quaker Girl*.

When Lehár arrived at Daly's for rehearsals he was welcomed by all and happy to be there. He felt at home. This was no battlefield now, but a part of his kingdom, where he ruled jointly with George Edwardes. The rehearsals were happy; everyone was cheerful and confident. They were right. When Lehár took his position that First Night he had no qualms at all, no lurking doubts; he approved everything. The welcoming roar from the audience told him that he was practically sure of another big success. And the show went magnificently. The score was luscious, delicious—the sparkle of champagne, the tang of Tokay, and the coffee and cream of Vienna. It stole over the senses, it set the feet beating. At the end there was a wonderful reception, with calls for all, and a special salvo of cheers for Franz Lehár.

He had done it again. It might have been different; it might not have lived up to the expectations roused by the *Widow*; it could easily have been an anticlimax. But Lehár did not know the meaning of such things. He gave always of the best; he aimed always at the highest target; and he had again hit it plumb in the centre. And for him that First Night was even more exciting than usual. For Their Majesties King George V and

Queen Mary came to see *The Count of Luxembourg*, at its First Performance, a rare and signal honour. They sat in the Royal Box, or rather the
Royal Boxes, for two were made into one. They were delighted by all
they saw. At the end the King sent his Equerry to bid Lehár come to the
box to be presented and to receive the Royal congratulations. Lehár was
in a state of panic. It was not at the thought of the Royal meeting, but
because he could not find his hat, and to appear before Their Majesties
without his hat was to him sacrilege and *lèse majesté*. Nobody, least of all
himself, was ever clear as to whether, in the confusion, he took his own
or somebody else's. But he was received very graciously, and the King
spoke in German to him the whole time. Lehár spent some time in
London on that visit, with his sister Emmy, Mme Papházay. They stayed
at the Carlton, which was now his favourite hotel.

During the course of the run the Guvnor gave him a party, a reception on the stage of Daly's, in the Grand Ducal set. It was held during
the afternoon, and masses of celebrities came to visit the great celebrity
from Vienna. Lehár got to know what it must be like to be the President
of the United States, so many hands did he shake. He was delighted with
everything; he chatted as well as his limited stock of English allowed; and
his charm made everyone his friend. He asked to be allowed to make a
little speech. He had had it written in English, and he delivered it in that
tongue. Silence fell upon the crowd, and the orchestra—the Daly's
Theatre orchestra—seated in their pit, stopped playing and stood up to
hear what the *Maestro* had to say. What Lehár did, and what Lehár said,
was quite typical of him. He went down to the footlights; he beamed
upon the orchestra, and he thanked them for playing his music with such
skill and understanding. He was grateful to them, he said, and he was
proud of the privilege of having conducted them. It was the true musician
speaking to those who recognized him as such—and every word he said
was sincere.

As usual with all George Edwardes shows, there were changes in the
cast as the run proceeded. Daisie Irving played for Lily Elsie when she
was on holiday, Huntley Wright was succeeded by Lionel Victor, and
Gladys Guy took over from May de Sousa. Bertram Wallis, who was
magnificent, played right through the run. *The Count of Luxembourg* was a
resounding success, but knew no big anniversaries with souvenirs. It ran
for just 340 performances. You cannot have a *Merry Widow* every time,
not even if you are Fortune's Favourite—and London's favourite too—
like Franz Lehár.

CHAPTER TWELVE

Gypsy Magic

W ITH his debt to the Theater an der Wien discharged (and at hand-some interest!) by *The Count of Luxembourg*, Lehár was now free to complete *Zigeunerliebe*, which was produced at the Carl Theater in Vienna on the 8th January, 1910, and greeted with the acclaim that its revelation of new aspects of its composer's talent merited. In London, under its announced title of *Gipsy Love*,[1] it was eagerly awaited. People had heard that in this play Lehár's music soared to the heights, that it was in the region of Opera, that it was the best he had ever composed. They were impatient for this new show, for Lehár was the man who gave them, musically, what they wanted when it came to romance. That melody of his, with its throb of the heart, its underlying beat of passion and its sensuous, seductive slow waltzes—it was the very life-blood of Waltz Time, the Waltz Time in which they still lived.

They did not abate their delight in their own composers, of which they had many; but in that particular brand of the illusion of the Theatre, this magician who could make them feel romantics themselves, who could make the women respond with sparkling eyes to his love call, who could make the reserved Englishman almost throw away his formality and feel like singing a serenade beneath a balcony—well, there Lehár was King. He was monarch of the waltzes of Waltz Time, the genie who could make reality of romance. So when the announcement was made that his new operette *Gipsy Love* was to open at Daly's Theatre on the 1st June, 1912, in the height of the Season again, in the marriage month, in the month of the roses, all seemed right with the world.

George Edwardes was confident of success. He and Lehár had been in conference as to alterations suitable to London, and Lehár had made no difficulties at all. He knew London now as well as it knew him. And

[1] "Gipsy" is the spelling (or mis-spelling) used in the title of the English version.

he knew George Edwardes; he had every confidence in him. What the Guvnor said was agreeable to Franz Lehár, whose judgment of men was as good as his judgment of melody. They met in Paris. Edwardes took over the version of the play which Captain Basil Hood had prepared for Daly's. It differed very much indeed from the book of *Zigeunerliebe*. In fact, Hood, who had made many alterations in *The Count of Luxembourg*, had for *Gipsy Love* written what amounted almost to a new libretto. On the Continent, the Second Act had been a representation of a dream of the heroine's. Edwardes knew that dream plays were no good to the more matter-of-fact British, no matter how easily the Viennese or Berliners might accept them. Hood knew that, too. In this country a play which is partly in the form of a dream is almost foredoomed to failure. British audiences like to see things actually happen; and when they have been watching something with interest and find that it has just been a dream and has no substance, they feel that somebody has taken a liberty with them, that they have been fooled.

So Hood threw away that dream, not only at Edwardes's command, but out of his own knowledge, too, and showed the dream action as reality. Nor did Lehár object; the work was done so well, the scene was so cleverly constructed, his music fitted in so perfectly, that he thought it an improvement himself. He did more than that. He broke his usual rule that the operettes had to be played as he had composed them, with nothing added. For *Gipsy Love*, although no other composer was allowed to touch the score, Lehár himself did some new music, some new songs, which the continental playgoers never heard. Lehár did them for Edwardes, for Daly's and for London.

Gipsy Love, as produced at Daly's on the 1st June, 1912, was in three Acts, the First being in the Garden attached to a Roumanian Palace—no dodging the actual name of the country this time, as with "Marsovia", and no pandering to Paris as the most suitable background. This was a play about gypsies, so it went to Roumania. The Second Act was in a tavern or wineshop, a place of resort for the gypsies, and the Third was the Summer House of the Roumanian nobleman whose Garden had supplied the First Act. All these scenes were things of beauty; they glowed with colour and romance. Edwardes lavished money on them and on the costumes. They were worthy, as indeed were all his productions, of the company which was to appear in them and the music which would bring them to life.

There were some new faces in the company. There was no Lily Elsie this time. She had married and she had left the stage, and whilst everyone's good wishes went with her they missed her very much. What would have been her part, Ilona, daughter of a nobleman named

Dragotin, was to be played by Sari Petrass, whom Edwardes had imported. She was Hungarian by birth, from Budapest, where she was born in 1890. She was only twenty-two when she played lead at Daly's, a pretty girl, full of charm and with a delightful voice. Not a very strong actress, perhaps, she made up for it in beauty, personality and singing. She married an Englishman, Gordon Crocker. London liked her, and she liked London. She adorned the stage of Daly's as she adorned its restaurants, where people gazed at her, and as she adorned Rotten Row, where she rode daily. She loved horses and could ride like an Amazon, though that was the only Amazonian thing about her. Poor Sari Petrass —her end was tragic. She was drowned in the Scheldt when the car in which she was travelling with a friend plunged into its waters in 1930.

No shadow of that hung over her at Daly's in 1912. The part she played was the pivotal one. The well-born Ilona was engaged to a gallant Roumanian soldier, Jonel, but was swept off her feet by a handsome romantic gypsy, fled with him, throwing all to the winds for love, only to find when she got amongst the gypsies that they were not quite what she was accustomed to, and that the wonderful lover—Joszi—was by no means all she had thought him. She was saved—virtue and reputation intact, of course—by the timely intervention of an English lady, a woman of the world, called Lady Babby, who happened to be at the inn when Ilona arrived there with her gypsy. Lady Babby sized up the situation and restored Ilona to her irate father's care and the arms of her true lover. That, in short, was the plot. It gave scope for situations, of which Basil Hood took full advantage; it gave scope for comedy, drama and romance, and once again the magic of Lehár's music endowed the characters with life and reason; it seemed to run in their veins and inspire them.

The irresistible gypsy, Joszi, who stole away Ilona's heart was played by a new Daly's favourite. It has been mentioned that during the run of *The Merry Widow* Joseph Coyne took a holiday. In his absence during the autumn of 1908 the part of Prince Danilo was played by a young actor named Robert Michaelis. This newcomer made a far deeper impression on the audience at Daly's than is the lot of most of those called to take the place of stars. From the moment of his first entry, slim, black-haired and supremely elegant in the white gloves and opera cloak of the frolic-some Prince, he held his audience by the force of his romantic personality.

Robert Michaelis had been born in 1884 while his parents were in Paris, and had been educated there and at Dulwich College. He had learnt singing in Vienna itself from Signor Bottelli; and if this continental background accounted for the touch of fire in his acting, his handsome, clearly cut profile and charm of manner would have been enough of themselves to give him a place among what were then known as the "matinée idols". His first London engagement had been as a singer at the Palace Theatre of Varieties in 1903, and since then he had toured in musical comedy and also made two appearances in New York.

His English reputation had thus been, so far, mainly provincial, and to step from there into the shoes of such a West End favourite as Joseph Coyne was not a challenge that the first good-looking young actor to hand could have successfully accepted. Robert Michaelis did so, though inevitably when his Danilo is compared with Coyne's old-time enthusiasts for *The Merry Widow* enjoy taking sides. In truth Michaelis was a little hampered by the obligation of following his predecessor's reading of the part. His instinct would have been to put more passion into it, whereas he had to copy, as best he might, the whimsical and jerky mannerisms by which Coyne had expressed the Prince's annoyance and frustration, and had also to sacrifice his attractive singing voice and, like Coyne, speak most of the music. That, in spite of these handicaps, he scored such an individual success proved him a highly gifted artist. When at Christmas Joseph Coyne returned to the cast of the *Widow*, he was given, as was right and proper, a tumultuous reception. But this was no vote of censure on the actor who had been filling his place. Everybody hoped that Robert Michaelis would soon be seen at Daly's again.

This hope was gratified when *The Merry Widow* was followed in 1909 by Leo Fall's *Dollar Princess*. Indeed, George Edwardes spoilt his patrons, for he gave them both Coyne and Michaelis in the same programme. Coyne had a part far more to his liking than Prince Danilo had ever been, that of a young American heir to millions, who falls in love with a lion-tamer posing as a Russian Countess, and is made to believe that she is a Nihilist with a bomb in her handbag, sent to kill him. And Michaelis played the English hero, Freddie Fairfax, an Edwardian Petruchio with a gold cigarette-case instead of a whip, who tames the millionaire's haughty sister, the "Dollar Princess", by imperturbable politeness and that twinkle in the depth of his dark eye with which Michaelis always knew how to escape the fatuity which is the snare of the stage's handsome heroes.

The Dollar Princess left Michaelis an acknowledged West End star, and his myriad admirers had next the privilege of seeing him in all the proper trappings of the romantic hero when Oskar Straus's *Waltz Dream*, which had been a failure at the Hicks Theatre in 1908, was given a new production at Daly's in 1911, with Lily Elsie and W. H. Berry. Glamour could hardly go beyond the point to which Michaelis carried it in the figure of the hero, Lieut. Niki, magnificent in his white cavalry uniform, and steeped in love and melancholy. Straus's celebrated waltz might have been written round such a Prince of operette; and yet there was never a touch of the saccharine about him, but always the saving glance of humour to keep the character virile.

Michaelis was one of the best lovers the musical stage ever possessed. There was nothing stiff or restrained about him. He knew all about the art of love-making. He attacked the love scenes as if he were indeed infatuated with the girl who played opposite to him, and he made his acted love seem very real to the audiences who watched. So often, even in straight plays, love-making fails to convince, especially the passionate, fiery love-making of the gypsy or the romantic. There are not, and there never have been, very many Lewis Wallers about, whose understanding of this art is quite complete. There are, of course, many ways of making love on the musical stage, each of which has had its experts. There is the rather stiff, English way as exemplified by Hayden Coffin, although he was American born. This way was to rely very much on good looks, the situation, and the voice—to sing to the girl about love rather than carry it to her. There was the Joseph Coyne way, the wistful, diffident, lightly quizzical and comedy way, disclosing a love which could flare into an outburst as unexpected as convincing, and then retreat behind the mask again, awaiting its next chance. There was the eminently masculine way of Bertram Wallis, who made love in the grand manner, always master of the situation, knowing that the girl must fall into his arms. And there was the romantic ardour and attack of Robert Michaelis, who had every attribute a stage lover, either of musical or straight plays, could possibly have, and was also a master of "timing".

He knew how to sweep the girl off her feet, and how to embrace her; for he understood that the way to make love is at short range, so that the beloved can be taken into the arms almost before she is aware of it, with no reaching out and stretching, no chance of giving the audience— even a well-bred and intelligent audience—that temptation to titter which so often affects British playgoers. No matter how intent they are, they are always self-conscious when it comes to watching love-making and passion. They mean no harm, but they are always embarrassed if there is the slightest excuse for them so to be. So speed is the thing, proximity— the girl embraced, her lips locked to the lover's, and all over before the audience can draw breath or feel uneasy! The *fait accompli* holds them; it is just the moment before which is dangerous. Few indeed are the actors who can achieve this. Waller never failed, and Michaelis was the Waller of musical comedy. Another thing was in his favour—that he liked playing love scenes, which is two-thirds of the battle. Also he believed in them, and that is the remaining third, for he communicated his belief to his audiences.

Of the Daly's stalwarts in *Gipsy Love* there was Fred Kaye, in his usual elderly staccato part; there was Kate Welch; pretty Madeline Seymour (Pretty? Beautiful Madeline Seymour!), now advanced to speaking rôles; there was dainty and adorable Mabel Russell; and above all there was W. H. Berry. He played Dragotin, a Roumanian noble, the father of Ilona. He was, of course, a play in himself. He was his own conception of what a Roumanian noble should be, as complete a personality as he had been as Nisch in *The Merry Widow* and as Brissard, the artist, in *The Count of Luxembourg*. His nobility was immense; he trod such heights that the low people beneath him were ants. His dignity was tremendous; his capacity for rage, wonder and amazement far-reaching. He could be the kind father or the irate and outraged parent, and he was both; he could unbend to the humble and be haughty to his equals. He could let loose the vials of his wrath in the most serious yet side-splitting manner, and he was quite convinced that he was irresistible to the ladies, especially the English Lady Babby, who was a stranger to his land. He invited her to visit him, and her polite reply, "I am delighted to accept your invitation," was to him fraught with hidden passion, with complete surrender. He believed in phrenology; he had had his bumps told and had been assured that had he chosen he could have rivalled Bismarck; that there was Blood and Iron in his character. He believed it too—even if he got a bit mixed, being a comedian, and being Bill Berry, and referred to these two ingredients as "Bovril and Bedsteads". Still, he always got a laugh, and had his usual topical song; this time it was called "Home Again".

But the newcomers also were important. There was Harry Dearth, one of the best singers in the country, a man who could sing any type of song, character, sentimental, comic or religious, who was equally at home in Oratorio and on the concert platform or (as he soon proved) on the stage at Daly's. Although not a good actor, for he could never subdue his own personality (Who wanted him to? It was a personality of charm), yet he was a tower of strength. He came to Daly's straight from a masque by Sir Edward Elgar, in which he sang St. George. He had not in musical comedy the same ease as he had on the concert platform. There, he would lean against the piano, often with his hands in his pockets, and let that magnificent voice roll out. He could put into a song a wealth of expression, but he could not act it. It was a matter of face and vocal powers. But this did not matter. He was at Daly's to sing Lehár's music, and sing it he did, divinely. One of the most versatile vocalists of his day—his rendering of the youthful rustic who was "sore afraid of a single maid" and his singing of "Awake, Beloved!" were both matchless —his voice could act, but his body could not. But his artistry and charm made up for it. He was universally popular, on and off the stage.

In the play Fred Kaye, who played Dimitrie, had a son, Kajetan, and

that part was played by Lauri de Frece, now a comedian of the front
rank, who excelled in parts demanding shyness or simplicity. He had made
a big success at the New Theatre in a musical play called *Amasis* with
an ancient Egyptian background, in which his part had been the Keeper
of the Crocodiles. He had gone on steadily from there, and he had made
a big impression with Ada Reeve in a musical version of *The Palace of
Puck*, originally produced at the Haymarket, but in its musical form known
as *Butterflies*.

In that piece he had played a chauffeur. He possessed, he told his
audiences, a brother who had found work upon a farm, but (the chauffeur
told us) "He'd never been upon a farm before." As a farmer's boy that
brother was a failure, and the failure culminated in his misunderstanding
of the art of rearing chickens. They were found starved to death, little
lifeless balls of yellow fluff. The farmer, pained and surprised, said he
supposed his farmer's boy had fed them? For answer, he got a look of
blank amazement. Then that young man informed him that he thought
they lived on milk, so he had left it to the hen—for he'd never been upon
a farm before. To hear Lauri de Frece sing that song was to remember
it—and him—always. He was a true grotesque, a true clown, with a mien
usually sad, surprised and downtrodden, full of embarrassment and shyness, yet able to blossom forth under females' smiles, as it did in this case
under the charms of Jolan, Dragotin's niece, played by another Daly's
favourite, Mabel Russell. In *Gipsy Love* Lauri de Frece added greatly to
his laurels.

The part of Jonel, Ilona's accepted lover, the dashing Hussar, was
sung and played by Webster Millar, also a newcomer to Daly's, rather a
small but very neat man, with a good-looking face, a nice manner and a
pure tenor voice of quality. Rosina Filippi, as good an actress as ever
walked the stage, and a grand teacher of the art, too, played Julesa,
Ilona's nurse, and played it as well as she had, before then, played the
Nurse in *Romeo and Juliet*. She lifted every scene in which she appeared
and gave it substance and reality.

But there was one more newcomer—to Daly's, not to musical comedy
or to London—and that was an adorable woman who was an idol of the
public, who had been given her first chance by Edwardes when she was
a girl, had taken it, had leapt to stardom overnight, had for years been
the very embodiment of the Spirit of the Gaiety Theatre, where she was
Queen, had recently charmed all London at the Adelphi as a Quaker girl,
and who now came to Daly's to bring a spirit of diamond-like brightness
and sparkle into the exotic atmosphere of its romance. Her name was
Gertie Millar. She played the Englishwoman Lady Babby. . . . What a
team of experts, of performers of lustrous, starry quality, Franz Lehár had

behind that curtain when on the night of the 1st June, 1912, he once more stepped into the conductor's stand, to conduct his new operette *Gipsy Love*!

And what a full-throated roar of welcome he got from the Londoners assembled in the theatre! There titles with the dust of years of nobility upon them rubbed shoulders with, or at least sat in adjoining stalls to, the princes of the Turf and the world of Sport. Here were the people encountered in that most exclusive domain, the Royal Enclosure at Ascot. And it was almost as difficult to get into the stalls at a Daly's First Night as to tread that much-desired turf on the historic Heath. Perhaps Daly's was a bit more democratic, for the real talisman for admission was to be a friend of the Guvnor's—the accolade of good fellowship and sportsmanship combined. So one would see Dukes and Earls, Lord Lonsdale prominent in the latter rank; W. B. Purefoy, fast friend of Guvnor George, whose long, pointed nose marked him out for recognition, and who knew all there was to know about the points of a horse or a play; Fallon, the famous trainer, and Major D. J. Edwards, another; Harry Slowburn, one of the best-known bookmakers of his day; Colonel Newnham Davis, journalist, librettist of the Empire ballets, *flâneur*, gourmet, authority on food, supporter of the widely read *Pink 'Un*, whose pen-name was "The Dwarf of Blood"; and, usually in a box, Alfred de Rothschild. Jockeys would be there—Danny Maher, who married a Daly's girl named Dora Fraser; the Hartigans, one of whom was Edwardes's son-in-law; and both the Griggs. Another regular First-Nighter at Daly's was Lady Duff Gordon, who was "Lucille", the celebrated and fashionable dressmaker, as well. Medicine was represented especially by Sir Anderson Critchett, the eye specialist, Sir Milson Rees, the throat specialist, and Harry Forsyth, about the leading dentist of his day; and such was the Guvnor's care of his companies that those three eminent men looked after, if need be, the eyes, the throats and the teeth of all the people at Daly's.

But indeed the celebrities were countless. The Guvnor was in his usual box, the O.P. stage box, watchful as ever under those seemingly sleepy lids; the upper circle glittered as usual with jewels, if anything in greater profusion than did the stalls; and the pit and gallery were gasping with excitement. The talk and the chatter ceased as the sturdy figure of Lehár was seen, and he received a welcome which assured him of the goodwill, the esteem, indeed the affection, in which he was held. London was grateful to this man for warming its grey winter nights with his melody, for giving an extra sparkle to its spring, and an added glow to the sunshine of its brief summer. . . . Again, the poised baton, the beat, the sweep of the melody, and *Gipsy Love* had begun.

The rumours playgoers had heard of the quality of the music had not been exaggerated. Here was the longest reach Lehár had yet made in his grasp towards Opera. Here was music, pleasant, delightful, tuneful, lilting and pulsing with emotion—yet on a higher plane than that which Lehár had given before. It was real Lehár, of the true vintage, with the added mellowness of experience—and Success. That audience adored it all. They cheered the fine song given to Harry Dearth; they delighted in Berry's topicalities with their lilting tune, they loved his duet with Gertie Millar. Here were two artists who matched each other, who knew their job and how to play together. In Berry Gertie Millar had found a comedian who was as well suited to her as had been Edmund Payne, her old partner at the Gaiety. She could give her words every point, every inflection; so could he. And those words, by Adrian Ross, were worth hearing too. Not one syllable was missed, for these two understood diction. They kept that trifle, light, gay, and most melodious, "You're in Love", dancing in the air. Sari Petrass also was a success, and her song "A Little Maiden" stopped the show, for it was one of those genuine Lehár slow waltz tunes.

The audience followed the story with interest; they revelled in the love scenes between the carefree, fascinating gypsy of Michaelis and the captivated Ilona, and when he sang his song, again a slow waltz, it seemed as if *The Merry Widow* had a real rival. They laughed at the comedians, all of whom scored big hits; they were held by the scene between Lady Babby and Joszi, when the clever Englishwoman defeats the shallow and fickle, yet very charming, gypsy and opens Ilona's eyes. How extremely well Michaelis and Gertie Millar played that scene, for he was a good actor, and Gertie could switch to drama with a sudden tenseness and grip that always surprised! The end was triumph for all. It was waltzes, waltzes all the way—the comedy duet had been a waltz too—and Lehár had conquered again. London was his willing captive, and Waltz Time was further enriched.

Gipsy Love was acclaimed. And Gertie Millar had proved herself as much at home at Daly's as ever she had been at the Gaiety. She, the lady of laughter, died only recently. Her passing seemed to her friends like the blacking out of a light, like the sudden cessation of the gurgle of a stream. She was the greatest musical comedy star this country ever possessed, for what she might lack to some slight degree in one way she amply made up for in others. In range and versatility she had not an equal, and for real sparkle and *joie de vivre* nobody came near her. After *Gipsy Love* she was a Queen of Daly's and a Queen of Hearts everywhere.

There were calls for everyone; shouts of "We want Edwardes!", a brief reply from him, and cheers like the thunder of the surf for the man who had done it again, the man who now won his third success at Daly's, whose music was better than ever, with a more opulent note in it, a richer texture and a deeper colour—the "Puccini of Operette", he has been called—yet with all the fizz of champagne and the charm of Vienna. Franz Lehár was now the wearer of a triple crown and undisputed King of Waltz Time, the rhythm to which that world of 1912 moved.

Outside in the summer night the happy throngs went homeward; the cars and the carriages purred and rolled away. Men stared before them, beauty in their eyes, maybe humming, maybe whistling the melodies or what they had caught of them. Women sat silent, still clasped by romance. The girls and boys of the pit and gallery were starry-eyed with happiness; this was indeed, they hoped, what life would be like for them. Older couples linked arms, perhaps held hands, their youth renewed, their hearts beating faster, for that was the magic which Lehár could compass; and that young disciple of his, who sat in the pit, in the gallery, and sometimes managed to afford a stall, dreamed that perhaps one day he might do something like it too. Ivor Novello's dream came true as well.

Gipsy Love ran for 299 performances—a good run, but not so long as *The Count of Luxembourg* and nothing like so long as *The Merry Widow*, of course. It had not indeed quite the same popular appeal. Lovely and musicianly as the score was, and full of luscious romance, it was not quite so easy to memorize, not quite so easy to whistle, as that of *The Merry Widow*; and that was a grave thing in the days when people whistled from sheer pleasure at being alive; whistled tunes, not strange, piercing discords, as happens now when there is any whistling at all. *Gipsy Love* was a thing for connoisseurs more than the populace. Indeed, at the end of Lehár's lifetime, in 1943, under the title of *Garaboncias*, it was to be transformed into a Grand Opera and played in the Opera House of Budapest.

There were other reasons, too, why *Gipsy Love* was not quite the success its predecessors had been in London. Sari Petrass, charmingly pretty, fine-voiced and intelligent, was not a Lily Elsie; Robert Michaelis, excellent actor, singer and romantic, had not quite the curious charm of Joe Coyne. Bill Berry, ripe comedian, had a big appeal—the British always love the comic best—but what was lacking here was the atomic energy, the vast, overwhelming attack and command of George Graves. Nevertheless Gertie Millar pulled them in. Sometimes even she, used as she was to it, could not face the mob at the stage door, and slipped in and out by the front entrance; there was a corridor behind the box-office at Daly's which took you backstage. But, still, *Gipsy Love* was a success, a very big artistic success. It had showed a Lehár with all his old compelling charm; it foreshadowed a Lehár with even greater things to come, a Lehár climbing victoriously out of operette into Opera.

When, however, he returned to Vienna after that triumphant First Night

Richard Tauber, the great tenor who sang so many great rôles in the later Lehár operettes, including *The Land of Smiles* and *Paganini*, in London

Richard Tauber as Prince Sou Chong in *The Land of Smiles*, the Lehár
operette produced at Theatre Royal, Drury Lane, in 1931

he did not dream that *Gipsy Love* was to be the last time he would occupy
the conductor's chair at Daly's; that it would be the last time for many
a year that his music would be heard there; that, indeed, the Waltz of the
World was drawing to its close—and that another kind of music would
replace it. . . .

In that year of 1912 few people—in England at any rate—saw the
real danger ahead. Life went on as it had gone on for years, in the memory
of most people indeed. The year 1912 was not a specially memorable one,
but there were signs and portents. The previous year had seen a sudden
crisis. Germany had interfered in something which did not concern her,
or so France and Great Britain thought. Her gunboat *Panther* had no
right at Agadir. There had been a quick gasp of tension; storms had
covered the sky with tropical swiftness; War—almost unbelievable War
—seemed to hover. France and Germany began to swing into action. A
speech by Lloyd George at the Mansion House left the world in no doubt
about which side would be Britain's, and the clouds dispersed, the tension
slackened, the world breathed once more.

But the Crisis had been; it could come again; war between Great
Powers was not a thing of the past in Europe. The British half believed,
half derided the challenge of Germany to their supremacy. When they
thought of it they also thought of the British Navy, and all seemed right
with the world. Besides, there was the *Entente Cordiale*; that clever old
man King Edward VII had engineered that; he knew what he was doing.
Was there not an alliance, too, between France and Russia? Germany
would never dare! . . . England was not asleep. It was all right. . . . On
with the dance! . . . On with the days and nights of Security. . . .

But it was not quite all right outside the coasts of this island. There
was actually a war in Europe in the year 1912, although Britain, generally
speaking, paid little attention to it. For it was a Balkan war, an affair of
those comic-opera countries which the English did not regard as civilized
and hardly believed were part of Europe at all. Comic-opera countries—
yes—had not Lehár himself poked fun at them in *The Merry Widow*? Had
they not figured in so many light operas and musical comedies? Could
they be taken seriously?

In 1912, however, Greece, Montenegro—*The Merry Widow* again!—
Serbia and Bulgaria had combined against a common enemy, Turkey.
Contrary to expectations, they had given the Turks, for whom the British
always had a soft corner in their hearts, a good hiding, and this had
mainly been accomplished by the remarkably good fighting and general-
ship of the Bulgarians. Turkey had been almost completely driven out of
those parts of Europe which she still retained and upon which during
centuries she had left her mark. Macedonia and Thrace were freed from

K

Turkish rule. When peace was made and it came to dividing up the spoils, Bulgaria, who had done most of the work, grabbed most of the prizes. True to comic-opera principles the little nations who had been allies a few weeks before rushed to fight each other again. Turkey saw her chance, jumped in and took back Adrianople and a bit more. Bulgaria was shorn of much that she had gained and left sullen and resentful, feelings which were to burst into flame at a later date. . . .

In this land much was going on. There was the tragedy of the sinking of the *Titanic*, the greatest sea disaster in history up to then. The first Alexandra Rose Day was held, and that beloved and widowed Queen drove through a London which wore her flower in such numbers that it seemed as if a pink mist had broken out. King George V, newly on the Throne, attended Henley Regatta in his Royal Barge. Herald of the future, a giant airship (or so it seemed then) lurked in a hangar at Wormwood Scrubs. Nor was that the only portent of change, of gathering speed, of the opening of the mechanized age, for at that year's Derby the horse-driven vehicles were only in a tiny majority over the motor-cars. The winner at that High Festival of the Horse was Tagalie.

Machinery swept on; science showed its paces; seaplanes hovered over the Solent. But the Navy was the Navy, and the bluejackets still wore, in summer, those broad-brimmed straw hats which were the most favoured headgear for children of the period. The American Navy visited us, and the British gazed in astonishment, not unmixed with amusement, at the sight of sailors in kid gloves. Death removed General Booth, the founder of the Salvation Army, and the Duke of Fife, husband of the Princess Royal.

Down in peaceful, rustic Oxfordshire there was a small, unimportant building, rather like a shack, which was the springboard from which the advancing machine age would take a great leap forward. It was called "The Oxford Garage", run by Mr. W. R. Morris, who also made and repaired cycles. From that small place came a revolution in the motor industry, and a title and millions for Mr. Morris, whose name became a household word. There was trouble in Ireland, but the public did not care much about that. They were used to it. It seemed strange to them that they could control a fifth of the globe but never satisfy Ireland. Home Rule was the issue again, and a tall, dark, grim man, named Carson, one of the most brilliant King's Counsel of the time, was telling the world that Ulster would resist to the death; indeed, a "cold" religious war was already in progress. . . .

In Lehár's own world, that of the Theatre, much was happening too, and the Theatre, as always, mirrored the trend of the world around it. Speed was gathering there too; acute observers (rare in the Theatre at any time) might have read the writing on the wall. Anna Pavlova had come to the Palace to enchant, to bewilder, to create a furore by examples of the art of the Russian Ballet, so different from the ballets then being shown at the Empire and the Alhambra. Revue was surging forward steadily, and challenging both operette and musical comedy. And prominent in that department was a dainty, bewitching blonde, with big blue eyes and a lovely figure, whose reputation was more vivid than her art, for she had cost a King his crown. She was Gaby Deslys, and she shocked whilst she delighted Londoners. Her hats were beyond reason—but she never got them on the heads of every woman, as the Merry Widow had done. King George V commanded his loyal Music Hall Performers to appear before him, and they did so, with immense fervour and *réclame*, at the Palace Theatre.

But more significant than all this, riding on the tide of revue, was a new type of music, a new type of rhythm, coming, not from Paris, not from London, not even from Vienna, but from America. It was called Ragtime. Albert de Courville put it in the forefront by a revue called *Hullo Ragtime!* at the London Hippodrome. Ethel Levey and Shirley Kellog were the stars. This curious type of melody—if melody it could be called—interested and amused the British. Just a craze, of course, they said, but quite funny, and they sang "Yiddle Up, Fiddle Up, On Your Violin" and "Everybody's Doing It" and began to get the hang of syncopation. Very funny they thought it—but of course, just a passing whim, not really music, like the waltz. But jazz bands blared and made them laugh when they saw men walloping tin cans and making weird noises in place of the throb and wail of the strings. And then came a song, "Alexander's Ragtime Band", and before anyone knew it, Ragtime, syncopation, was accepted, was implanted, was indeed challenging the Waltz—a portent of the changing, quickening times. There were many other signs as well. The cinematograph had come to stay; it was crude to a degree, but people went to it. But, still, these things seemed mere ripples, and life went on still in Waltz Time as 1912 changed into 1913.

Lehár brought nothing to London in that year of change, of the dawn of change. The security of the Victorian and Edwardian eras was hastening to its end, but few people realized it. Dress was becoming more informal, but had not reached the depths of today nor anything like it. Fewer middle-class people wore the silk topper; more the bowler or the straw, and more still the Homburg. The morning coat was ousting the frock coat for ceremonial use, and soft collars and coloured shirts were common wear. The motor was now predominant, horse-driven vehicles becoming more and more rare; the last horse-bus had gone in 1911, but on the south side of the Thames there were still horse-trams. Women's skirts were getting shorter, they no longer trailed along the ground. A Frenchman named Pégoud had actually flown upside down for a fraction of time; it was described as "looping the loop". People thought it was wonderful; nobody guessed to what it would lead. There was still unrest and trouble in Ireland; the mutterings there had become an audible growl.

Women were demanding Emancipation, the Vote. The Suffragettes were militant and causing havoc. Indeed, they caused tragedy when one of them, Emily Davison, upset the King's horse, Anmer, in the Derby and was killed. To try and upset the Derby, a thing sacred by tradition, was considered terrible, and people wondered what would happen next! Apart from that, it was a sensational Derby, for the favourite Craiganour, first past the post, was disqualified, and the race given to Aboyeur. And the Downs were thronged with motor buses.

The Balkans were in the news again, a tragedy there marring the comic-opera atmosphere, for the King of Greece was assassinated. And a famous comedian, Harry Fragson, whose real name was Potts, figured in a murder too; he was killed by his own father. . . . Morals seemed to be tottering, for an "unspeakable" word had been used on the stage of His Majesty's and loudly cheered!

The cinema was progressing now. Personalities were making themselves felt there. Men like John Bunny and Max Linder had been the pioneers; but now came something fresh, something more vivid. A little Englishman, working in American films, began to get right to the front of the screen, began to be talked about and looked out for; his individual make-up, the bowler hat, the baggy, patched clothes, the splay feet, the little cane, that make-up which was in direct descent from Arlecchino the first Clown, was a definite hall-mark. His sad expression, his woes and troubles, his antics and his supreme gift of clowning were a sure draw in those ill-contrived, flickering but improving spools of celluloid, and his name was Charlie Chaplin. There were other names, too, which made a mark: Florence Turner, Maurice Costello, Leah Baird, Helen Costello and Marie Dressler. This, the newest form of the drama, was following the traditional lines of the older form, that of the Theatre; the star system was breaking through, as it always must because the public wills it; the actors and actresses were becoming as important as the play.

In the Theatre itself in 1913 *The Marriage Market* was filling Daly's, with music by Victor Jacobi. It came not from Vienna but from Germany. In the cast were Gertie Millar, Harry Dearth, W. H. Berry, G. P. Huntley, Robert Michaelis, Tom Walls, Avice Kelham, Elise Craven and Sari Petrass. *The Girl on the Film* was at the Gaiety, with Madeline Seymour in the lead; *The Girl from Utah* at the Adelphi with

A rehearsal for Lehár's *Paganini* at the Lyceum Theatre, London. *Left to right*: Sir Charles B. Cochran, who produced the play; Richard Tauber (at piano); Sir Alan P. Herbert and Reginald Arkell, who wrote the English book and lyrics

Richard Tauber (*left*) and Franz Lehár at a rehearsal

Ina Claire, from America, Joe Coyne, Phyllis Dare, Gracie Leigh, and Edmund Payne, no longer at the Gaiety, and in that play playing his last part. *Within the Law* was a big success at the Haymarket, with Mabel Russell, of *Merry Widow* fame, making a tremendous hit. Henry Ainley was playing in *The Great Adventure* at the Kingsway, Cyril Maude in *The Headmaster* at the Playhouse, a starlit revival of Sardou's *Diplomacy* was packing Wyndham's with a cast which included Arthur Wontner, Norman Forbes, Owen Nares, A. E. Matthews, Lady Tree, Ellis Jeffreys, Gladys Cooper and Gerald du Maurier. Matheson Lang was startling London by his magnificent acting as *Mr. Wu*, with Lilian Braithewaite as his leading lady.

At the dances, public and private, the Waltz was already being challenged. There was the *Veleta*, and there was a new dance, the Tango, which was all the rage. There were some funny things from America called the Bunny Hug and the Turkey Trot—not popular as yet, but still, they had arrived. And then came that year of Fate, for the whole world, and for Fortune's Favourite, Franz Lehár . . . 1914 dawned. It saw the first woman to fly as a professional, a Mrs. Buller. The *Empress of Ireland* sank in the icy, fog-bound waters of the St. Lawrence River, taking to their doom Laurence Irving and his wife, Mabel Hackney. Madame Caillaux, wife of a French Cabinet Minister, shot a journalist who was assailing her husband.

The Suffragettes kept up their battle for the Vote, and in Mexico Civil War was raging. There were threats of that nearer home, for the crisis between Ulster and the South of Ireland had become acute. Led by Carson, who had among his assistants holding the rank of "Galloper" in his irregular army, a prominent politician, whose name was F. E. Smith, Ulster grew threatening. Unrest was abroad, and then, when June shone over the world, the British Fleet paid a visit to Germany, to Kiel. The two fleets, German and British, eyed each other, the old, full of tradition and victory, the new, anxious to try its strength, and thinking of its toast, *Der Tag*! Still, nobody knew how near that Day was to be. But the menace of Germany was now better appreciated; the Germans were challenging in all directions; their monster liner *Vaterland*, largest in the world, had just been launched. The British Fleet returned, and the First Lord of the Admiralty, Winston Churchill, assembled it at Spithead for a great review. Twenty-two miles of warships lay across the sea for their King to inspect, and for the world to note their strength. . . .

CHAPTER THIRTEEN

Sunset of an Epoch

IN spite of the sinister portents mentioned in the last chapter the whole of this pre-War period was a dazzling phase of Lehár's career. He had become so famous that he was even represented as a character on the stage in a farce by Léon and another. In 1910 he had the triumph of seeing three of his pieces running simultaneously in Vienna, and all of them successes—*Der Graf von Luxembourg* at the Theater an der Wien, *Das Fürstenkind* at the Johann-Strauss Theater, and *Zigeunerliebe* at the Carl Theater. To these was added in the following year *Eva*, with a book by Willner and Bodanzky. Like *The Count of Luxembourg*, this piece has a Parisian setting. It tells the love story of a factory girl and a wealthy industrialist, her employer. Of course, she married her boss—or did she? The question seems to be left slightly open; but operette at this period was still bound outwardly at least to observe the proprieties. *Eva*, from the passionate colouring of its music, has always been especially popular with Italian audiences.

And all the time the conquest of the world by the Widow proceeded without a check. After so sensational a success in London her début in Paris might well seem overdue. It took place at last in 1909 at the Théatre Apollo in a version prepared by those popular French playwrights G. A. de Caillavet and Robert de Flers. The name of Henry Meilhac also appeared now for the first time on the bills, for his heirs-at-law had taken care that this should be so. (The agreement that averted proceedings in the courts was drawn up by a shrewd lawyer from Lorraine, called Raymond Poincaré, a name that throws across Lehár's bright world a dark shadow of things to come.) Yet despite the five authors now claiming credits, and in spite of the fact that the Widow herself was Parisienne of the Parisiennes, the French version does not sparkle quite as much as we should expect it to do. It is rather a surprise to discover that "Missia

Palmieri" (which is now the Widow's name) is an American from the Far West, though brought up in the long-suffering fatherland of Prince Danilo, and that she is directed to speak in "an English accent, tinged with Slavonic"! The accent, however, is explained when we note that the original Paris Merry Widow was an English actress, the statuesquely handsome Constance Drever, who had played the Ambassadress for a time at Daly's in London, and was later to create there with immense success the heroine of Oskar Straus's *Chocolate Soldier*. Her powerful voice, trained for Grand Opera, was her chief asset, and was, no doubt, fully appreciated in Paris.

It is amusing to discover that those two foppish French noblemen and shameless fortune-hunters known in London as in Vienna as "M. de St. Brioche" and the "Marquis de Cascada" have become respectively a Belgian and a Guatemalan—apparently no Frenchman might be a ludicrous figure on the Paris stage of 1909!—and that some attempt is made to utilize Ambassador Popoff for a skit on the Machiavellian or Bismarckian diplomatist; political caricature has an irresistible attraction for the French pen. The amorous passages of the story receive, as was to be looked for, full value in the familiar vein of Parisian cynicism; but how the rather frivolous French lyrics ever got fitted to Lehár's passionate music is a problem not easy to solve. No doubt the singers dealt with it in their own way, but it is rather like swallowing a fish-bone to find "There once were two Princes' children" converted into "Jean-Pierre adorait Jeannette", and the name of Maxim's banished from Danilo's celebrated song—in Paris of all places!

The score of *The Merry Widow*, however, could carry a worse libretto than this through to victory; and, no doubt, there would be ground for the same sort of complaint about most of the versions that in all the languages on earth have filled the theatres of the world. Mr. Forbes Winslow in his book *Daly's* states that at one time the *Widow* was being played nightly at over 400 theatres in Europe alone. It was played in Belgium, in the Scandinavian lands, in Constantinople and in Trieste (where it was actually booed by angry Montenegrins and Yugoslavs, a novel experience for Franz Lehár!) A souvenir from Australia, where it was an amazing success in 1908 on its first production, shows that the cast included that truly delightful artist Carrie Moore as Sonia; Andrew Higginson as Danilo; Florence Young as Natalie; Victor Gouriet as Popoff; Reginald Roberts as Jolidon; E. Nable as Novikovich; W. S. Percy as Nisch; Jessica Deane as Olga; A. Hunter as the Waiter and Gladys Turner as Frou-Frou (called there Fifi). Maudie Thornton was S. Africa's first Sonia.

Its New York success was another triumph. *The Merry Widow* was the play which never failed—although so often expected to do so. In America not only Merry Widow hats but Merry Widow cigars, chocolates, corsets, beefsteaks, dogs and beer cellars became the craze. There was a version in the Arabic tongue, and an exploring party to the Zambesi and the Victoria Falls found the Merry Widow there before them. Hanna or Sonia or Missia, the photographs of her impersonators show every variety of feminine charm, blonde or brunette, slim or full-figured, stately or playful, aloof or alluring; the faces she has worn belong to every national, almost to every racial, type. Imagination pursues her further and sees her in the yellow skin of China and the black sheen of the negress. Did such things happen in reality, or only in the cartoons of the popular Press? . . .

Anyhow with three such sources of income as *The Merry Widow*, *The Count of Luxembourg* and *Gipsy Love* to supply him, Lehár could now forget the pinched life of the *Militärkapellmeister* and the privations of the not yet successful composer. He could surround himself with that atmosphere of beauty and luxury for which the artist and the musician crave, a noble infirmity (if it be an infirmity) from which Wagner was no more exempt than the composers of operette. In 1908 Lehár had bought a handsome house in Vienna, No. 16 Theobaldgasse, on a commanding corner site, better suited than his former modest dwelling to his new status. The ground floor was let to the Composers' and Authors' Society for offices; the second was Lehár's private flat; the third his librettist Dr. Willner's; while the top story became a kind of museum, where were collected the various trophies of Lehár's career—wreaths and addresses, special conductor's batons presented on occasions of honour, photographs of all the famous players who had appeared in his works, illustrated souvenirs marking the 100th or 300th or 600th performance of different pieces of his, collected programmes, all the milestones of a composer's progress.

The place, it will be seen, was a workshop as much as a residence. Lehár's more intimate dwelling was at Ischl. First it was at the Rosenvilla, round which there still hung something of the magic of great composers who had inhabited it before him—Meyerbeer, Brahms, Joseph Joachim—and where his mother died, to his deep grief, in 1906. Then it was in the beautiful classical pavilion, formerly a ducal residence, with its sculptured triangular pediment, its balustraded coping and stone urns, which stands on a little quay beside the glancing River Traun (now called Quay Lehár) and which after 1911 was his favourite place of work as well as his real home for the rest of his life.

This villa, thanks to Lehár's own taste and that of his wife, became, as the years passed by, an artistic treasure house in the lavish and eclectic style favoured at the epoch. From a somewhat severe entrance hall in the

style of a hunting lodge, with antlers on the walls and a chandelier gracefully carved with leaping stags, a staircase led to the upper floors, which
could, however, be barred at the top of the first flight by a pair of exquisitely wrought iron gates, locked by Lehár himself when he wished
to retire for uninterrupted work. The principal rooms were, in the taste
of the day, crowded with pictures, antique furniture, statuettes, and every
type of elegant *bric-à-brac*; and there must, in the bright mountain sunshine and the reflected radiance of the snows and glaciers, have been an
opulent glitter from the gilt picture-frames, the polished bronze *appliqués*,
and the gold haloes of the Saints upon the walls. This would be softened
by the warm tones of the Old Masters and their disciples, whose paintings
filled nearly every inch of wall-space. Van Dyck, Kremserschmidt,
Amerling glowed there, as well as landscapes of the Biedermaier school,
matching the richly brocaded furniture of all periods, Renaissance,
baroque and Empire.[1]

Such a collection would have been out of its period if it had not had
a strong ecclesiastical flavouring, and the splendours of Southern Catholic
art are everywhere apparent. Besides the Holy Families and other religious themes in oils, we find a beautiful wooden Madonna and Child of
the 18th century, and a Tyrolean sacristy cupboard of the baroque period,
inlaid with painted reliefs of the Nativity; while delicious little plaster
cherubs (*putti*) are even made to adorn the elaborately ornamented
Jacobean sideboard that was presented to the Master at Daly's in souvenir
of the success of *The Merry Widow*. . . . The Theatre, after all, could not
be left out, and Lehár felt no disharmony in mingling these *objets d'art*
with his favourite photographs of actors and actresses, which he set in
profusion upon the carved desks and inlaid tables.

If in his earlier days Lehár had known neglect, and in his Army life
had suffered slights, the world was eager now to make amends for all
that. He was sought after, honoured, even adulated. Indeed, the crowd
of visitors and the mass of invitations became embarrassing; the telephone
was always ringing, and so was the front-door bell. Telegrams came in
an endless stream, begging for his presence at the first performances of
his pieces in different countries, and the letters (which he was scrupulous
to answer, with old-world courtesy, in his own hand) made piles upon
his table.

It became a real problem how he was to find time and privacy for
his work, and it was, no doubt, this pressure on his nerves that led him
to take what might seem extravagant precautions to prevent interruption

---

[1] A charmingly illustrated catalogue of the contents of the Villa, which Lehár left in his
will to the town of Ischl and which has been turned into a Lehár Museum, has been issued by
the Municipality.

when he was composing. He preferred the dead of night for working in, and he almost literally immured himself in his work-room. Each house he lived in was so arranged, or if necessary reconstructed, that penetration to his private apartments was absolutely impossible unless he himself unlocked the doors leading to them. Most astonishing of all to those who cannot understand an artist's idiosyncrasies is the fact that his wife, to whom he was devoted until the end, did not live with him. She always had her own establishment, either in an adjoining house or, later, in his more magnificent Vienna residence, the Schikaneder-Schlössl, in a self-contained part of the building, cut off from his living-rooms. This was no sign of disunion, but a necessity of his highly strung nature, to preserve his solitude.

Among the more pressing disturbers of the Master's privacy, but not the most disagreeable, were the innumerable singers, actresses and dancers craving for a part in his pieces or at least an audition. Many are the tales of the ruses by which they managed to get past the guard of the faithful servant who kept the doors—perhaps Lehár did not always loyally second his sentinel on these occasions! It is impossible that the legend of any composer of operette should not have its full tale of amorous encounters, but in Lehár's case the atmosphere of *bonnes fortunes* is even more pervasive and glamorous than usual.

After all, he was pre-eminently the composer of tender and passionate love-strains, and he was reputed to have declared that all his heroines were in some sense drawn from life—and from his own emotional experiences. A man like Franz Lehár could not but be credited with countless conquests; but it is worthy of remark that all the anecdotage about his *affaires* is of a chivalrous and delicate character, and that the story not infrequently ends upon a humorous note, recalling his father's comments upon Franz's youthful misadventures over "noble passions". What simplicity and good nature were revealed for instance in the story of the two Parisian midinettes who, after long waiting at the stage door for a glimpse of the Master, were rewarded—amazing honour!—by an invitation to lunch in a restaurant the next day. (Both of them, for if two be company three is safety!) Lehár answered their naïve questions about how he thought of his tunes, and the rest, and before leaving wrote on the back of the menu not only his name but a few bars of music. The beginning of some waltz that never went further can it have been? . . . Anyhow the delighted girls carried it away and it has never been found since.

A situation more difficult to handle was created by the lovely unknown to whom he opened his door himself, and who announced that she was from Königsberg in distant East Prussia, and that she had come because she "must come" to him after hearing his music. No, she didn't want to go on the stage; she was married; but she had had to come to the creator of *The Merry Widow*. The solution was not romantic, but all to Lehár's credit. It was a discreetly worded telegram to the husband.

Most characteristic of all, however, is, perhaps, the tale of the lovely girl encountered upon the deck of the Channel steamer on the crossing to England. She was, it appeared, a mannequin from a great Paris house; so Lehár found it prudent to be a traveller in gramophone records. They made a *rendezvous* to meet in a restaurant in London, and the mannequin and the salesman got on so well that another meeting was arranged. But before this could take place Lehár went to a reception at a large and fashionable West End mansion. He had not met his hostess before . . . but he recognized her only too well. . . . They behaved as strangers, and that was the end, except that he was anxious to make the incident the plot of an operette, but was dissuaded by Willner, who said it was too old!

The simplicity and good nature revealed in these stories make their appearance again in other often-quoted anecdotes about the Master. One of the most famous of these tells how, just before the production of *Wiener Frauen*, he was persuaded by some friends in the theatre to take a walk through the part of the Prater which is used as a fairground. On one pitch the attraction was a "phonograph", the early forerunner of the gramophone, in those days an astounding novelty. Lehár paused a moment to listen—and was worse than astounded. For what the machine was playing in its shrill tones on the cylindrical record was nothing else than his own "Nechledil March", the big hit, as he hoped, of the coming production, never yet heard in public! "What's that?" he cried, horror-struck, to his friends. "Oh! Only some old March or other!" was their casual reply. "But no!" cried the outraged composer. "It's my big number in the new show! How did it get here?" The showman deferentially assured the gentleman that it was a very well-known Hungarian melody, and Lehár, with his head whirling, hurriedly bought the dreadful cylinder . . . to hush the matter up! He could hardly believe it when the joyful laughter of his friends disclosed that they had made the cylinder secretly themselves, and "planted" it in the Prater with the connivance of the showman.

There was always, says E. Decsey, something of the great child in Lehár, and this was proved again only a day or two later, when, after the first performance of *Wiener Frauen*, he was waiting with anxiety in a café for the first editions of the morning papers. One of the same merry companions proffered the telephone number of an agency where early copies of all the Vienna journals would already have arrived and the manager would surely oblige by reading some of the criticisms to him. Lehár rushed to the telephone kiosk and made his request. A polite voice asked for a minute or two to fetch the papers, and then, beginning with the all-important *Neue Freie Presse*, read out such a series of slatings as no composer of operettes had ever yet had to endure. Lehár tottered out of the kiosk completely shattered . . . into the arms of his delighted friends, who had perhaps scarcely hoped that they would be able to play a second trick on him so soon after the first!

He took it all in good part, as he did his little misfortunes in love, which cannot, indeed, have deeply afflicted a man surrounded by so much feminine homage. He had, after all, a right to that homage as part of the kingship he had won for himself, for had he not gathered up and placed upon his own brow the crowns of Johann Strauss, of Millöcker, of Suppé and all the hitherto famous Viennese composers of light opera? He had completed the victory of the native operette over the French *opéra bouffe*, and had lived to see Offenbach surviving almost solely as the composer of *Tales of Hoffmann*, romantic music drama rather than operette. Perhaps there was a lesson and a beckoning for Lehár here. . . . But at present he headed a brilliant Viennese galaxy which included Leo Fall of *The Dollar Princess*; Oskar Straus of *The Chocolate Soldier* and *The Waltz Dream* (the melody of which, with its endless silken windings and unwindings, seems to be trying to draw into itself the quintessence of every Viennese waltz with a sweetness that almost cloys, as Lehár's music never does); and other such names as Eysler, Kalman, Ascher and the rest.

None of these, however, could usurp Lehár's place, and his biographer does not claim too much for him in saying that he embodied the spirit of an epoch. He was, he always declared, a product of the age of Franz Joseph, an age with many of the features that characterized the Edwardian era in England, already described in these pages. In both countries Society was still based on class distinctions, was wealthy, carefree, luxurious, bathing in pleasure as its natural element, preferring splendour to art, perhaps, and comfort to strenuous achievement, yet inspired by graceful sentiment and true to standards of gentlemanly behaviour. To this epoch Lehár gave the music that at once expressed and refined its feelings and ideals.

It was an era that looked as if it must last for ever, so firmly based it seemed. To the discontent of the masses and the darkening of the European situation it paid little heed. There might be sabre-rattlings from Berlin; dangerous policies driven forward in the Balkans by the unscrupulous Foreign Minister of the Austro-Hungarian Monarchy, von Aehrenthal; signs of crisis from Turkey, where the Sultanate had collapsed and a revolutionary Committee had taken over the Sick Man's

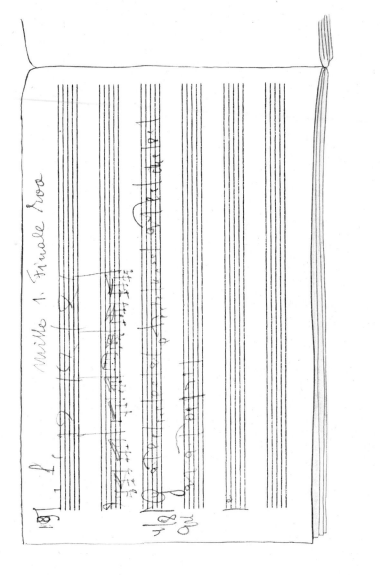

Actual size reproduction of one page of the pocket book carried by Lehár into which he jotted ideas for melodies as they occured to him. The excerpt is a passage of music in *Eva*, one of his operettes

Franz Lehár amongst the treasures of the Schikaneder-Schlössl

heritage, for the possession of which the Great Powers were manœuvring. Who could seriously believe, however, that the clock was to be set back in Europe, the bright lights to be extinguished, the gay tunes to quaver into silence? Lehár's round of triumph continued, and his next work was entitled *Endlich Allein* ("Alone at Last"). It was produced on a February evening . . . and the year was 1914.

Endlich Allein had not come into being without birth-pains. It has been noted that the want of suitable subjects for his music was a continual worry to Lehár, and sometimes this anxiety became more than he could endure. His principal librettist at this time was Dr. Alfred Maria Willner, an interesting character who found no inconsistency in varying his work as a light opera librettist with the composition of mystical poetry expressing his deeply religious instincts. Perhaps, however, the difficulty of combining these two activities was one of the causes that made his production of books for light operas slower than Lehár could bear.

One summer night at Ischl Lehár's patience gave out. In such moments he could be terrible; the kindliness and courtesy that he showed to all around him in ordinary life vanished when he felt himself artistically frustrated. In such moments his collaborators shook in their shoes; and, indeed, it used to be said that when one of his works was at last ready for production his librettists were ready for a mental home.[1] Past were the days when he had had to go round, cap in hand almost, beseeching well-known writers to choose him for their composer; now they thronged round him, begging him to choose them for his librettists. The unhappy Dr. Willner was therefore aghast when, with glowering eyes, Lehár informed him that unless he brought him a subject on the following morning he would "go to Unterach". This was a fearful threat. Unterach, not far from Ischl, was where Victor Léon was staying. If Lehár returned to him, it was all up with Dr. Willner.

In despair he wandered out into the streets of Ischl, and entering the church prayed on his knees to every saint whose image stood there for help . . . for inspiration. Then he returned to his rooms, resolved to pass the night in solitary meditation, hoping that thus the spirit of invention might visit him. And as he thus sat, gazing out upon the aloof mountain peaks and the remote stars above them, alone at last after the anguishes of the day, the long-sought-for idea flashed upon him. Alone at last! . . . Not a poor author of operettes, but a pair of young lovers who climb a peak together to escape the turmoil and frustrations of the world below!

---

[1] One of his librettists, after a prolonged and gruelling session with him that lasted up to midnight, went home exhausted and flung himself upon his bed. At 3 a.m. the telephone shrilled. "You don't mean to tell me," cried the indignant voice of Lehár, "that you've been asleep!"

Alone at last! The next morning Willner was back at Lehár's villa, tempting him with the idea of something really novel in operette—a whole act to be played by these two characters, alone above the world. Lehár was enthusiastic: he did not go to Unterach, and Willner was saved! Promptly the operette *Endlich Allein* was written.[1]

For many years Lehár was accustomed to call *Endlich Allein* his favourite work. This must have been, at least in part, because it presented, under the beautiful symbol of the lovers climbing to the summit of the mountain, his own deep-seated longings and impulses towards a purer idealism. The piece opens, operettishly enough, in a Swiss hotel, where we learn that the lovely American heiress, Dolly Doverland, is to be married for the sake of the title to the son of an impoverished Count— a bargain that suits both fathers. It does not, however, suit Dolly, who plays truant, and slips off to climb a neighbouring height alone with a handsome young guide. The next act, of which the scene is laid among the Alps, is entirely occupied with the adventure of the two, who as yet scarcely know that they love. In the course of this long, lyrical interchange, as the sunset gradually flushes the scene, occur the famous songs:

> *Es steht vom lieben so oft geschrieben,*
> *Wer nie geliebt, ist ein Narr geblieben*[2]

and *"Schön ist die Welt"*—("Fair is the World")—one of the best known of Lehár's compositions.[3]

Dolly realizes her love when the young man takes a deadly risk to gather the *Edelweiss* she has been longing for: but though they stay the night together up there, while "The mountains stand in silver light", the young man respects her innocence, and they return without even an explicit declaration of passion. That in the Third Act we descend from the heights to the land of operette again, and discover that the "Guide" is really a young Baron and an admirable match for the heiress, while the son of the impoverished Count is only too glad to get out of the engagement, having placed his heart elsewhere, does not matter. What matters is the exquisite music which Lehár composed for the mountain scene, embodying so perfectly the solitary spirit of the peaks.

---

[1] *See* Peteani, pp. 122–124.

[2] "It has so oft been writ of Love that he who has never loved has stayed a fool!"

[3] *Schön ist die Welt* was made the title of the revised version of this piece, brought out after the First World War in 1931. The lovers were then raised to the rank of a Crown Prince and a Princess, and there was a good deal more comedy in the hotel scenes, into which a *thé dansant* and Tango atmosphere was introduced. But the original score was substantially unchanged, except for additions, and the mountain scene was retained—though a portable wireless warned the lovers that their disappearance had been remarked! On the whole scarcely, it would seem, an improvement.

It is a thousand pities that this beautiful work of Lehár's has not been given in England, either in its earlier or its later, more sophisticated, form. The reason may be the difficulty of finding in this country singers of light opera who could sustain the prolonged duet that constitutes the Second Act. In Vienna the heroine was played by Mizzi Günther, giving fresh proof of her versatility, for a part differing more widely from the Merry Widow could hardly be imagined. The disguised young Baron was played by the handsome and talented Hubert Marischka, whose fame was already beginning to mount until as actor, singer and producer he became one of the leading personages of the Vienna stage.

On the 28th July, 1914, while the tender and meditative melodies of *Endlich Allein* were still sounding, a shot rang out which echoed round the globe. It was fired in one of those comic-opera Balkan states, at a place called Sarajevo . . . and the Archduke Ferdinand of Austria was dead, he who was heir to that straggling mass of countries, races and creeds which was the Austro-Hungarian Empire, shapeless, rickety perhaps, but still a buttress of the peace of Europe. That shot sent the world hurtling into war. It meant the end of the great days of Europe. Gone were security, placidity, leisure, beauty and peace. That shot was to take millions of lives and masses of treasure, to alter maps, to change the course of history. Its echo killed George Edwardes, and the Edwardesian Empire came to an end. Its crack broke the ancient friendship between Austria and Britain and made Franz Lehár technically an alien enemy. He might— he did—live to write many, many more waltzes, but the world was never to move in Waltz Time again.

CHAPTER FOURTEEN

The Second Flowering

NONE of the countries that entered the War of 1914–18, probably, realized that the issue would be for them not the usual fruits of victory or penalties of defeat, but the end of a world. And on no place did the catastrophe fall so crushingly as on Vienna. Thanks to the fanatics and doctrinairies of Nationalism, the Hapsburg Empire, that indispensable support of Central Europe, was dissolved into a mosaic of small States which were to prove in the end unable to resist either the new Nazi German Empire or the Communist dictatorship of Russia, while Vienna itself was left the derelict and overgrown capital of a tiny Austro-German Republic.

Want and hunger now stalked the streets that had been bright with prosperity and gaiety; the music of the great Imperial and Royal Army, like its gorgeous uniforms, lingered only as a dream; the vast parade grounds were empty; the Hofburg and other residences of the Monarchy rang hollowly to the footfalls of tourists. On the palace walls of the exiled or ruined nobility the stucco was flaking; the Grand Avenue of the Prater lay unmarked by hoof or wheel; drained of its life-blood by the cutting of its industrial arteries and by galloping inflation, the haggard capital was sinking into a lethargy of death—to be broken presently not by the lilt of the waltz but by the mutter of machine-guns. Vienna had become the city of the grey Danube.

That was the title of a waltz that Lehár composed at the time—*An der grauen Donau*. Few indeed can have felt the blast more chillingly than he. The world that had toppled was essentially his; he had been its acknowledged interpreter and the King of its music-makers. From the very moment when the guns opened up he had felt the shadow fall across him. He, whose most intimate nature was kindliness, joy, and delight in the pleasure of living, could never find the harsh notes needed to celebrate

The workroom in the Schikaneder-Schlössl

Feeding his goldfish in the pond which he kept full of them in the
Schikaneder-Schlössl; and consulting the astrolabe in the grounds of the
Schikaneder-Schlössl

strife and destruction. He had the ordinary patriotism of the decent man, and after being for so long attached to the Austrian Kaiser's Army, he could not be without sympathy for his former comrades now marching to fresh ordeals. But he felt no impulse to compose a "war operette"—even though his old collaborator Victor Léon was making a soldier on leave the hero of a new libretto—and such war songs as he wrote expressed the tragedy rather than the exaltation of the struggle. The most note-worthy of them were his setting of Zwerger's pathetic poem *Ich hab' ein Hüglein im Polenland*, a woman's lament over a distant grave, and the tone-poem called "Fever", which reflected, no doubt, his experiences at the bedside of his brother Anton, whom he helped to nurse back to life after a dangerous wound.

In the War-time Theatre the operette *Der Sterngucker* (*The Star-Gazer*) had failed, and his only success had been a Hungarian piece entitled *Wo die Lerche Singt* ("Where the Lark Sings"). This story of a Hungarian village girl who is seduced into going to Budapest by a painter who wants her to be his model, only to be betrayed by him and to return to her native wilds "where the lark sings", surely masks the composer's longing for escape to the scenes of his childhood from the iron age into which his time was passing. As the old grandfather sings in the play:

> *Was geh'n mich an die Leute in grosser Welt?*
> *Meine Welt, das sind nur zwei,*
> *And'res ist mir einerlei, einerlei!*[1]

With the restoration of peace, accompanied by the delusive hopes that every revolution creates, there was a short period of feverish enjoyment in Vienna, and it seemed for a while as if the ghost of the old gaiety had returned to haunt the scenes where it had once flourished. Lehár would have been glad to satisfy this nostalgic craving, and to offer the consolation of golden dreams when the bitter realities began to pierce through the brief illusions of the post-War years. But the task of recalling to life a dead world was beyond him or any composer; nor could the deeper develop-ment of his gifts which he was always seeking be promoted by reviving the echoes of the past.

None of his works of the period immediately following the War, neither *Die Blaue Mazur* (*The Blue Mazurka*), nor *Die Tangokönigin* ("The Tango Queen") adapted from *Die Ideale Gattin*, nor *Libellentanz* (played in England as *The Three Graces*), nor the more ambitious *Frasquita*, with its Spanish setting, the most successful of all, nor the really clever musical

---

[1] "What matter to me the folk of the greater world? In my world there are but two. The rest is all one, all one to me."

farce *Clo-Clo* (in which Louise Kartousch won a personal triumph as a
Parisian dancer compelled to pose as the unacknowledged daughter of a
provincial Mayor, her "gentleman friend", in his home), made an impression comparable to that of Lehár's best works before the War or were
reckoned to add anything to his status. It began to be whispered that
Lehár was a survival, that he was written out. . . . And then in 1923, on his
birthday, Fortune, who had seemed to be neglecting her Favourite for an
unduly long while, gave him a present such as he had through these last
years been vainly dreaming of.

He was suffering from a slight attack of influenza and to pass the
evening took up a manuscript that a friend had sent him. It was the
libretto (by a hand not disclosed) of an operette on the life of Paganini,
that enigmatic genius of the early 19th century, who by his weird looks
and deliberate mystifications had earned himself the title of "the devil's
violinist". The opening tableau, showing a group of peasants outside the
inn of an Italian village listening fearfully to the strains of an unseen
violinist floating through the windows of a half-ruined pavilion on the
edge of a wood, at once fired Lehár's imagination. Was he not, too, a
violinist, trained in the romantic Hungarian tradition? Was he not, too,
a magician, who had laid a spell upon his times? Had he not been, like
the Italian *maestro*, a great lover of women? Nicolo Paganini, in some sort
his own *alter ego*, seemed a subject fallen from Heaven for his pen.

He continued to read the libretto with increasing enthusiasm; the influenza was forgotten, while he sat at the piano, already jotting down
themes and settings for the lyrics. It was morning before he had done, and
already an Act and three-quarters had been composed in outline. The next
thing was to telephone the friend from whom this precious windfall had
come, and to ask who the author of the book might be. The answer was a
surprise. *Paganini* was no first effort by a gifted beginner; it was the work
of a man already widely known in Vienna and outside it both as author
and composer. He was also a personal friend of Lehár's.

Paul Knepler and Franz Lehár had first met when the former was
doing his service at the age of nineteen in the regiment of which Lehár was
Bandmaster. The young soldier had composed a waltz and dedicated it to
the Colonel, who received a copy of it with pleasure, and was graciously
pleased to order that it should be played at a forthcoming regimental ball
in Vienna. On the night, as the moment drew near for the number of
Knepler's waltz to go into the frame beside the bandstand, he received an
urgent message to go round and speak to the Bandmaster. Lehár, receiving him with an air of consternation, announced the appalling news that
his waltz had been forgotten—it had not been packed up with the other
music to be played at the ball, and it was too late to search for it now,

especially as the Band Sergeant in charge of the library was on leave for the evening!

Knepler was shattered. His début as a composer was annihilated . . . and what would the Colonel say, who had expressly ordered his waltz to be given? Lehár proposed a way out of the dilemma . . . the only way. The band had with them the music of a new waltz of his own which they had been practising and which had never yet been played in public. Would Knepler agree to this waltz being performed under the name of his? But, Knepler objected, the Colonel had read the score of the other! . . . Lehár smiled and reassured him: the Colonel would not notice any difference. So the Lehár waltz was played, and at the end Private Knepler received a wild ovation. . . . As indeed he well might. For the title on the front page of the piece for which he was receiving the honours was "Gold and Silver", and only a few nights later it would be acclaimed at the Princess Metternich's celebrated fancy ball. "For a quarter of an hour," Herr Knepler ruefully relates, "*I* was the composer of 'Gold and Silver'." Lehár, however, whispered into his ear as they went out, "*My* tune was not so bad, either."

This had been years ago. Now Herr Knepler had won a name as the author-composer of an operette, *Josephine Gallmeyer*, written round the life of a star of Viennese operette who might be called "the Marie Lloyd of Austria", and another entitled *Wenn der Holunder blüht* ("When the Elder Blooms"). On his *Paganini* he set great store, and had already, besides writing the story, composed some of the music. It must have been with misgivings that he allowed his book to be shown to Lehár, whose demands in artistic matters were always urged with an irresistible energy; and now, it seemed, his suspicions were justified. His friend *must* have *Paganini*, just as years before he had told Victor Léon that he *must* have *The Merry Widow*. It was a sharp disappointment for Herr Knepler; but after hearing some of Lehár's projected settings, he was only too glad, as an artist and a friend, to surrender his claims. It was a fine testimony to his admiration of Lehár, and Herr Knepler met with his reward in the world success of the operette in which he remained at least a partner.

Paganini tells the tale of the love of the Duchess of Lucca, Napoleon's sister, Anna Elisa, for the fascinating fiddler, whose music she hears one day while she is hunting. It is a foredoomed passion, since not only the Duke, her husband, but her all-powerful brother, the Emperor, are determined to drive Paganini away from Lucca, or to arrest him if he refuses to go. Anna Elisa saves him from the guards under General Hédouville sent to seize him, and even follows him in gypsy disguise as far as a smugglers' inn upon the frontier. But the last word is renunciation, perhaps because the Duchess remembers her duty . . . even more probably because she has already been given only too much cause to realize that the "devil's violinist" will never be faithful to a woman. His famous theme song,

Gern hab'ich die Frau'n geküsst,[1]

is no jest, but the expression of his deepest nature, and he will remain true to one mistress only . . . his violin.

An operette with an unhappy ending! Another defiance to venerable tradition. But Lehár must at all costs have his freedom, and in *Paganini* his genius had taken on a new lease of life and soared away from old *clichés* and conventions. The romantic passion of these lovers could not be expressed within the existing framework of the musical stage. What was Lehár composing—operette or Opera? He did not care. As an eminent critic was one day to remark, "It is well known that there are now three kinds of dramatic music—Opera, operette and Lehár!" And Ernst Decsey pronounced that "*Paganini* is the best that Lehár has so far written".

It was the opening of a new epoch in Lehár's career . . . and he was fifty-five years old. But it was even more than that. It was the beginning of a new artistic collaboration that was to sweep the world in an unheard-of triumph. In Vienna, when produced at the Johann-Strauss Theater in 1925, *Paganini* had had but a modified success; it had lacked the ideal interpreter of the title-rôle. But when, in the following year, it was brought out at Berlin this want was made good. For the Paganini was Richard Tauber.

It would be difficult to exaggerate what the discovery of Tauber meant to Lehár. Taken in conjunction with the happy chance that had given him the *Paganini* libretto, it marked the great turning-point in his career. He had been fully aware since the War of the problems confronting him. He was as conscious as anybody of the changed times, and he was resolved to win over this new world in his own characteristic way—by striving to do better and better, to compose on a higher level, without sacrificing that personality of his which had expressed itself so clearly in his earlier works. He still sought tirelessly for libretti which would yield the right kind of inspiration; he still refused steadfastly to put out work that did not satisfy his own standards, or to "write down" to a deteriorating taste. And among his chief needs was that of a voice—a singer who would do for him all that Caruso had done for his friend Puccini. And in Tauber he believed that he had found him. "He and I are brothers without the luxury of blood-relationship," Lehár used to say in after-years. There will be much more

[1] "Girls were made to love and kiss."

to tell about his friendship with the great tenor in later chapters; here it is enough to note that after Tauber's prodigious success in *Paganini* at Berlin, Lehár made the German capital his centre of operations. Indeed, it was inevitable that for theatrical productions on the grand scale Berlin, still wealthy and unravaged by the late War, should take the place of impoverished Vienna. And Lehár was soon to find there in the brothers Fritz and Alfred Rotter producers of rare quality and imagination.

His first piece given in Berlin after *Paganini* was *Der Zarewitsch*, described as a "romantic operette", though it had been better called a "music-drama"—but it was becoming progressively less and less possible to find a term under which to classify Lehár's works. *Der Zarewitsch* was drawn from a historical drama of that name by the poetess Gabriela Zapolska. As soon as Lehár saw this play in Vienna in 1925 he realized that it was a subject for him. Russian themes had always been congenial to him, since the faraway days of his first Opera *Kukuschka*. He told his friend and librettist Béla Jenbach over the telephone that same night that he wanted *Der Zarewitsch*—only to have his hopes dashed by the news that the rights were already sold to the composer Künneke. Jenbach, however, was resourceful. Without a word to Lehár he took the train to Berlin, whence two days later he was able to telegraph that Künneke had paid Lehár a fine compliment. He would give up the rights in *Der Zarewitsch* to him.

This work, of which the text was written by Jenbach and Reichert, was produced in Berlin on the 21st February, 1927, but has never been given in England. Perhaps the psychological theme is not one that could, according to our ideas, be satisfactorily treated in a musical play. Alexis, the Crown Prince of Russia, is a woman-hater; but since he must shortly marry according to his rank and responsibilities, his father and the Court judge it essential that this inhibition should be overcome. They can think of no better way to effect this than to introduce a beautiful young girl, Sonia, into his apartments, disguised as a Circassian soldier. Alexis, however, who has already confessed his passion for solitariness in a song that is now famous, "A soldier stands on the Volga's shore", is impervious to the temptation. Yet, to spare Sonia the disgrace of failure, he consents in the kindness of his heart to let her have the show of success, and visit him freely in his rooms.

The result is what is to be expected. But when the chilly Prince at last falls in love it is only to be told that he must marry elsewhere . . . and that his Sonia is a light-o'-love. There is a first separation, then a secret reunion of the lovers and flight into Italy. Thence, however, the Zarewitsch must be recalled by his duty to his people, for the news comes that his father is dead and that the Throne awaits him.

This story, with its strong characterization, its sex psychology, its mingled Slav and Italian atmosphere, and its philosophy of renunciation, might have been expressly written for Lehár, the serious Lehár of these post-War years, while at the same time it offered a magnificent opportunity to Tauber, whose voice, with its wonderful *piano*, excelled in scenes of love and pathos, and to Rita Georg, who played the heroine. There was no doubt from the first about the success of *Der Zarewitsch*, which firmly established the new Lehár in general favour.

His next important venture was of a more daring character. Two librettists, Dr. Ludwig Herzer and Dr. Fritz Löhner (the latter one of the most accomplished writers of lyrics of the day), had suggested to Lehár the idea of putting Goethe on the stage. It is difficult for English readers to appreciate the audacity of the proposal. Dr. Willner had been in hot water enough years before for making a stage figure of Schubert. But Goethe! The idea of making Shakespeare a hero of musical comedy conveys but a faint idea of the sacrilegious air that clung to the notion of a singing Goethe on the boards! For Will Shakespeare, when all is said, was but a poor player, but Goethe was a Privy Councillor, a poet in official robes—was it not almost *lèse majesté* to take liberties with such a figure? Lehár however was not deterred by the storm of criticism that broke loose when the project became known. He had faith in his own integrity and high purpose. He knew that he was equal to treating a dignified theme without cheapness or frivolity. . . . If any of his listeners had not yet appreciated that, he was ready to convince them.

Nor was his Goethe to be the mature poet in all his literary and official dignity, the canonized national poet of Germany. The authors had chosen for their book an episode of Goethe's youth, his early love for Friederike, the daughter of the Pastor of Sesenheim. This village idyll is displayed in the First Act, while in the Second the accustomed conflict breaks forth. Goethe is summoned to the Grand Duke of Weimar's Court to take his place there as poet and dramatist, and to develop his heaven-sent gifts for the benefit of his country and humanity. In the conflict between love and vocation Goethe is for choosing fidelity to his village flower. But Friederike is a maiden of heroic mould, and when she learns from the poet's friend Weyland what a future he is abandoning for her sake she steels herself to drive him away onto the path of greatness, even though to do it she has to flirt and pretend infidelity to their love.

In the Third Act, nine years later, the poet, crowned with success and honours, revisits Sesenheim, to find Friederike still unmarried, and to learn, now that her sacrifice has accomplished its purpose, that she had done it all for him and had never wavered in her love. But it is too late to turn back, and once more the lovers must part—yet again the theme of renunciation that sounds so loudly in Lehár's later works concludes the piece. Certainly Lehár had by now completely buried the superstition that a "happy ending" is essential to light opera.

Friederike was produced at the Metropol-Theater, Berlin, by the Rotter brothers, the first work of Lehár's that they put upon the stage. Käthe Dorsch played the name part, and Tauber played Goethe. The ethereal tenderness and delicacy of Lehár's score, containing such gems among love songs as "Maiden, my Maiden" and "Wayside Rose", and expressing the spirit of the period with such fidelity, both in its rococco elegance and in its naïve Alsatian folk melodies, were at once appreciated by the Public, though critical carpings over the "sacrilege" did not cease. But they will not be remembered so long as this enchanting idyll of young love and human sadness, which perhaps discloses more of the intimate soul of its composer than any other of his works.

From the old German atmosphere of *Friederike* Lehár returned for his next piece to the exotic. It was to prove the only case perhaps in which a revision of an earlier work won a triumph denied to the original. Among the pieces that Lehár brought out in Vienna during the early years after the First World War was one entitled *Die Gelbe Jacke* ("The Yellow Jacket"), played in 1923 at the Theater an der Wien. Its subject was the love of a Viennese Countess for a Chinese diplomat, whom she follows to his native land to become his wife. But there she finds that "East is East", and that her beloved is ready, as a condition of becoming a Minister, to comply with the Chinese law requiring him to take a wife from his own people and relegate his European Countess to an "unofficial position". She refuses to accept the condition and returns, home-sick, to Vienna, whither her Chinese lover follows her, but in vain.

For some reason *Die Gelbe Jacke* was not a success in its original form, but when in 1929 in a rewritten shape it was brought out again as *Das Land des Lächelns* (*The Land of Smiles*) at Berlin, with Tauber as the Chinese hero, Prince Sou Chong, it was a very different matter. Although there was not much new in the score, the rigorously revised text, especially Dr. Löhner's lyrics, seemed to give the operette fresh value, and there was Tauber for the first time to give effect to the songs "*Immer nur Lächeln*" and "*Dein ist mein ganzes Herz*", which, known to the English-speaking world as "You are my Heart's Delight", has taken place with the "Gold and Silver Waltz" and the "Merry Widow Waltz" as one of the three Lehár tunes with which everybody on the globe is familiar.

The years 1925 to 1929, which gave us *Paganini, Der Zarewitsch, Friederike* and *Das Land des Lächelns,* may be reckoned the great creative period of Lehár's life, the time when his genius, matured by age, came to full fruition. We have now to trace the fortunes of Lehár in England during these years and the reception that his latest works met with over here.

Before doing that, however, a few words on Lehár's relations with the art of the film may end this chapter. Those odd, jerky shadows on a screen that had amused the world half-contemptuously in the days when *The Merry Widow* was young had made great strides in the two decades that followed. They had improved in clearness and coherence; they had acquired spectacular and dramatic quality; they had given rise to a great comic genius; but they had not yet found a voice. Yet even the "silent" films early attracted Lehár, who, as a rule, was not given to welcoming novelties. Mme Peteani gives a most entertaining account of how, in those "silent" days, he was persuaded to appear on the screen himself, and in the character of "Franz Lehár"! He found the rigours of film-making at that period more than he had bargained for (especially the melting heat of the lights), and though this biographical screen-play was given a gala opening for the benefit of the Vienna Red Cross it does not seem to have made cinema history. Another film on Lehár's life was screened in 1929.

Versions of *The Merry Widow* and other operettes of Lehár's were, of course, seen on the cinema during the era of silent filming; but it was not until the talking film was perfected at the end of the 1920's that anything like an adequate presentation of his works could be achieved. The new series began with *The Land of Smiles*, in which Tauber appeared, to be followed in 1932 by *Friederike*, with the charming Mady Christians in the title-part. A version of *Der Zarewitsch* disappointed Lehár by its departures from the original story. The film of *Frasquita*, however, satisfied him far better, and the actress who played the gypsy heroine on the screen with brilliant success, Jarmila Novotna, was afterwards to create the name part in the last and greatest of Lehár's works upon the stage. Lehár himself was shown conducting the overture. *Paganini* was filmed under the title *Gern hab' ich die Frau'n geküsst*, and Jeanette MacDonald made the success that was to be expected as a singing Merry Widow of the screen.

But Lehár's interest in the cinema was not limited to the adaptations made of his existing works. He also composed between 1931 and 1936 original scores to four films. These were *Die Grosse Attraktion*, a conventional tale of back-stage love between a dancer and an Opera singer, in which Richard Tauber was the star; *Die Ganze Welt dreht sich um Liebe* ("All the World Turns on Love"); *Grossfürstin Alexandra* ("Princess Alexandra"), a spectacular Russian romance, designed as a vehicle for Maria Jeritza, in which Lehár was disgusted to find music by other composers blended with his own, and which was a failure; and *Es War einmal ein Walzer* ("There was once a Waltzer"), perhaps the only important one of the group. The beautiful and talented Marta Eggerth played in it, and it contained a notable waltz called an "English Waltz":

Es war einmal ein Walzer, es war einmal ein Wien!
Es waren schön're seiten, doch die sind längst dahin . . .[1]

The librettist who wrote these lines in 1932 had a prophetic instinct. It is impossible in reading them not to think of *The Dancing Years*, in which Ivor Novello, writing on the very edge of the gulf of 1939, celebrated that "one-time" Vienna in romantic story and romantic song, and unconsciously foretold much of the end of Franz Lehár's own life history.

On the whole it must be owned that Lehár's incursion into the world of the film was a disappointment to him. Mme Peteani is right in concluding that "Lehár did not conquer the Film; it was the Film that conquered Lehár". In fact, at the time when he gave his energies to it, it was not yet ready, as Stan Czech says, to collaborate with an artist of his rank.

[1] "There once was a famous waltzer,
There once was Vienna town,
We once knew happier moments,
But they long since have flown!"

CHAPTER FIFTEEN

The Return to London

THE War of 1914–1918, which made Lehár technically an enemy of this country and its people, kept him and his works from the British stage for nine years. Anything more absurd than the idea of Lehár as a foe of Britain cannot be imagined. But it was considered patriotic over here to ban all works by German, Austrian and Hungarian composers—and the same would have applied to those of Bulgaria and Turkey, had there been any. Even the music of such masters as Beethoven and Wagner was packed away. Yet there were never, at any time during the War, hard feelings against Austria. In fact, few people ever considered that we were fighting Austria at all. Germany was the foe. The British liked the Austrians; there had been long friendship between the two countries, and indeed the two races have much in common. But there it was; they were on the wrong side, so they must suffer.

It was not until 1923 that a play of Lehár's was again seen in London, and it was a revival of *The Merry Widow*. Naturally, the Widow came first in British affections; she always did. And that delectable lady came back, most suitably, to Daly's, in 1923. Evelyn Laye played Sonia, Carl Brisson was Danilo, W. H. Rawlins was Nisch, Derek Oldham Jolidon, Ivy Tresmand was Frou-Frou and Nancy Lovat Natalie. George Graves was once again the Popoff, and Kate Welch reappeared in her original character of Praskovia. Others in the cast were Clifford Seyler, G. Somers Bellamy, Claude Goodchild, Ronald Adair, Stanley Randall, Edwin Dodds, Cecily Saxe-Wyndham and Laurie Newton. With Graves in fine form, the attraction of Carl Brisson, and the talent and beauty of Evelyn Laye, the revival ran for 239 performances.

It may be mentioned in this place that, when revived again at the Lyceum in 1924, the *Widow* ran for 214 performances, with Carl Brisson as Danilo, Nancy Lovat as Sonia and again Graves as Popoff.

Brisson, an excellent performer with a large following, also toured the play, and another Sonia with him was Helen Gilliland. Jack Hylton revived *The Merry Widow* at His (now Her) Majesty's in 1943, despite the fact that once more Austria was in a war against us—much against her own will—with Madge Elliott as Sonia and Cyril Ritchard as Danilo, and it ran for 302 performances. It was revived yet again at the Coliseum in 1944 and at the Stoll Theatre in 1952. On that occasion Peter Graves played Danilo, Jerry Verno was Popoff and Margaret Mitchell was Sonia. . . .

But the post-War London to which Lehár returned in 1923 was a very different one from that which he had known and loved, and which had loved him and his music, when last he had faced it with *Gipsy Love* in 1912. That War had altered London, as it had altered the world. It was a much poorer and sadder London than in the days of Waltz Time, and although it still remained popular the Waltz no longer ruled, any more than the world still moved to its measure. The post-War Public was very unlike that of pre-War days. It had been through a furnace, but it cannot be said that it had been refined in the process. What had been melted out of it was the feeling of security and prosperity; and although it had won the War, it had been so extended that the belief in its own invincibility was no longer so immovably fixed in its mind. It had made tremendous sacrifices, and had given the cream of its youth; and there was hardly a family which did not show gaps in its ranks, which had not some lost one to mourn.

It was now living largely on its nerves; it was living fast and not thinking more than it could help. It was not content to enjoy its leisure as it had done of old; it had to be rushing about; it had to be febrile and "madly gay"—and above all it had to be dancing. But not the Waltz— or not the Waltz in the old waltzing way. For the tempo had entirely changed, even more than the characteristics of the race. The War of 1914–18 had much to answer for. It took away the riches; it took away the Golden Sovereign, and replaced it by paper—as flimsy as the standards of the times. The old-fashioned family life had gone; the old standards of morality and respectability, the courtesy and respect, the discipline of the home—these were things of the past. This had been a War for Freedom, and its survivors, certainly the younger portion of them, decided that freedom meant licence and rackety behaviour. The sexes were equal; so down with the old restraints on behaviour and on language! Let joy be unconfined; let all try to be "Bright Young Things", and emulate the pace of the youthful, post-War version of what had been known as "the Smart Set"! Sentiment, which had been prevalent during the War years, was completely jettisoned. Its place was taken by a brittle gaiety which

never rang true. Nobody wanted to go home, least of all to stop there—
no, on with the dance!

And the dances were different, for now America set the tune of them.
The ease and grace of Vienna were swamped in the jungle of Jazz. The
times were out of joint, and Jazz was music out of joint; so it was
eminently suitable. Couples on ballroom floors, who had once striven for
elegance, now either pranced, capered and dipped, or just walked around.
You did not have to learn dancing; just walk in time to the music and
hug the girl as closely as possible. Women, always the slaves of fashion,
followed the spirit of the times in their dress, their general appearance.
Skirts became shorter and shorter; legs were no longer mysteries, but
something for everyone to behold; there were no secrets of sex now. It
was a world which had emerged from the madness of War into a Peace
which it made as crazy. Values had shifted; the rich had become the New
Poor, and there was a Newly Rich Class, who had made money out of
what was then looked upon as Armageddon. Industrial unrest followed
stagnation in trade, once the short post-War boom was over and people
found that the paper money did not go nearly as far as the old golden
sovereign. Prices soared—but what matter? Let's have a good time, to
make up for the lost years! Let's go jazzing; let's be gay!

Indeed, it was not the world of Franz Lehár. Although London had
escaped the dreadful grip of poverty which held his Vienna in its strangle-
hold, still, it was not the London for sentimental melody, for the slow,
swaying Waltz with its grace and beauty. London wanted to shake its
shoulders and its hips; it preferred negro dissonance to the melody of a
maestro; it loved the groan of the saxophone better than the throb of the
violin. . . . The 1923 revival of *The Merry Widow* had been no test of how
Lehár would appeal to this new world which was so very different
from the one he had conquered. *The Merry Widow* had memories, was,
indeed, a classic, a milestone on the road along which musical plays had
travelled. The testing time was to come in 1924 when the first work of his
which had not been seen here before was presented, not at Daly's but at
the Empire Theatre.

It was a completely new start for Lehár. George Edwardes was dead,
a victim of the War; the old régime had gone, and the presenter of the
new work was, so far as this country went, a product of the War Years, a
strange, odd little man called Joseph Leopold Sacks. He is now a legend in
Theatreland, and scarcely, if at all, remembered outside of it. Yet, in his
brief years of success, he bestrode the London Theatre like a miniature
Colossus. It was a very different man who directed the return of Lehár to
London from the one who had first introduced him—there was a great
gap between George Edwardes and Joseph Leopold Sacks.

Joe Sacks could neither read nor write. A Russian or Polish Jew (he himself was not sure of his nationality), he had been taken to South Africa, then the land of promise, when a child, and put in the care of an uncle already there. He went to school for a short time, but could never learn the mystery of reading, let alone writing. He ran away and joined Fillis's Circus when that celebrated institution visited Johannesburg. He did odd jobs, swept up, appeared as a boy clown, sold bananas and the like in the menagerie, and he got on. He had no distractions, this boy who lived in his own world, to whom all print was meaningless. He concentrated on his work; he did not mind the hours, it was all one to him; and at the age of fifteen he was assistant manager. He could rise no higher because of his illiteracy.

Fillis brought his show to London in 1899, to Earl's Court; it appeared in the Empress Hall as *Savage South Africa*. Joe Sacks came with it. A big success was followed by a tour, but the Boer War broke out, and the circus broke up. Joe Sacks, having saved money, took a holiday. He saw life in London, he saw life in Paris. Then, in 1900, he got back to Cape Town. From then on his story is like a romance. This is not the place to tell how he and a partner erected a little theatre in Cape Town for the troops, made a fortune, lost it when their hall was destroyed, made another taking their show all over the war zone to play to the troops, and disbanded only when Peace was signed, after playing to the British High Command and the Boer High Command on alternate nights!

Sacks found himself back in Johannesburg with £28,000 to his name. He went into the hotel business, and made a profit. He went into show business; he made money, he lost it, he made it again, and he lost it again. He found himself in London with a handful of money and a contract with Sir Harry Lauder to appear under his management in South Africa. He persuaded Lauder to take the same terms to appear in a revue in London. It succeeded—and Sacks sold out. With his profits, and £500 which a man thrust upon him the night before he sailed, and which turned itself into £33,000 for that lucky speculator, he went to New York.

There he bought a play, a musical play, because he liked the colour in which the score was bound, and another because he could not have the first unless he bought the second. He bought a third before it was completely written, because he knew the composer. The first was *The Lilac Domino*, the second *Shanghai*, which was produced at Drury Lane, and the third *Going Up*, an immense success at the Gaiety. But this story need only concern itself with *The Lilac Domino*, because Sacks, helped by a man of the Theatre who knew him, got this play produced at the Empire, Leicester Square, against great odds, and with great success.

The Empire, world famous as a Music Hall, had suffered a severe blow during the First World War when its Promenade, its greatest attraction, was closed. That man of the Theatre who knew Joe Sacks suggested that it should again became a house for musical plays, as it had been when first built. He got Joe Sacks in, with *The Lilac Domino*. The change was justified. Joe followed up this start by his success at the Gaiety, and launched out in all directions. But he had a soft corner in his heart for the Empire. He produced another big success there in *Irene*. At one time he had seven successes running in London, this curiously ugly little man, who had a smile like sunshine, a charm with which he could dazzle, a capacity for weeping gallons of real tears when he chose to turn on the tap—a trick which got him out of many tight corners—who spoke almost a language of his own, not too easy to understand—to him a "show" was a "saow" for instance—and who was quite illiterate. True, he did eventually manage to make certain marks upon paper which were generally accepted as his name. But he had courage, the tenacity of his race, a firm belief in his lucky star, and a judgment of "saows" second to none of his time. This was the man who brought back Lehár to the London Public at the Empire Theatre.

The play was *The Three Graces*—originally called in its own language *Libellentanz*. The book by Carlo Lombardo and A. M. Willner was adapted by a young man who had been born in Hendon and educated at Charterhouse, and who was endeavouring to become a playwright in the intervals of playing and watching cricket. His name was—and is—Ben Travers, now the acknowledged master of the difficult art of writing farces. It was produced by Tom Reynolds, an Irishman, whose sister had married Robert Hale, the great comedian, and who was therefore uncle to Binnie and Sonnie Hale. He had been one of George Edwardes's producers, and had taken many of the Gaiety shows to America for the Guvnor; he was a delightful and most colourful character. Reynolds was one of the two men in whom Sacks placed some trust—for he really trusted nobody—and on whom he relied, the other being the man who got him the Empire and the Gaiety. Sacks was delighted to have the Lehár work; he knew all about Lehár, although he could not pronounce his name. He went to the Continent to see him—that meeting must have been worth seeing!—and he came back full of it all.

He gave *The Three Graces* an excellent production. Joe and Phil Harker painted the scenery, and Comelli, on familiar ground at the Empire where he had designed so many dresses for ballet, was responsible for the costumes. There was a splendid cast, which included Maidie Andrews (who succeeded Sylvia Leslie), Vera Freeman, Winifred Barnes, Jack Pierce, Harry Pringle, Stephen Frayne, A. Scott-Gatty, Eric Lovell, Pope Stamper, Ralph Roberts, who had been the Waiter in *The Merry*

Widow, but here played a sort of policeman, Morris Harvey, that extraordinary mimic and very gifted comedian, one of the original Follies, and Thorpe Bates, originally a concert singer, but with a long list of stage successes behind him by this time, including *The Rebel Maid* and *The Maid of the Mountains*. He possessed a magnificent voice, good looks, a fine presence and was a very useful actor as well. The chief comedian was W. H. Berry, who played the part of Bouquet, a comedian, and so experienced no difficulty at all, except that he turned the character into a study of W. H. Berry, which, as he was a comedian himself, did not matter.

But the trouble with *The Three Graces* was a cumbersome, top-heavy, over-complicated and perfectly incredible story. Ben Travers did his best with it, and managed to infuse it with life and comedy and amusing lines, but . . . but it belonged to the London of Waltz Time, not the London of Ragtime and Jazz.

Under its original title, *Libellentanz* ("Dance of the Dragon-Flies"), this operette had had a libretto written by an Italian author, Carlo Lombardo. In writing the score for it Lehár had utilized themes from his unsuccessful *Sterngucker*. When produced in Milan in 1922 it had made a great appeal to Italian audiences; but in a German version by Dr. Willner it had not pleased Vienna any more than its English adaptation was to please London. It introduces another "merry widow", but she has not the charm of the original one, and has to take part with two merry wives in a very theatrical and unconvincing plot. The three dragon-flies (or Graces), while in the city of Nancy, try for amusement to sting with the darts of love a young sportsman they encounter in the Duke of Nancy's Park. The sportsman is arrested by the game-keepers as a poacher and taken off to the Castle for judgment; but unfortunately the ducal residence and the ducal domain are at the moment in the hands of a rich vulgarian, Mr. Piper, who has lent money to the Duke.

Piper is concerned with amateur theatricals, not the obligations of his position, and is preparing with the help of the comedian Bouquet to put on in the Castle a sort of Offenbachian revue *From Olympus to Montmartre*. The three Graces are promptly enlisted in the company, and when it turns out that the poacher is none other than the Duke in disguise . . . well, it is hardly necessary to carry the story further. His Grace has only to pick out the widow.

The music was, of course, Lehár; it has some delightful numbers; but this, London felt, was not the Lehár of *The Merry Widow*, of *The Count of Luxembourg*, of *Gipsy Love*. There was even a fox-trot, but it did not grip and sway the people with the old magic. It seemed, indeed, to the majority of the young folk that this old magic, of which they had heard so much, was lacking. It was nice, oh yes! in an old-fashioned way. There was that waltz, and the song "Gigolette", and of course old Bill Berry knew how to sing that topical number "Coonah", but . . . well, this might please Father and Mother, but give us, said the young, the Americans . . . give us this fellow Irving Berlin. Vienna was not for them.

It would have been delightful to record a big and triumphant comeback for Lehár after his War years of banishment. But that was not the case. *The Three Graces* ran only from the 26th January to the 10th May, 1924 —Lehár's shortest run yet. Truly things were altered; the War had taken toll. With the magic of Edwardes behind it, his genius in cutting, his complete understanding, the fate of *The Three Graces* might have been different. But these new people in control did not understand Lehár and his *métier*; the Empire was not the place for romance; and that was that.

There was something else, too, of which the people were perhaps not quite aware, but which was there, nevertheless. In place of the old feeling of confidence and security had come a feeling of fear. It was hardly realized, it was pushed to the back of the mind; but War, which had smitten England so sorely, might come again. The British knew all about the slogan that the conflict in which they had been engaged was a War to end War, but in their innermost hearts they did not really believe it. They had won a great Victory, they and their Allies, but they found themselves poorer, not richer.

The spoils were great on paper, maybe; they included reparations and great tracts of land added to the Empire, which still existed and was apparently secure. But the basic ideas of Englishmen were shaken. Victory had not brought success and their standard of living was changing. There were still many shortages, still high taxation, still high prices. The great majority of them had expected that when the battles were over they would resume the life they had once led—and probably be better off. They found that they had been wrong, very wrong. Business was bad; markets had vanished; other markets, once dominated by them, were now shared by rivals. Many of the products of which this race had been the supreme, indeed almost the only, makers had, perforce, during the War been made elsewhere, and so there were new competitors, lost monopolies. The old days had gone, the days which had seemed so changeless, and were never to return. The English had to reorientate themselves. And it seemed that with those old days had gone the true melody of music; modern taste wanted something more primitive, something wilder, more akin to their disturbed minds.

Thus it looked as if with the old days had gone the music of Lehár. You could not give wild cocktail parties, dash about frantically in high-speed cars, dance in exotic, scanty costumes to his waltzes. You needed Jazz for

Lehár in his lovely salon at the Schikaneder-Schlössl

Top: Signing an autograph late in life, for an admirer, at Zurich. *Left*: At the keyboard, a characteristic picture

that. During the War, women had assumed trousers—and were loath to part with them; that did not go with Viennese grace, either. The whole way of life, the general upheaval, the breaking out of Woman from her guarded seclusion, her participation in manly habits, her entrance into what had been a masculine world, even into the saloon bars, none of this matched Lehár's melodies.

And he had come back to a different Theatre. Gone were the actor-managers who had given the Victorian and Edwardian Theatre its rich stability. Gone was George Edwardes, the inventor of Musical Comedy, the master-producer who was himself stable and secure in his two great theatres. Nowadays the Theatre had become a Tom Tiddler's ground where speculators, knowing nothing of the true dramatic art, rushed in to pick up the gold. The War had made a boom in theatres; people wanted to forget, to dodge reality, to escape, and here the Theatre performed its true job. It cannot be said that it did it with Quality, but it supplied what the people, uncritical in their insecure hold on life, really wanted. Farces like *A Little Bit of Fluff*, heart-throbs like *Peg o' My Heart* and *Daddy Long Legs*, these were the thing. And of course revue—for revue gave girls, legs and colour.

That was just what the boys from the trenches had wanted; it had been, in the current phrase, "the Stuff to Give the Troops". They did not want to hear about War, these warriors with such a short while to live. They wanted something that the horror of the trenches could not give them. And who shall blame them for that? So they flocked to revue—at the Palace, at the Hippodrome, at the Alhambra. They could not see enough of *The Bing Boys*; they all sang "If You Were the Only Girl in the World". That is the way of the British in war-time—fight like hell, but leave the battle behind when on leave! The music of Nat D. Ayer, of Jerome Kern, the music of British Frederic Norton for *Chu Chin Chow*, that super-spectacular pantomime-*cum*-Eastern romance, were the big successes. What place had Lehár in this set-up?

That young disciple of his, Ivor Novello, had, indeed, made a start. He had written the big Song of the War, "Keep the Home Fires Burning"; he was breaking into revue and musical comedy, but not as yet on the Lehár lines. The older people clung to the shreds of their youth, to its taste and its ways. The younger folk rushed ahead. American ways were becoming popular, American plays and above all American films. That young man Charlie Chaplin was top of the world, but as yet the Talkies had not come to implant or regraft American idiom on its own parent stem. Meanwhile, Lehár was in eclipse.

He was having his own troubles, too, as this book shows. But he knew that he must change with the world. He was reaching out for a

M

higher method of expression, and, above all, he wanted libretti to give him inspiration. His Vienna had gone. Germany had been beaten, but not smashed, and that virile race was soon on its feet again. Berlin had accordingly become his headquarters.

This showed not only his shrewd business sense, but his determination to have only the best—the highest standard possible. Austria had suffered far more in the War than Germany, although she did not deserve it. True, she had fired the first shot, under great provocation; but it was Germany's War, Germany took advantage of that opportunity. Quite recently, whilst this book was being written, on one of those discussion programmes given to the public by Television, a young man who was not alive when that War was being hatched and fought said in all seriousness that Germany had not been the aggressor, had not engineered the War. It had, in his estimation, been thrust upon her. A man who had lived all through that War, observed every move, fought and been lucky enough—extremely lucky in at least two cases—to escape with his life, was nearly sick with rage. Germany wanted what this nation had got; she prepared for years; she built her huge navy, the army she had already; and she waited her time. He remembered a postcard which he had purchased in that apparently peaceful land as far back as 1909, which showed a small German lad, in a sailor hat, seated in a tub with a broom tied to it, afloat on the ocean. In the background loomed the shapes of vast battleships. The legend was *Unsere Zukunft liegt auf dem Wasser* ("Our future lies on the water"). It was sold by the German Navy League. He brought it home and people laughed. Germany fought and Germany lost; but Austria lost more than Germany, for those delightful, cultured, gay people were not, are not and never have been for ages, militant or victorious.

However, in Berlin resurgent Lehár could get his shows staged as they should be staged, could command his audiences, could express himself in terms of the Quality which was his standard. Vienna starved while Berlin revelled. Lehár, with his musical message to deliver, as has been said, must find the best means of proclaiming it. And the best sounding-board available was Berlin.

He did not give up London. His name still had power. There was *Clo-Clo* at the Shaftesbury in 1925, in which, for the first time, his music was combined with that of a British composer, Max Darewski. And in the same year, at the Prince's Theatre, came *Frasquita,* which was solely his work. This was presented by Robert Evett, the Jolidon of the original production of *The Merry Widow,* now a Manager striving to carry on the George Edwardes tradition. He put up a brave fight for Daly's; he had a vast success in *The Maid of the Mountains*; but in the end modernity, in the form of the late James White, ex-bricklayer from Rochdale, who flashed

across the theatrical firmament dazzling all by his millions, beat Robert
Evett in Lehár's old London home. But much good the Theatre did to
James White; it proved crazier than his own methods of finance. He
committed suicide, going from Daly's Theatre with the bottle that contained his key to the Future. . . .

Frasquita had the immense advantage of José Collins as its leading
lady. She had risen to stardom at Daly's; she had been leading lady in
The Maid of the Mountains in 1917, a British show which for length of run
beat Lehár's *Merry Widow*, attaining 1,352 performances. She had with her
in *Frasquita* at the Prince's Thorpe Bates (who had been in *The Three
Graces* and at Daly's in *The Marriage Market* and the record-breaking
Maid of the Mountains) and Edmund Gwenn. But *Frasquita* was not a
success although it was so well done. It came at a bad time, and it was too
much of the other days.

The failure of *Frasquita* was a bitter blow to Evett, as it was to José
Collins. For she had, in that play, one of the best songs of her career and
one which she loved singing. It was "Serenade", a thing of real beauty,
the English words of which were by that first-class lyric-writer Reginald
Arkell. One song cannot make a whole play—or it could not in those days
—but it can, and does, keep its own individuality and go on being sung
after the play is forgotten. So it has been with "Serenade". José Collins
tells of it in her own exciting life story, and one feels the heartbreak of the
artist when she writes, "The worst play so often contains the best song.
Such is Life". Such too is the Theatre.

The trouble was again chiefly the libretto. *Frasquita*, as has been noted,
was the most popular of Lehár's immediate post-War pieces in the
1920's; at the Opéra Comique in Paris, in particular, it won a distinguished
success. But it does present a thoroughly conventional set of operette
characters and situations. The scene is in Barcelona, and there is the
gypsy dancer, Frasquita, the young French traveller whose uncle wishes
him to marry his daughter, Dolly, and the inevitable "friend", Hippolyt.
At the cabaret where Frasquita dances Armand is robbed of a gold
cigarette-case and (so imprudently in an operette!) accuses Frasquita of
the theft. She is innocent and determines on revenge. The revenge—you
have guessed!—is to make Armand fall in love with her . . . and spurn
him. Armand falls heavily to her blandishments (while Hippolyt takes the
chance to steal the charming cousin, Dolly), and when he finds he has been
duped proves as irreconcilable as Prince Danilo until the Third Act is
completed. There are tunes from *Frasquita* that are still sung all over the
world, but as a play, however cleverly adapted, it did not break the spell
of ill-luck Lehár was having in England.

Two more years were to elapse before a new piece by Lehár came to

London, and then he was back where he had started, at Daly's. It was a very different Daly's, though, from that which Lehár had known before. James White ruled where the Guvnor had had command. He sat in the same office, giving parties, gambling, drinking, sometimes all through the night, and always doing vast deals, and planning new productions about which he knew nothing but thought he knew everything. He would have able lieutenants and countermand all their orders, override everybody—until Fate overrode him. But it was under his régime that Lehár's music came back to Daly's, although Lehár himself did not come.

The name of the play was *The Blue Mazurka* (*Die Blaue Mazur*). It was doomed to disaster from the very first. White engaged a couple of people for the leading rôles who could hardly speak any English. They had to be got rid of during the provincial try-out which the play had, and native artists were engaged for London. The original book was by Leo Stein and Béla Jenbach. The English libretto was by Monckton Hoffe, a first-class and practised dramatist, but one who shared with Richard Brinsley Sheridan the habit of very slow delivery of his manuscript, and who was, also, very much better at original plays than musical comedy adaptations. The lyrics were from the graceful and fanciful pen of Captain Harry Graham. Money was lavished on the dresses and the scenery, and Robert Courtneidge himself, a king of musical comedy, produced. The cast included Gladys Moncrieff, Wilfred Temple, Clifford Mollison, Lester Matthews, Jack Kelvin, Eric Roland, Arthur Claremont, Herbert Maule, Nat Lewis, Cecil Pearce, Billie Hill, and two famous Lehárians, Bertram Wallis and George Graves. But not even they could do anything with *The Blue Mazurka*. The music was lovely; it was real Lehár; yet there was little or no response from the Public. Indeed, the most popular number was an interpolated song—"The Black Lancers"—composed by Herman Darewski, the brother of Max. One wonders if Lehár knew about that. Fifteen years before, Lehár's score would have swept *The Blue Mazurka* to success; now all the play could do was to limp along for 139 performances from the 19th February, 1927, to the 18th June, 1927. So far as London was concerned, Fortune seemed to be deserting her Favourite. . . .

Three more years elapsed before another offering by Lehár was placed before London. It was now 1930, and the times were troublous. The German menace was rearing its head again, and in this country things were far from well. There were crises, industrial and financial. The old stability had gone for ever. There were signs that the hitherto close-knit bonds of Empire were slackening. A man called Gandhi was determined to get independence for India—the bright jewel of the Imperial Crown. There had been elections which had returned Governments without a working majority, and Labour had been sent to Westminster to govern, but not with a clear majority, for the first time. In other words, a Social Revolution had taken place.

In that state of things, with the gradual tightening of money and the Gold Standard sliding, Lehár again made a bid for British ears. And with what exquisite music!—the music of *Frederica*[1], produced on the 9th September, 1930, at the Palace Theatre. This musical play, which has already been described, was adapted from the original of Ludwig Herzer and Fritz Löhner by Adrian Ross, who did not write the lyrics, as had been his wont, but left that department to Harry Pepper. The music was, of course, all Lehár, without interpolations. In the cast were Leonard Russell, Florence Vie, Dorothy Monkman, Vera Lennox, Jack Stephens, William Kendall, David Henley, Reginald Renaud, John Renton, Roddy Hughes, Phyllis Beaden, Gwendolin May, Dorothy Crofts, Joyce May, Clare Lindsay, Beryl Harrison, Kathryn Holt, Betty Burke, Dorothy Whelan, Emily Gardner, Ena Roscoe, Frank Freeman and Cecil Musk. The title role was beautifully played and sung by Lea Seidl, who was to make her real conquest of London in *White Horse Inn*, and the part of Johann Wolfgang Goethe was played by Joseph Hislop, the celebrated concert and Opera singer. *Frederica* was given a beautiful setting, and was produced by Felix Edwardes—no relation to George Edwardes. The First Night reception was splendid; there were scenes of enthusiasm, calls for all concerned, and the highest praise for the music. The Press was most enthusiastic. Yet *Frederica* ran for 110 performances only.

Admirers of Lehár might well ask what was happening to him. Was he losing his grip? Was he finished as a composer? They had the answer ringing in their ears—the music of *Frederica*. The trouble was not there. The fact was that the times were out of joint, and, as yet, Lehár was not the man to put them right. The period from 1930 to 1939 was a downward slide. The uneasy Peace was drooping again towards War. It seemed that there was no room for melody or romance. And yet, as those years continued, that disciple of Lehár, Ivor Novello, rose to his greatest fame with romantic story and music. Truly, the world of the Theatre is full of contradictions. The line between success and failure in the crazy land of Make-Believe is narrow; the reasons for success as incredible as those for failure. Such a very little thing can turn the scale.

Something was said in the last chapter of the importance to Lehár of his discovery of Tauber. The moment has come to return to that subject. What Lehár needed in the middle 1920's was a singer who could render the more truly Operatic music he was now composing, a voice, in fact, of Operatic quality, having in it the throb and surge of the Lehár scores and of the strong sex *motif* always running through them. He did

---

[1] *Friederike*.

not particularly want an Italian, for he did not write in the Italian style. What he wanted was a Teutonic voice having in it the passion of the South and the desire of the gypsy. And it had been while listening to some gramophone records that he had found it. It was the voice of Richard Tauber, then an Opera singer, and a man who was more than just a singer, who was an accomplished musician, and, as he afterwards proved, also a composer.

Richard Tauber had been born in Linz, in 1891, so was by birth an Austrian. He had music and the Theatre in his blood, for his father, also named Richard Tauber, had been General Manager of the Stadt Theater, Chemnitz, in Saxony. The younger Richard studied music at the Conservatorium, Frankfurt-am-Main, in Germany. He was training to be a conductor and he did actually become one, and a good one, at the early age of eighteen. But he had other views about himself; he wanted to be a singer. His father thought that a precarious job; conducting, he maintained, was better, safer and surer.

But young Richard got his way after a good deal of trouble, and studied at Freiburg under Professor Carl Bienes. He went straight into Opera in 1912 at the Dresden State Opera House, singing Tamino in *The Magic Flute*. The music of Mozart suited his vocal gifts and his personality. He was a success, and very shortly he was leading tenor at Dresden. By 1920 he was singing at the State Opera House in Berlin and also at the State Opera House in Vienna. He sang at those two leading Opera Houses from 1920 until 1923, and then Lehár secured him. His first Lehár operette was *Frasquita*, but the big triumph came, as has been recorded, with *Paganini*.

He was an enormous success everywhere—when he sang. For he developed not only a temperament (he had always had that) but a habit of often, far too often, being "off"—not singing when he should have done so. He was popular, he was very successful, and thanks to Lehár he was earning big money. It is to be feared that he did not treat his new musical godfather too well. Lehár, who could look after himself, would be very severe with him, and Tauber would go back and sing—until the next time. The trouble was that his voice was just right, that he was the supreme singer of Lehár's music. Lehár knew it. And so did Tauber. But these two men, who had musically so much in common, both of whom had been conductors, both of whom were musicians to their finger-tips and skilled composers, had nothing in common in their characters.

Lehár was correct, precise, careful, a man who did his duty as he saw it, and who would fulfil a contract to the last gasp, even if that had been his dying one. Tauber was careless, with all the artist's vanity and complete self-obsession, seeing things only from his own point of view, and considering himself before anything or anyone else. There were rows, arguments, recriminations, but the two remained friends. Both had an enormous attraction for women. How Lehár dealt with his mass of adoring females has been told. Tauber was clay in their hands. He surrendered —and he often paid dearly for it. Frequently it was not only his love they wanted, but his money as well. And they got it. One charmer was particularly careless. She was always losing the expensive trinkets he gave her—the rings, the brooches, the necklaces, the bracelets—and plunging into an anguish of tears over the terrible loss. Soft-hearted Tauber dried her eyes and replaced the missing article. When the *affaire* ended, that lady had "two of everything".

Lehár was always well dressed, dapper and smart. Tauber was the reverse. True, he had good clothes; but he did not wear them well. He was at his best in unconventional attire, in what are called "sports clothes", or in his shirt and trousers at rehearsal, with the inevitable monocle stuck in his eye, to add incongruity. No traditional English "Johnny" of the old school was ever more tenacious of his monocle than Richard Tauber —off stage. It was as much a part of him as the famous and quite amazing *piano* in his voice.

Lehár was punctilious about time, never late, always on the moment, often a bit early. Time and Tauber were complete strangers. The clock had nothing to say to him. He took little care of himself, or his voice, in his younger days. He turned night into day; he did himself very well, and he lived every moment. He liked wine, he loved women, and song was part of him. He was not a handsome man, despite his attraction for women. He was short and thickset. He did not move or walk gracefully. He had a habit of swinging one leg round after the other, and of keeping one arm crooked and close to his side, the fingers bent like talons. He was not a very good actor. But he was a better actor than most tenors, and certainly than any other tenor of his day.

There was charm in the man, despite his bad habits, his dreadful unreliability, his temperament, his sudden rages and quick recoveries, his lack of presence and looks—in spite of all there was charm. He knew how to exert it; he knew exactly when and where to do it. He had a smile which had a sudden, boyish charm of its own. And he had a sense of humour, too. He did not like facing up to troubles—troubles which he himself had caused. He would sulk and run away like a naughty boy. There was not much that was lovable about him. He had been married, and the marriage had been dissolved. That was nothing. . . .

But when he sang—he was transformed. Then the magic of his voice, with its fire, its passion, its sex appeal, its trumpet note and its quiet, almost whispered *piano*, which nevertheless reached the furthest recesses of the

largest theatres, Opera Houses and concert halls of the world, and
sounded like those horns of elfland faintly blowing, made you forget the
man, his awkwardness, his gaucherie, indeed, and surrender entirely to the
music he gave you. And nobody could write music to suit that voice as
could Lehár. Nor could anyone sing Lehár's music like Tauber. It was a
combination of composer and singer fraught with the most splendid possibilities. Among its achievements was to be the reconquest of England for
Lehár.

CHAPTER SIXTEEN

Up to the Skies

DESPITE the short runs of the later operettes of Lehár in London, his fame and his power there did not weaken. The plays may not have succeeded, but the music always did. It was played by orchestras, and innumerable people bought records of it to play over and over again on the gramophone, which was now exceedingly popular—quite a craze, in fact. Radio had become part of daily life, and Lehár's music constantly went over the air. Theatre Managers, the most optimistic of men, would always bid for a composition by Lehár—there simply must be another *Merry Widow* coming sometime.

In the early part of the year 1932 a young man named Stanley H. Scott hastened to Vienna to see Lehár, and to secure one of his plays, *The Land of Smiles*. He also wanted to secure that tenor whose success in it had echoed even in this country, which pays little attention to what happens, theatrically, on the Continent. Stanley H. Scott wanted both the play and the tenor; nor was he the only Richmond in the field. But he had a card up his sleeve which he thought would be an ace of trumps. He could offer Lehár a production at Theatre Royal, Drury Lane. Now Mr. Scott was a newcomer to the Theatre, unused to its ways, its pitfalls and gins. He loved the Theatre life, and he loved the people. He had dabbled a bit, and had been pretty lucky. He had once had his name up as presenting a show in conjunction with Joe Sacks, but, either by luck or judgment—more the former than the latter—had managed to defer putting up any capital until the show had actually been produced. It plunged to disaster on its first night, and Stanley Scott emerged scatheless in pocket.

He was an extremely self-confident young man, given to wishful thinking. To him, to conceive an idea was to consider that idea carried out. He did not mean any harm by this; he was quite convinced he could do anything that he thought of; and it was this confident assurance of his which prevailed upon George Grossmith, then General Manager of Drury Lane, to promise him that he could have that Theatre of Theatres for *The Land of Smiles*—and Richard Tauber. Drury Lane was not doing well. It wanted a success. This seemed to be just the thing required. Grossmith was a most experienced man of the Theatre, especially where musical plays were concerned. He had been for years a pillar of the Gaiety and a right-hand man of George Edwardes. He was not only himself a great star of musical comedy, but an excellent writer of libretti too. Also, for years, he had been the senior half of the production firm of Grossmith and Laurillard, which had many successes to its credit. "G. G.", as he was to most people who knew him, liked the sound of this new idea, and he badly wanted an attraction for Drury Lane, never the easiest theatre to fit. So off went Stanley Scott hot-foot in pursuit of Franz Lehár. Unknown he might be to that great man; unknown indeed he was in the Theatre. That did not daunt him. His over-enthusiastic mind saw the whole thing complete. He could hear the First Night cheers, the sound of money pouring into the box-office.

He found Lehár and he discovered he had rivals. He was not the only one who wanted *The Land of Smiles* and Richard Tauber. But he got them. He got them because he could promise that the production would be at Drury Lane. Stanley Scott had a way with him—until you knew him. He was tall, dark and good-looking in a rather ruthless style; there was a faint resemblance to the film star von Stroheim. He had very good manners and address, a very good tailor, and he knew how to wear his clothes. And, as has been said, he had supreme self-confidence. He was the typical product of the post-First War world. His life was bounded by the Theatre, the cabaret, the smart restaurants and hotels, the dance floor and the night clubs. First Nights, suppers and dancing, parties, champagne and hectic gaiety—that was his world. That, he imagined, was the world of the Theatre. Like so many others he thought that because he knew a lot of theatrical people he knew all about the Theatre. He thought that because he could tell a success from a failure at a First Night, his judgment was impeccable. He was not the only person under that delusion and he was not the last. He saw himself as The Great Impresario. And when he formed a mental picture like that it was real to him. He was married to the daughter (an exceedingly charming lady) of a very rich man indeed, and he lived in a very nice house in St. John's Wood. This time he got what he wanted again; he signed up Lehár and Tauber for *The Land of Smiles* at Drury Lane.

He took offices in the Strand, and started to work. He got one or two people around him who knew something about the job in hand. He began well indeed. For Harry Graham wrote the English book and lyrics from the stage story which Ludwig Herzer and Fritz Löhner had contrived from the original piece by Victor Léon, *Die Gelbe Jacke*—and Victor Léon was one of the librettists of *The Merry Widow*.

Stanley Scott wanted publicity for this show—and for himself. He loved publicity—what theatrical person does not? To them it is their life's blood. Despite what so many people say, there is hardly one soul in this world who does not like publicity—unless it is the sort which they cannot control, and is unflattering! Then, of course, it is not publicity at all but a "dastardly attack". Stanley Scott wanted the controlled sort. So he betook himself to a man who specialized in it, whose name loomed large in the publicity world of those days, and asked him to undertake the job. The Publicity Man agreed to do so. He was, at that time, publicizing about twelve important West End theatres and running another; he was also managing the newly built Whitehall Theatre, which he had opened for the American dramatist Walter Hackett, in order that Hackett's wife, Marion Lorne (in her own line there was nobody like her), should become an actress-manageress and appear in her husband's plays.

That Publicity Man had done every job there was to do in the Theatre. So he knew what was good publicity and what was bad. He was as well known in Fleet Street as in the Theatre. His office was an informal club in which, every night, all the scribes who wrote about the Theatre could be found—or almost all of them—and a good sprinkling of other journalists, to say nothing of Editors, as well. You could meet everyone there, everyone who was anyone in Fleet Street, Theatre, Films, Literature, Sport, even Finance and Commerce. It had members who were bank managers and members who were policemen. Prizefighters sat and listened whilst Opera was discussed. Members of Parliament and even Cabinet Ministers were no strangers. It was unique, and distinguished visitors to London were always brought along. Stanley Scott had been there, and that was why he wanted its founder to handle his publicity.

Now, that Publicity Man knew all about Drury Lane. He had very old family connections with it; he had worked there himself. He had quarrelled with the man who had controlled its destinies just before George Grossmith—perhaps it would be better to say that the man had quarrelled with him—and, except as a member of the audience, he had not set foot in that theatre which he loved for just on ten years. But he knew what it wanted. He also knew Franz Lehár, from the days of *The Merry Widow*.

He did not, however, know Tauber. But then, nobody in this country knew him, except the people who had bought his gramophone records—

sung in German—and who raved about his voice. The Publicity Man secured all the records, played them over, and was more than satisfied.

He knew then how to handle the story. He knew all about the post-War plays of Lehár and their failure to attract, but he also knew the reason. He knew, too, that Lehár's music was better than ever, and that it still held the middle-aged enthralled. Lehár for the middle-aged, then, and Tauber for the youngsters—that was the plan of campaign. The Publicity Man got what material he could about Tauber, and it was scant. He wrote to Lehár for more. The answer came in living form—not Lehár, not Richard Tauber, but Tauber's brother, a charming man with a beard and an air of distinction, who could not speak English but brought an interpreter, and who announced that he was "the little Tauber". He and the Publicity Man got along famously together.

That Publicity Man, however, did not believe all he was told. He made his own enquiries through contacts on the Continent, and he found out about Tauber's unfortunate habit of being "absent on parade". He kept this knowledge to himself, but it was to stand him in good stead. He had his campaign prepared. He told Stanley Scott to keep his mouth shut. A wrong word at the wrong time and the publicity would be ruined. He knew that Scott met many of the gossip writers; he knew he would chatter; and he knew how an "exclusive" in one paper would ruin his story. He had to frighten Stanley Scott pretty severely. And when he saw the likelihood of Scott's silence coming to an end—he knew it would be of short duration, for the excited, enthusiastic young man was bubbling over—he put out his first general statement just in time to prevent damage. He kept it up with stories of all kinds. The name of Tauber became well known. More people bought the records and approved the voice, which was what the Publicity Man wanted. And gradually the time for Tauber's arrival and the start of the rehearsals drew near.

By this time Tauber, *The Land of Smiles* and, of course, Lehár had become what is known as "news". Not front-page news, but still news, and of sufficient importance to get space in the Press. The Publicity Man hoped that Lehár would come too, and bring over this tenor he had made so famous in Europe, but Lehár could not. So Tauber alone would have to do.

The Publicity Man did not want to "overboost". He knew the dangers of that. Scott ranged London proclaiming the glories of his show and how the success would be staggering, but none of that got printed. It was only heard in the purlieus of Theatreland—where they know what such things are worth. The Publicity Man had done what he wanted. He had got his man talked about; but he had never proclaimed a furore, a miracle, a smashing success. What he had done was to awaken a desire to hear this man, which was all he wanted. If Tauber was a success when he sang, that would be fine; if not, least said soonest mended. The Publicity Man knew full well how dangerous was over-expectation.

Stanley Scott had made himself an office in Drury Lane Theatre. He was not content with it as it stood. He turned it into the dream of a Florentine nobleman. It was all Florentine furniture, mirrors, couches, chairs, and lanterns on the end of poles, and everything was red velvet and gold lace. The last thing you would expect to happen in that office was work—and you would have been right in your expectation. Stanley Scott entertained there lavishly; champagne popped whilst he told of the wonders to come. And then the day came for Tauber's arrival. Scott went down to Dover to meet him. Before he left, the Publicity Man besought him not to overdo it. He knew his man, so he begged Scott to keep well within the bounds of truth, not to tell Tauber that London was his willing slave already, that thousands of "fans" would be at the station to meet him. Scott wanted to take all the Press down to Dover with him, but the Publicity Man would not hear of this. He wanted two bites to his cherry. He agreed to a couple of Theatre Correspondents whom he could trust going, but no more.

Nor would he go himself. He would be at Victoria Station with the cameramen, the most important people in the world of publicity such as he desired. He asked them all to come. He knew his difficulties, especially the difficulty of getting a picture of a man—and by no means a handsome man—into the papers. But he relied on what he had done already, and on Drury Lane Theatre, to overcome that. He relied on one thing more—the friendship of the cameramen. For he was a friend of them all; he always looked after them, made their jobs as easy as possible, was on Christian name terms with them all. They responded by calling him either "Bill" or "Mac", neither of which happened to be his name, but he did not mind; being a sensible, humble sort of man only interested in results, he answered to anything. So he hoped for the best, and did not expect very much.

He got to Victoria Station in plenty of time to meet the train bringing Tauber and Scott to town. To his amazement, the station was simply packed with people, great crowds of them. He could not quite make it out. He did not think his publicity had been as good as all that! He found his cameramen in a group. They told him, very crossly, that the officials had informed them that they would not be allowed on the platform. What was the game? Would he see about it? He would. He sought out a high railway official who was a friend of his. The official was co-operative inasmuch as he disclosed the reason for the crowds. "You know the King of Spain has abdicated?" he asked. The Publicity Man did know that. "Well, he is on the same train as your singer," said the Station official;

"it is supposed to be a secret but it's leaked out, we don't know how. That's why the crowd is here, and that's why cameramen are not allowed on the platform."

The Publicity Man pleaded his case. The official gave it friendly consideration. "Alfonso is in the middle of the train," he said; "your man is in the rear. Supposing I let you take your chaps on to the platform, will you do your best to keep them away from the King?" The Publicity Man promised he would do his best. He looked the official straight in the eye, and the official also regarded him steadily. They understood each other. "Right!" said the railway man. "I'll take you and your crowd through myself. But remember—the rear of the platform only!" The Publicity Man collected his photographers. They listened to what he said. They all trooped after him and the official on to the platform. He was profuse in his thanks to the friend who had helped him. Then he spoke to his "boys". "Now look," he said, "I've got you on here. I can't stop you taking pictures of the King, but I do expect you to come back to me and take my man too—lots of him!" They all laughed, and promised. The train steamed in, the crowds surged to the barriers. The cameramen rushed; their cameras flashed and clicked. . . .

The Publicity Man found Tauber and Scott standing at a window of the last coach. Both were wearing smiles of delight. He got them out, Tauber staring round him with pride. The photographers returned. Pictures were taken, lots of pictures—Tauber waving from a window, Tauber on the engine, grasping the controls, Tauber shaking hands, Tauber being patted on the back by two rather astounded members of the public off the train, who had not the slightest idea what it was all about. They had been rushed into it by the Publicity Man—who turned on charm and persuasiveness—and as they were ladies and good-looking, they had not the slightest objection to their photos being taken; they were all smiles at that. . . . There were so many cameramen and such a fuss that now quite a crowd did gather, and Tauber was at last packed into his car —a final picture looking out of the window and waving—and that was that.

Stanley Scott enquired of the Publicity Man how he had managed it, and was asked what he meant. "Well," said Scott, in a relieved voice, "I am afraid I ran away with myself. Tauber seemed a bit downcast at Dover, and I told him all London would be at Victoria to meet him. How did you get that crowd?" The Publicity Man told Mr. Scott, and also reproved him for doing what he should not have done. But he breathed a prayer of thanks to King Alfonso, who had unwittingly saved his tenor from disappointment. His luck had been in. And Tauber never guessed the truth. He thought to the last it was all for him.

Later that evening, the Press met Mr. Tauber at the Hyde Park Hotel, where he was staying. It was the usual kind of Press Reception, but very well attended. Tauber sat in a chair and stared at the Press, who stared back at him and partook of refreshment. The Publicity Man said his little piece and invited questions. It used to be hard to break the ice at affairs of that kind, but the Publicity Man had a friend upon whom he could rely to start things going. That was A. T. Borthwick, of the *News Chronicle*, a fine journalist and a charming, kindly man, and on this occasion, as on many more, Borthwick started things going. Tauber proved a good talker, and the Conference went very well indeed. A lot of space was given to Tauber in the morning papers.

The next day rehearsals were to commence. Tauber arrived in a big white car at the front entrance, not the stage door. He got out, went up the steps of the theatre into the noble vestibule, walked straight to the box-office and shook hands with the Manager thereof and his assistants. Those, he said, were the men with whom to be friendly—they took the money! The company was assembled in the Foyer, that lovely specimen of Regency architecture. With them was the producer, Felix Edwardes, who had done many shows at Drury Lane, and reproduced many more from overseas. The stage was required for the scenic arrangements, so the first rehearsal was in the Foyer.

Renée Bullard, a beautiful singer from Vienna, had been specially imported for the part of Lisa, the leading lady, and pretty little Hella Kürty was to play Princess Mi, which she had created at the original production at the Metropol, Berlin, and played also at the first production in Vienna, at the Theater an der Wien. There were also George Bishop, a sound and reliable actor, Lena Halliday, J. Neil More, Walter Webster, Phyllis Edwardes, Dorothy Crofts, Gwen May, Dorothea Ronald, Dorothy Cooper and David Henley. Important parts were played by George Vollaire, as Captain Gustave von Ploetz; Bruce Winston, the very fat actor, as Chi Fu; and W. Cronin Wilson, a straight actor of repute, who had played many West End leads and had been with Lewis Waller, as the old Chinese Prince Tschang.

There were also members of the Press, anxious to chronicle this important occasion. They were removed, with tact, from the Foyer as soon as they had had a look round and had met the principals, because it was not necessary, from the Management's point of view, that they should see the actual rehearsal. It is almost always better that they should not. They had got their story and mostly had drifted away, but one or two had stopped, gossiping with the Publicity Man on the Grand Staircase. Suddenly a figure burst past them, sobbing as if its heart would break. It was Hella Kürty—and something was wrong! That was evident to everyone. The scribes scented a news story, but the Publicity Man got in first. He ushered them into Stanley Scott's office in all its Florentine splendour, and left them there until he could find out what was going on. He soon found out—and kept the trouble to himself, explaining it as just a little outburst of nervous temperament and smoothing it all over. Then, Stanley Scott seeing fit to produce champagne, the contretemps was soon forgotten. But it was the first discordant note in a series of rehearsals which were far from calm and peaceable. However, Drury Lane was, in those days, watertight for news, and when there was trouble not even Stanley Scott dared gossip.

Meanwhile the demand for seats was a big one. Those who had seen the show in Berlin or Vienna raved about it. Those who had the records wanted to hear the real thing, and everyone wanted to hear a new operette by Lehár. Walter Hackett, the big American dramatist who looked like a bison, had seen this show on the Continent and he told all London of its glories and of Tauber's voice. Tauber came to the Whitehall Theatre, where the Publicity Man was Manager, sat in the Royal Box, and was introduced to the audience, who cheered him. At the Whitehall was the latest and best panatrope possible to be got. So after Tauber had been introduced, the audience was informed that they would hear some of his songs on records. The panatrope chose that evening to go wrong for the only time in its career, and instead of the voice of Tauber, dismal churrings and croakings were all that could be produced.

The First Night at Drury Lane drew near. So far Tauber had just "walked through" the rehearsals—when he had been there—and had not sung a note. Those who had neither seen him act nor heard him sing could not form any idea of what he was going to be like. The dress rehearsal arrived. There was everything as it should be, with the magnificent Drury Lane orchestra under the baton of that prince of conductors and musicians, Ernest Irving, a man who not only knew all about music but had a will of his own and was not afraid of speaking his mind. The curtain went up. Except for the Directors and staff the vast auditorium was empty. But naturally, the show was to go through "as at night". Every one wore his or her costume, everyone was made up. All except Tauber. He just "walked through" and went through the motions of singing . . . wearing his street clothes.

So the First Night arrived. Drury Lane was packed with a smart, fashionable audience on that evening of the 8th May, 1932. Expectation ran high. This was going to be exciting. Hopes beat in the hearts of those responsible for Drury Lane itself, too. Things had not been too good there lately; indeed, they had not been good at all. Since *Show Boat* in 1928 there had not been a success, except Julian Wylie's pantomime, and that

The last phase—a very late picture of Lehár, worn out by his troubles and sufferings during the Second World War

"You are my discoverer". Photograph given to Victor Léon, librettist of *The Merry Widow*, bearing, besides this inscription, themes from Lehár's works

Top: Immortal Melodies. Lehár
conducting a concert of his works.
Left: The Mortal Remains. Grave
of Franz Lehár at Ischl

perforce was seasonal. There had been *The New Moon*, *The Three Musketeers* and *The Song of the Drum*, the first two from America, the third home-made. None had done well; *The New Moon* had run 148 performances, *The Three Musketeers* only 240. Sir Alfred Butt had left the Lane after the production of *The Song of the Drum*, which ran for 131 performances, although the comparative failure of the play had nothing to do with his retirement. Gone were the days of *Rose Marie* and *The Desert Song*. So there were prayers in the hearts of the Drury Lane staff that Lehár and Tauber would break the spell of bad luck, for the big musical shows just mentioned had had much to recommend them, yet they had not done the trick.

The curtain rose on *The Land of Smiles* and disclosed a beautiful scene in "The House of General Count Lichtenfels" in Vienna. There, as a guest, came "Prince Sou Chong" from China—and that was Tauber's part. His entrance had been awaited with impatience by the audience, and now he came. They saw a rather short, thickly built man in evening dress, with a Chinese make-up of yellowy-sallow hue on his face. They saw a rather ungainly walk and gestures. It was not quite what they had expected; there did not seem much romance in this new thing of Lehár's, nor in this new tenor!

But Tauber soon had them under control. For he opened his mouth and he sang; it was one of Lehár's loveliest melodies, "Patiently Smiling",[1] and he sang it beautifully. Nobody saw the gaucherie any longer—nobody cared about that; this voice had already got them. Tauber played a little scene with Lisa (Renée Bullard) leading up to their duet "A Cup of Tea", and that—a light, sentimental, semi-comedy duet—was given a fine reception and an encore. Things looked very good indeed. The Publicity Man, never an optimist where theatrical affairs were concerned, had his hopes. He had the place filled with cameramen and they were doing their job. No "flashes", but they were taking pictures all the same. An official of the theatre came to protest about them. They were disturbing the audience, he claimed. "You get out of this," snapped the Publicity Man. "You haven't had an audience for so long that you don't know what disturbs them. These chaps are going to help get you one in future." He had his way; he knew when to call his men off, and he knew they would not overdo it. That Publicity Man won. He was feeling good. He had not entered that theatre officially for ten years to that very night, and was not going to be robbed of his little triumph.

And the audience were *not* disturbed; they were too intent on the stage. Tauber sang a serenade, "Beneath the Window of My Love", the passion and sex in his voice awakening a trembling response from the female section of his audience, and then the Finale, the love finale between Lisa

[1] *Immer nur Lächeln.*

N

and Sou Chong, brought the First Act to a close amidst cheers. So far, so good. The audience buzzed; the critics were friendly; and the experienced knew that, in the catch phrase of the day, "they'd heard nothing yet", for Lehár never packed his gems into the First Act. It looked as though Fortune's Favourite had found his own London fortune again, and was bringing fortune to Drury Lane as well. Tauber's name was on every lip, praise on all sides. The bar bells gave their warning, and the audience did not hang about as usual; a good eighty per cent hurried back to their seats.

The curtain rose on the Second Act and they found they had left Vienna for China. They were in the Palace of Prince Sou Chong and it was a dream palace, it had all the colour and romance of China; it had the velvety sheen and softness of lacquer, the waxed delicacy of a magnolia flower. It breathed the very scent and mystery of the Celestial Land, and was a very lovely scene indeed, painted by Alick Johnstone on the premises, in the great Paint Room of Drury Lane itself. In this scene the story unfolded, the opposition of wise old Uncle Tschang to his nephew Sou Chong's infatuation for Lisa the beautiful Viennese, the dalliance of little Princess Mi with her Viennese beau von Ploetz—but what did the story matter? Here was Lehár in operatic vein, pouring out rich, sweeping, embracing melodies, of a texture they had not heard from him before, and here was a Voice—the voice of Tauber, who could give those songs what they needed.

The audience was sitting forward, not losing a note. They drank in "What Has Given You This Magic Power?", a duet by Tauber and Renée Bullard. They encored Hella Kürty's dainty song "The Only Thing I Care About", and they gave a double encore to her duet and dance with George Vollaire, "I Love You and You Love Me", a comedy number delightfully rendered. It was clear that Hella Kürty had made a big personal success. *The Land of Smiles* was scoring heavily, and Tauber was, to all intents and purposes, established. He looked so much better and so much more impressive in his Chinese robes than he had done in his European evening dress. His voice was magnificent . . . magnificent, all agreed. . . .

And then, he took the stage alone. He seemed to fill it completely as he stood there and faced them, and he looked a real Chinese Prince. There was a glint in his eye as Ernest Irving's baton waved and from the orchestra stole notes which sounded like golden drops. Then the figure on the stage began to sing, and something gripped that audience. This, they knew instinctively, was the moment—there was an invisible spell coming over them from that man who had seemed so odd but who now was so commanding. They hushed to a dead silence as, very quietly but with infinite tenderness and appeal, he sang, for the first time, the refrain of "You Are My Heart's Delight".

He sang the refrain; he swept into the verse; the love throbbed out of him towards that Western lady of his heart. He was laying bare his soul, his depth of being, as, in phrases of Oriental imagery, yet with the simplicity of all lovers, he painted her picture in verse and music. As he told her—unseen—that she had cast a net around him, and bound him by a magic spell, that was just what he was doing with his audience. Seldom has there been such stillness in a theatre, seldom such withheld breath, seldom such pent emotion as while the beauty of the voice and music held them prisoners in its thrall. Then he was singing the refrain again, giving it all his power, all his passion, until at the end the voice went right away into the distance, and seemed like an echo in a mist of golden romance as it murmured, softly but with perfect clarity, the last three lingering words "I Love You".

For a moment or two he held it, looking straight out to the audience, who were silent as if stricken dumb. Then he turned and walked towards the exit—and the floodgates were loosed. Winds at gale force, tidal waves dashing against sea walls, surging crowds acclaiming heroic conquerors—that was what it sounded like. The very walls of centuries-old Drury Lane seemed to tremble at the impact of the applause. This was Triumph. Tauber turned; he bowed and bowed, and the cheering continued. There were almost frantic yells of "Encore! Encore!", as if he might not do it again, and he must—he must! . . . Tauber still stood there bowing and bowing; and then with a smile—with almost a comedy twist of his body and a swing of the leg—he went back to the centre of the stage, and sang again.

It seemed as if he would never be let go. Every time he tried to make his exit the applause and calls were louder and more deafening; every time, just before his exit, he did that same odd twist—which now made them laugh—and got back to the centre of the stage, to face them four-square and sing for the delight of their hearts. He sang it in English, in German, in French, in Italian—in every language he knew—and this further delighted the enraptured audience, who, it seemed, wanted nothing more than to sit and listen to this song all night. Nobody counted the number of encores. Over and over again Tauber sang, until at last he shook his head with a broad smile, and really made his exit. And even then they could not get on with the piece. If ever a show was "stopped", in stage parlance, and stopped by one man, that show was *The Land of Smiles*.

But was it really Tauber alone who had done it? Most decidedly not. Granted he sang with perfect artistry, it was the song, the music, which gave him the chance so to do. Franz Lehár was again Fortune's Favourite. This was his music, this was a Lehár that nobody had heard before.

Previously he had conquered by a waltz, the natural rhythm, the musical voice of Vienna. But the world no longer moved in Waltz Time and nobody knew it better than Lehár. So, for his great appeal, the Waltz had gone and here was—what was it, a ballad, a serenade, a love song, an aria? What did it matter? It was a marvel. Instead of luring them to move to its grace, as the waltzes of Lehár had done, this song, this melody, bound them to their seats, with its real throb of the heart and its tremendous passion—a passion poised for outburst, but held in because the loved one was not there to make all complete. It was the floodtide of overwhelming love, driven by the tempestuous winds of passion, and rearing its head like a great breaker, just about to loose itself in full force and carry all before it. Lehár had expressed all that. He had given the feeling of the disjointed mind driven by the senses, of the beating pulse, the racing heart, the mist before the eye, the tensing of the muscles; and then by contrast had come, with almost magical effect, the last few notes in that *piano* voice of Tauber, his greatest possession, his greatest trick if you will, but used in such a supremely masterly fashion by Franz Lehár.

This song had swept out and bound the audience by chains. It had crept amongst them fastening their fetters; it had played with their emotions in its almost staccato moments; and then tossed them about like trifles in its swell of sound. It had not lured its hearers into sensuousness, as the waltzes had done; it had just made them complete and abject captives. Waltz Time might be dead; but Lehár had the new formula— and here it was. What did the failures matter? What did the bad years count now?

It seemed that anything more would be an anticlimax; but the tempo of the piece quickened, the delicate Chinese romance became a broken melody, a shattered vase of porcelain, for Sou Chong lost his beloved Western lady. It could not be fulfilled, this hope of marriage between them; East was East and West was West; and, as the curtain fell, Tauber sang that matchless melody again, not the triumphant, expectant lover this time, but with black, broken-hearted despair. The dream was over; the melody a broken one; his heart's delight was gone. Operette had become Grand Opera. When the house lights went up and the audience came to themselves, they seemed dazed to recollect that they were just at a First Night watching a play. . . .

Lehár and Tauber—that was what one heard all through the interval. The Press, in the Press Room, showed unwonted excitement, asked questions, even went to the unprecedented length of discussing what they had just seen. Would the Third Act stand up? It did; it showed Sou Chong in his sorrow, a Prince before he was a man, and a Chinaman before all. It showed him hiding his grief, revealing only to little Mi, who shared his woe, a glimpse of his broken heart, facing his lost love and the world with inscrutable Oriental countenance; and then when alone singing that song he had sung before, "Patiently Smiling", and singing it huddled and stricken, with such utter sadness in its notes that tears were compelled. . . .

The scene at the final curtain was amazing. It was more like the decisive goal, scored just before the Referee's whistle at a hard-fought Cup Final. The noise resembled that of Wembley Stadium. People stood up and cheered; they stood on the seats and bellowed. They waved hand-kerchiefs; they let themselves go. Tauber and the company took calls; they all took calls; and then Tauber alone. They roared for a speech. He smiled—that wide, sudden, boyish smile—he glanced down at Ernest Irving, who had conducted so superbly, and instead of a speech he once more told them, in song, that they were his heart's delight. Then the orchestra swung into "God Save The King" and the house lights went up. An evening never to be forgotten.

Only one thing was missing, there was only one regret—that Lehár was not there to see this crowning victory of his. The news went to him by telephone; but his friends, and he had many in the house, felt a sense of personal sorrow that he could not have heard this London of his once again acclaim the man who had given them so much, and who had, this night, bridged the gap of the War years, thrown away his favourite and tried weapon, the Waltz, and conquered by that music of passion and romance of which he was King. Once again he was Fortune's Favourite —and at Theatre Royal, Drury Lane.

CHAPTER SEVENTEEN

Down to Earth Again

IN the morning the Press was wonderful. The Publicity Man's bedside 'phone was busy at an unearthly hour with journalists wanting interviews. He called them all to the Hyde Park Hotel, where Tauber was staying. Always an early bird, the Publicity Man was earlier than usual. He was at his office before 9 a.m., a time which does not exist in Theatreland. At about ten he sent a message through to Tauber to say the Press was doing him the honour of calling upon him at twelve noon. He did not disturb Tauber, but he left strict instructions that the message was to be given him as soon as he awoke; that it was of paramount importance; and that Tauber must not fail. He knew Tauber was not likely to be awake early— he knew about the party the night before—but he also knew that this most unusual Press gathering was one which must be carried through; a thing like this happened so seldom, and for Drury Lane's sake, for Lehár's sake and for Tauber's sake, it must be a success. To him, of course, such a thing was sacred. Fleet Street must have what it wanted; he had always worked by that rule.

Collaborating with the Publicity Man at that time was a journalist of front rank, whose paper had been amalgamated with another, and who was for the moment at a loose end. The Publicity Man had offered him this little fill-in, which was far beneath the journalist's merits, but was something to do. That man now holds a very high and responsible position in Fleet Street on one of the national newspapers with a colossal circulation. Together they went to the Hyde Park Hotel. There they asked if Tauber was about. He was not. Had he had the message? He had. What had he said? He had grunted. . . . They sent up a message to say they were waiting—and they continued to wait. The Fleet Street men and women began to arrive. Another message went up. No reply. It was now noon. An urgent message was sent—for the Press were there in force. The

Publicity Man explained all about First Night parties and subsequent exhaustion and begged indulgence. He sent a more urgent message at twelve-fifteen. The answer came that Mr. Tauber was not coming down. So the Publicity Man and his colleague went up to Tauber.

He was in bed. He was told what he was up against; he was spoken to pretty roughly when he seemed disposed to pooh-pooh the whole thing; and he was informed that if the two men before him went back and told the Press that he refused to see them—they who had done him a most unusual honour—he might as well take the next train back to Germany, Austria, or wherever he wanted to go, because they would see to it, those two who spoke to him, that he was flayed alive. And Mr. Tauber, in his dressing-gown, came down to see the Press, like a prisoner between two flinty-hearted warders. He put up a good show, although he looked terrible. And after half an hour he was allowed to go back to bed. It was a Saturday. The house was sold out; the second night Press were to come on the Monday; indeed, money was being turned away. The Publicity Man did not like either Tauber's looks or his manner. He got hold of Stanley Scott and warned him. Scott, drunk with success, said it would be all right. All the evening papers carried big stories and pictures, and the Sundays were constantly coming through for more news. So Saturday evening came.

An audience even more excited than that of the First Night sat in the auditorium. For the First Nighters had not known when they came in, but these people knew the treat in store for them. The Publicity Man was there early; he had horrible fears. He spoke to the Management. Precautions were taken, for H.R.H. The Princess Royal was to be in the Royal Box. Also, in case of trouble, they had a great throat specialist standing by. Tauber arrived in plenty of time, and went straight to his dressing-room. So far, so good. But still the more experienced had qualms. Then the blow fell. A message came that Tauber could not play; his throat was bad, the *piano* would not work, and Tauber without his *piano* —unthinkable!

Stanley Scott raged; the experienced men of the Theatre went into action. Round went the throat specialist, and a high official informed Tauber that it was imperative that he should sing. "In front tonight," he was told, "is our Princess Royal, the daughter of our King. Not to sing is *lèse majesté*—more, here it ranks as treason. I don't know what will happen to you. Your name will stink; you will have to fly the country; it will be complete ruin for you, because the specialist says you can sing, he guarantees it, and we shall tell the world so." There was a terrible scene; but Tauber sang, and sang as he had sung the night before. . . . It was another evening of triumph.

The "Libraries" (the booking agents) had plunged; the advance booking had never stopped all that day; and the Sunday Press was remarkable. Monday morning dawned, and it should have been cloudless. But down came the message that Tauber was ill. He could not—he would not—sing that night. And the house was sold out. The play had been produced on Friday, it was now Monday; here was a front-rank success, and here was the man who had made it so missing at the third performance. The understudy must play—at this short notice—but however good the understudy might be, he could not be Tauber, and it was Tauber whom the packed audience would be expecting. The understudy was quite calm and collected. He was ready to go on, he said; he knew the part, words and music. He was British and his name was Robert Naylor. He had a splendid tenor voice and he was a good actor. But—he was not Richard Tauber.

The Publicity Man did his best to keep the secret for as long as he could. Scott was chasing Tauber, who had gone into hiding, and it was not until the audience bought their programmes that they found the dreaded little slip, "Owing to the Indisposition of Richard Tauber, the part of Sou Chong will be played at this performance by Robert Naylor". There was a groan of disappointment. It is a most disheartening thing to be an understudy, however good you may be. You go on knowing that the audience don't want to see you at all, that they will give you kindly applause, but all the time wish you far away. The best you can do is to "keep the curtain up". Robert Naylor did that—and more. A good-looking man, his fine voice sang every note true as a bell; he got encores for "You Are My Heart's Delight", and his performance was excellent in every respect. Outwardly he was as calm as a cucumber; he was a real "professional". Inside he felt terrible, but he went through the job nobly. He got quite a little ovation at the end . . . and he deserved it.

Next morning Tauber's absence was front-page news. He was off for some days; business fell right away. What should have been a glittering success began to melt like a snowball in a thaw. Then Tauber came back. It was duly paragraphed, but momentum had been lost. There was doubt in people's minds—and how right they were!—for nobody ever knew when Tauber was going to sing. He did not seem to care. He had apparently no feeling for the play, the theatre or the great composer who had taken him from Opera, put him in the front of the world, and enabled him to earn so much big money. He had no thought of his own reputation, of his companions in the company, or of his manager Stanley Scott. He just did as the whim took him. The Publicity Man, with the aid of his friends in Fleet Street, ran a kind of daily bulletin, saying "Tauber will —or will not—sing tonight". Fleet Street had no sympathy for the tenor, but they helped the man who helped him. And they also began to print opinions of their own.

It was stark tragedy. Here was success thrown away by a man's whim. Here was a fortune being frittered; here was the return of glory for Franz Lehár being trampled in the mud. It might have been so different. Here was a success as great as *The Merry Widow* being sabotaged—there is no other word. Proof of what might have been was shown by the constant telephone calls to the theatre; was Tauber singing or not? If the callers could be assured that he was—and even this was difficult—then the place filled up. If not, it was half empty.

Celebrities came to see Tauber and were often disappointed. One night a woman who was world-famous attended the show, and Tauber was singing. She came with her husband. She had been, she still was, "The World's Sweetheart", although now that the Talkies ruled the screen she was seen no more thereon; she was Mary Pickford. She arrived like a Queen; she sat in the Royal Box with Douglas Fairbanks Senior. The Publicity Man took her round to see Richard Tauber. He conducted her across the great stage in the interval, and the stage hands lined up to get a glimpse of her. She bowed to them with a regality that true Royalty might have envied. It was indeed like conducting an Empress. And the journey back to the box was the same. She had an ovation from the audience as soon as they realized who she was. Tauber had the great dressing-room, the Number One Dressing Room of the World, where so many famous people have dressed. It did not seem to impress him; he did not seem to care.

And then, another blow fell. He was not only "off", this tenor, but he had gone—back to Vienna. Robert Naylor played on; Scott swore that Tauber would return. The Publicity Man, sick of the whole thing, went round to Scott's office to have a real show-down. As he went up the stairs, he met Felix Edwardes, the producer, coming down. Edwardes was all smiles. Scott had told him the arrangements, and they were fine. He gave the Publicity Man his blessing—his invariable custom—and passed on.

But the hard-boiled Publicity Man had grievous doubts. He told the ebullient but worried Scott that something must be done, some announcement made, or he would not be responsible for what might appear in the papers. Scott swore him to secrecy. It was all right. He had secured an even greater tenor than Tauber, who would be in London on the following Wednesday and would take over the part. The man who had to tell the world reflected. "It must be Piccaver," he said, and was told he was right. "But it is Saturday afternoon now," he objected; "how can he learn the words and music and open on Wednesday?" Scott informed him that Lehár had been teaching Piccaver the music for some time. Still the

Publicity Man had his doubts. "But the English script—and the business?" he queried. "Felix Edwardes has been with him for ten days, producing the new tenor," Scott said. Now, the Publicity Man had been speaking to Edwardes not ten minutes before. He told Scott so, and the poor man had nothing to say, except that he hoped . . . that he had been in touch with Lehár. . . . He had really meant no harm. He was trying his best. It was just wishful thinking. . . .

The Publicity Man walked out, back to his office. He put a call through to Lehár, and he got him. Lehár answered that he himself would bring back Tauber, and that Tauber would sing again. There was nothing in the Piccaver story. He, Franz Lehár, was bringing Tauber back; they would soon meet. How they did and what happened has been told in the opening of this book. . . .

But that second "First Night"—that second night of triumph at Drury Lane—could not save the day. The damage was done. *The Land of Smiles*, a born success if ever there was one, ran at Drury Lane only from the 8th May to the 18th July—a mere seventy-one performances—all because of the temperament, the bad sportsmanship, the complete unreliability of a tenor. But although Tauber had killed the operette he could not kill Lehár's music, and he could not kill the great song "You Are My Heart's Delight". That went into the national repertoire. That was heard on all sides, as indeed it still is. It was heard on the unlikeliest occasions. A pretty young actress died, in tragic and very unexpected circumstances. She was given a Memorial Service at St. Martin-in-the-Fields. As the mourners were rising to leave the church, the organist played a voluntary—and it was "You Are My Heart's Delight". He had been requested to play it by a great admirer of the actress.

Tauber, although he ran away from *The Land of Smiles*, could never escape from that song. He had to sing it always, all his life, before an audience would let him finish his entertainment. It became to him what the Prelude became to Rachmaninoff, what "I'll Sing Thee Songs of Araby" had been to Ben Davies, one of the haunting, never-to-be-shaken-off songs. There are many of them. Thus, although *The Land of Smiles* had failed to run, Lehár had succeeded. He had once again given this country a melody which it would never forget, of which it would never tire. It was financially a poor consolation to Lehár the business man, but it was a tremendous source of pride and happiness to Lehár the composer, Lehár the artist, and that was the Lehár who mattered.

Tauber came back to London and did concerts. He was as unreliable as ever. He was booked to appear at the Royal Albert Hall, and that immense building was sold out. He was still under the management of Stanley Scott, but the concert tour was sponsored by Lionel Powell, the big man in that branch of the musical world. The Publicity Man was still attached to the outfit. He had grave doubts about the Albert Hall affair. The concert was to be on a Sunday. On Friday the Publicity Man sat down to his typewriter and wrote his story for Sunday; he was quite sure of himself. On Sunday he went to the Albert Hall with a friend, and gave him instructions what to do in certain circumstances, on a sign from him.

The public streamed into the Albert Hall, and there was not an inch of space anywhere. Nor was there an inch of Richard Tauber. There was only half an hour before the concert was to begin. Stanley Scott was there, quite certain that Tauber would turn up. He was told he had better go and get him. He went, and—like the man in Itma—he came back. He had found Tauber having a late lunch. He had told him he must sing; there had been a row; and Tauber had thrown the cruet at him, rushed out of the hotel, jumped into a waiting car and driven away—it came out afterwards that he had gone to Richmond Park. There was nothing for it but complete cancellation.

This job devolved upon Eric Evennett, Lionel Powell's right-hand man, for Powell himself was desperately ill. Mr. Evennett walked on to the platform and faced that expectant audience. A sudden hush fell, like a foreboding of doom. And then he told them, plainly and simply, that Richard Tauber could not sing that afternoon, and that their money would be returned. Anything might have happened in the awful pause which followed. What did happen was a glance from the Publicity Man to his friend, who did as he was told. He shouted two words across that deadly stillness—a phrase which was in common daily use—"Buy British!" The angry, disappointed audience laughed, and began to go away, resentful, furious, but not making trouble. The Publicity Man went to the telephone and put over the story he had written on the preceding Friday; he had known what would happen. Tauber slunk out of London the following morning, with hard words about him in all the papers.

But let justice be done to him, nevertheless. He went to New York; he sang in the Town Hall there in October 1931, and had a big success— for he turned up. He came back to London in 1932, and sang in a revival of *The Land of Smiles* at the Dominion Theatre, today a cinema. His leading lady was that fine soprano Josie Fearon. In 1933 he appeared in *Lilac Time* at the Aldwych, playing Schubert in German. In 1934, at the State Opera House in Vienna, he was back with Lehár again, singing in *Giuditta,* the last work of the Master's, which must be given separate treatment in this book. And in the same year he appeared at the Theater an der Wien in an operette of his own composing, *The Singing Dream*. He came to England from time to time, and did an extensive concert tour in 1935. And let it be stated now, in fairness to him, that he had abandoned many of his old bad ways. He broke out very seldom; he was much more reliable. He made several films, and he was singing better than ever.

In 1937 Lehár once again challenged London with his music. He had not been defeated by the *débâcle* at Drury Lane over *The Land of Smiles*. He knew where the fault lay, and that it did not lie with him, or his composition. He knew the value of Tauber and his voice, and because that man could sing what he composed better than anyone else, he stood by him. Tauber had let down Lehár—but Lehár never let down Tauber. It was not in the man to do that. So it was with Tauber that Franz Lehár made his last bid for a big theatre success in London.

In 1937, when things generally were in a very doubtful state, when the Nazi menace was mounting daily, when Hitler, that evil genius of the world, was grabbing all he could, to his right and his left, and showing clearly that, appeasement or not, in him lay the threat to the peace of the world—that uneasy peace, really little more than an Armistice, which had existed since 1918—Lehár arranged with the leading showman of the time, Charles B. Cochran, to present his operette *Paganini* over here. Neither he nor anyone else at the time realized that this was to be the last new production of a Lehár play that London was to see. Yet history had, in a strange way, been repeating itself. It was in 1907 that *The Merry Widow*, Lehár's first venture in London, had been produced. In 1937, exactly thirty years afterwards, came his last. George Edwardes, the greatest Manager of his day, produced *The Merry Widow*; Charles B. Cochran, the greatest Manager of *his* day, produced *Paganini*. Edwardes's name on the bills meant a lot to the public, so did Cochran's. An Edwardes production, a Cochran production—both were hallmarks of Quality. And if Edwardes was having a bad time when he did *The Merry Widow*, so was Cochran when he handled *Paganini*. . . . But there the similarity ended.

The news of *Paganini* was a big "story". Cochran saw to that. It had all the elements which arouse public interest. Cochran, a supreme showman, and the best Publicity Man since Barnum, whipped up excitement over this forthcoming attraction. Richard Tauber was to appear again in a Lehár operette, singing a rôle which he had created on the Continent. It was announced that Lehár's music to *Paganini* was the best he had ever composed; the public were led to believe that it would transcend everything hitherto known. And beautiful Evelyn Laye was to be leading lady and to play opposite to Tauber. If ever a production had the promise of success, it was *Paganini* . . . before production.

The theatre was the Lyceum, and there was nothing wrong in that. It was a real Theatre, and it would hold the money. Cochran banged the drum, and the Public responded. Evelyn Laye, blonde, beautiful and extremely talented, went to Vienna to see Lehár. She found him completely charming, and no doubt he found her the same, for Evelyn Laye—"Boo" to her friends—is a grand, human, understanding person, helpful in all ways, with no side or conceit, a hard-working "Pro" above all, entirely of the Theatre. Lehár played her the music of *Paganini*, showed her great courtesy and kindness, made her feel an honoured guest, and, when she left, presented her with one of his greatest tokens of esteem—a medallion bearing his head in bas-relief. She must have impressed him very much (and there is every reason why she should have), for he was sparing of these marks of his favour. She treasured it and had it hung on a bangle. Recently, when she toured Australia, it was an object of the greatest interest to all who met her. Those medals of Lehár usually brought luck to their recipients. Lehár gave one to the Publicity Man mentioned in this book, and it is now an heirloom, or will be when the proud possessor passes on. . . .

Paganini was adapted for the English stage by A. P. Herbert (Sir Alan P. Herbert, not knighted then however) and that eminent writer for the Theatre and very popular personality, Reginald Arkell. The cast included Claude Farrow, Lawrence Hawtry, George Casselli, Billy Hartnell, Charles Barrett, Joyce Holloway, Jean Panter, Anthony Neville, George Hayes, Dorothy Hutchison, Maurice Brooke, Phyllis Hollis, Cathleen Boutall, and the stars were Esmé Percy, Charles Heslop, Bertram Wallis (the original Count of Luxembourg), and, as has been said, Richard Tauber as Paganini and Evelyn Laye as Princess Anna Elisa. The piece was staged by Tyrone Guthrie. If anything looked set for success, it was *Paganini*. Tauber had behind him all the *réclame* of *The Land of Smiles*, or rather of "You Are My Heart's Delight"—for the short run of the play was already forgotten. He was a best seller on gramophone records; his concert tours and his films had taken his name and voice everywhere. Evelyn Laye was the principal leading lady of the musical stage in this country. The two English authors were on top of their form —and there was only one C. B. Cochran.

But all was not well within the camp. It may be that Tauber was repentant for what he had done in *The Land of Smiles*. For he appeared to hold a watching brief for the composer, and to resist to the last ditch any alteration suggested to the work. Reginald Arkell says, very truly, that in those days, when the rights of a continental success were secured for London, little attention was paid to any clauses in the contracts calling for purity of performance and strict adherence to the story, and requiring that no numbers should be interpolated. Many alterations were made in *Paganini*, and Tauber resisted them all. In Arkell's opinion he wanted to work on a more or less literal translation of the original script, which of course he knew. He accepted the lyrics, but he resisted the new words, even where it was necessary to modernize the story to meet existing tastes, and to bring it into line with what the authors knew full well was the English idiom.

He reported everything to Lehár, who did not come to London, and Lehár, too, proved "sticky". Tauber and Lehár in a sense "ganged up" against Arkell, Herbert and Cochran; and although the arguments were on a friendly and most courteous level, Lehár held out to the end—aided and abetted by Tauber, who was probably trying to make amends. Lehár had probably never known about the interpolated numbers in *The Blue Mazurka*, or, if he did, was not going to have anything of the kind now. He manifested the utmost politeness, but also the utmost firmness in this matter. No interpolations, no liberties with the score, were to be permitted.

It is impossible to blame Lehár for taking this stand. Whatever altera-tions may be required in the book of an operette or Opera when it is produced in a country other than that of its origin, there can be no excuse for diluting the score—especially when the score is by a man like Lehár. Even the interpolation of numbers from other works by the same com-poser may be disastrous, as was shown in a recent clever production of Offenbach's *Tales of Hoffmann*, when the insertion of an extract from his *La Belle Helène*, written at a different period of his life and in quite a different style, had a most inharmonious effect. Much worse is it when the music of another mind is thrust into the score, whether the intruded numbers be good or bad. In the original London production of *The Merry Widow* there had been interpolations, easy to be detected, and Lehár was well within his rights in refusing to allow this to happen any more.[1]

Thus the production of *Paganini* was no smooth ride for C. B. Cochran. He was having a load of troubles at the time, and *Paganini* did not lighten them. One of the snags which had to be overcome was Tauber's idea of a suitable salary for himself. By this time he had done many concerts for which he received a very high fee indeed. He did not see why this should not be the basis of a theatre salary. His idea was that the personal fee for one concert performance should be multiplied eight times—that is, for six evening and two matinée performances. Logic may have been on his side, but the economics of the theatre were dead against it. That did not appeal to him at all. Figures were figures. If he was worth so much to sing

[1] He did not always like the drastic changes made, especially in America, in the plot and setting of his works, when, for instance, "You Are My Heart's Delight" was sung in front of a back-cloth of the Eiffel Tower! When told that the American public was different from the European, he hazarded the opinion that human beings have much the same reactions every-where (*Bekenntis*, pp. 5–7).

at a concert, he was worth so much to sing in a theatre; the fact that there was a company too to be paid had nothing to do with him. A figure was at length agreed, but the size of it made financial success for the play almost impossible.

Tauber may have been awkward with the Management, but he was very charming to Evelyn Laye, who says she found him most unselfish, willing to give way on almost any occasion, and often surrendering lines and positions which more grabbing artists might have considered their own. Reginald Arkell also has a memory of Tauber, which is characteristic. At rehearsals, when the tenor had just finished running through a song, he said to Arkell, "For that number I shall take four encores every night." Arkell gazed at him, doubtfully. He knew his Theatre very well, and he knew the public. "How can you possibly tell?" he asked. "You may have done so abroad, but you don't know if a London audience will react in the same way." Tauber nodded and smiled his boyish smile. "You will see, my friend," he said. "Four encores for that number—at every performance!" Arkell remembered that and watched. It came about just as Tauber had said. He would get applause, come back right away and sing it in French—then in German—then in Italian. It was the technique of "You Are My Heart's Delight" all over again. Tauber knew what to do to them.

Paganini was produced at the Lyceum Theatre, London, on the 20th May, 1937, with all the blaze and brilliance of a Cochran First Night. Everybody who was anybody was there—and quite a lot of nobodies too. Any Cochran show was assured of a wonderful First Night socially, and this time there was the additional excitement of Tauber and an operette by Lehár. The First Night reception was a good one, and notably applauded amongst the songs were "Girls Were Made to Love and Kiss", and "Beautiful Italy", for which Sir Alan Herbert had written charming lyrics. Yet the play did not succeed, Tauber, Evelyn Laye, the fine company, the staging of Tyrone Guthrie, the Cochran production and Lehár notwithstanding.

The real trouble was Tauber. It was not his voice or his non-appearance this time; rather it was his actual appearance. The British Public may not be musical—that is proverbial, but not essentially true—but it is realistic. It happened to know a bit about Paganini, the actual Paganini of history and fame. It knew that he was not a bit like Tauber, whose stocky figure did not resemble the sinister, emaciated, almost skeleton form of the celebrated and mysterious violinist. The public did not accept him in the part, although it highly approved his singing. On the Continent it had been different; there much more was taken for granted. Provided the voice was right, what did credibility or appearance matter? But the British were matter-of-fact. It mattered a good deal to them. They would accept a great deal in Grand Opera—that was another thing. There they did not have to believe in the story at all. But this tale had to be real; and here the strength of Lehár, who would only have a real, human story to inspire him, proved the weakness of the production. The public loved the music; they bought the records; they liked the selection; but they did not want to see the play.

Once again Lehár the musician succeeded, but Lehár the composer of operette failed. It was not the music that left the English audience cold, but the idea on which it was strung, and not quite the idea perhaps but its delineation. Cochran went to America, a disappointed man, and *Paganini* was withdrawn from the Lyceum on the 17th July, 1937, after sixty performances—Lehár's shortest run. Fortune had not attended its Favourite this time. . . . Yet it should be put on record that only in England has this charming operette failed to prove an attraction. Everywhere else its success has been great and has continued to grow. The calamities of the Second World War and its sequel have not interrupted its triumphs. The list of theatres in which it is played is every year a long one, and the number of performances in each place is impressive too. It seems possible that London made a big mistake in the summer of 1937.

Let the story follow Tauber, Lehár's finest singer, to his end. In 1938 he played at the Royal Opera House, Covent Garden, as Tamio in *The Magic Flute*, the part in which he had made his original operatic début, and also as Belmonte in *Il Seraglio*. He toured Australia and the United States with great success. He was back again in 1939 singing at Covent Garden as Hans in *The Bartered Bride* and Octavio in *Don Giovanni*, after which he toured the United States again and Canada, giving concerts. Then the Second World War broke out. Tauber had already cut himself off from Austria, from Germany, from Nazidom. He had nothing to do with that faith. Discord of such a kind was repellent to him, and, anyway, he was a decent man who believed in freedom and not oppression. He might be awkward, he might be temperamental (after all he was a great tenor), but he would have nothing to do with Hitler.

He worked nobly for this country during the War. He became a British subject in 1940, and appeared in a revival of *The Land of Smiles* at the Lyric Theatre, London, in 1942. Once again, Lehár was a technical enemy, but it made no difference to the British this time. They did not regard the Austrians as enemies, but as victims of Hitler, and there was no question of banning music by Middle European composers, unless they were modern and Nazi. The revival of *The Land of Smiles* came at a bad time for air raids, but once again Tauber thrilled his audiences with "You Are My Heart's Delight", and this time he did not stay off and miss performances, as he had done at Drury Lane. He had married a charming British actress, Diana Napier, and he was very happy. She was a great influence for good on him, and kept him to his engagements and to regularity of performance. He shed his old ways and became a thoroughly good fellow.

He seemed quite tireless, and he would come down to Drury Lane, then the headquarters of ENSA, whose job it was to entertain the troops, and do broadcasts for them, which went all over the world and had great propaganda value. There he would stand on that stage where he had made such a success—and thrown it away—smiling, joking, doing what he was asked to do, dressed usually in a shirt with a loose collar, a loose pair of trousers and suède shoes, singing as if possessed—always with the monocle in his eye. He became personally very popular.

In 1943 he showed London his quality as a composer. He appeared in an operette of his own composition, *Old Chelsea*, and succeeded in both rôles. One of his songs, "My Heart And I", won a great popularity. It was tuneful and melodious—but not another "You Are My Heart's Delight". *Old Chelsea*, with its Cremorne Gardens setting, had quite a success, and a much bigger one when Tauber toured the country with it. His leading lady in London was Carole Lynne, and an old woman's part was played with ripe comedy by that grand Irish actress Maire O'Neill. In the company, also, for a while was a girl who was to become a star—made so by that disciple of Lehár's, Ivor Novello. Her name was Vanessa Lee.

In 1946 Tauber again visited America, and in the same year, in London, he showed his gifts as a conductor—the rôle in which he had started his career. He conducted a revival of *Die Fledermaus*, called *Gay Rosalinda*, at the Palace Theatre, and proved that he was a very good conductor indeed. He died, quite suddenly and unexpectedly, in London in 1948, aged fifty-six years. He went in his prime, for he had never been in better form, spirits or shape than when he was stricken down. Nor had he ever worked harder or more assiduously. Had he done the same at Drury Lane in *The Land of Smiles*, Lehár would have had a success running for years. Richard Tauber was missed, for he had made very many friends and was popular on both sides of the curtain. There was no conceit, no side, no frills about him. He seemed just like a big, happy boy, enjoying life and enjoying laughter. He leaves a happy memory and an impression which time can never blur in the minds of those who heard him sing Lehár's greatest song—and can never forget it.

Since *Paganini* none of Lehár's later works have been seen on the British stage. His style, his method, his type of music, however, did not vanish in the overwhelming tide of modernism and the sweep of music from America. For Ivor Novello carried on the Lehár tradition—even to the adoration of Tzigane melody. He kept alive that type of music and that glow of romance to which Lehár had introduced London in *The Merry Widow*; to the end the *Widow* was Ivor Novello's favourite musical play. And now he, too, has gone to that shadowy land where doubtless his spirit has sought that of Franz Lehár, to lay a tribute at his feet; and where, probably, those two makers of music find themselves fast friends, and, maybe, have both achieved the ambition for which they were reaching out—the culminating triumph of a Grand Opera which would have earned world-fame. Lehár did indeed come very close to that in his last work, but this country has never seen it. Nor did Ivor Novello grasp his ambition of having a Grand Opera of his played at Covent Garden, with himself conducting it; although he gave a foretaste of what it might have been like in the last Act of his *Arc de Triomphe*. Well, the world is the poorer place. . . .

CHAPTER EIGHTEEN

The Crowning Work

DESPITE all the dazzling successes of his career Franz Lehár had never ceased to be conscious of an unfulfilled ambition. As a young man he had forsaken the security of a career in Army music to become a composer of Opera. Yet in all his life only one Opera of his had been produced—*Kukuschka* (later renamed *Tatjana*). He had been deflected into operette by the necessity of earning a living, and after *The Merry Widow* it had been hard to escape from the *genre*. But he had worked consistently to enlarge the borders of light opera and to raise its musical standards. It was no longer to be a frivolous entertainment, but a representation of real life through the medium of music. It had already become absurd to give the title of "operette" to pieces like *Frederica* and *The Land of Smiles*, and now in 1932 Lehár was to receive from Paul Knepler a libretto written in collaboration with Fritz Löhner, entitled *Giuditta*, which was to prove the last step in his ascent to the summit he had so long aspired to attain.

When Herr Knepler read the First Act of *Giuditta* to him, Lehár exclaimed, "This masters me!" (*Der Stoff bemächtigte sich meiner!*), and indeed it would be difficult to think of any libretto falling short of actual tragedy that has more dramatic power. The heroine—and the heroine is well-nigh invariably an all-important figure for Lehár—is a dancer of mingled Spanish and Moroccan blood. When the play opens she is living in a Southern seaport town married to a middle-aged man, a maker of birdcages, who is, not without cause, devoured by jealousy of his young and fascinating wife. To the port comes a group of young officers whose regiment is due to embark for North Africa, to put down a rising there; and while waiting to sail they visit the inn of the Golden Barque opposite the house where Giuditta and her husband live. Their leader Octavio, a young and handsome Captain, brimming over with vitality and gaiety, tells of his joy in life in a song, "*Freunde, das Leben ist lebenswert!*" ("Life is worth living, my friends!"), which is one of the most exhilarating and gladdening melodies that Lehár ever composed.

When it is finished the officers leave to see to the embarkation, except Octavio and his friend Antonio, a Lieutenant, who seeks to confide to his Captain the grief he is feeling at parting from the girl he wants to marry. But Octavio does not listen for long. From inside the house comes the voice of Giuditta singing of her longing and her desolation; and as Antonio at last goes off to rejoin the others, she appears in all her dusky beauty, set off by the bright colours of her Southern dress, a half-African Carmen, still wrapped in her dream:

> *In einem Meer von Liebe . . .*
> *In einem Meer von Lust*
> *Möcht' ich vergehen . . . versinken . . .*

To be "drowned in a sea of love!". Passion is the whole being of this creature, and she knows nothing and cares for nothing but the intoxication of love. For Octavio the sight of her is fatality, and he is from this moment enslaved. "*Schönste der Frau'n,*" he implores her, "Loveliest of women",

> *Wenn alle Sterne glühen,*
> *Sollst du von Liebe träumen . . .*
> *So wie im Märchen!*

Under the stars they will dream their dream of love, "as in the fairy-tales!". Octavio entreats her to fly with him; she hesitates, but before he goes he begs her to follow him to the harbour. She returns to the house, and as Octavio departs with a last glance at her dwelling the word "Giuditta!" falls from his lips and is overheard by her husband, Manuele, who has just come home. A violent scene of recrimination follows, at the end of which, crazed with jealousy, Manuele casts his wife off and shuts himself up in his house. With a symbolic gesture Giuditta opens the bird-cage that hangs before the door and sets the little prisoner free. . . .

In the next Scene we are in a North African garrison town, where Giuditta and Octavio live together in a secluded villa, drowned in that sea of love of which she had dreamed. She dances for him, she sings for him; there is nothing to trouble their bliss, but the possibility that at any moment the order may come for Octavio and his regiment to leave the garrison for the front. And in the third Scene, a camp outside the walls, by moonlight, where Octavio is sitting with his friend the young Lieutenant Antonio, we learn that the order has come. They are to march against the rebels at dawn; but Octavio has not yet had the courage to tell Giuditta of their coming separation, and Antonio realizes that it is doubtful whether he will have the strength to put his duty before his love. The distant song of the soldiers, giving cynical warning that absence makes the heart grow fonder—of somebody else, is torture to him; he cannot bear the mocking refrain:

> *Dann muss sie einen andern küssen,*
> *Kann ja nichts dafür!*

"She must kiss another lover, there's no other way." Left to himself, he breaks out into the song, *"Du bist meine Sonne!"* ("You are my sun!"), a number that throbs with all the tenderness and passion that Lehár is capable of putting into his music. Here at last is the full expression of that enthralment to love of which "Vilya" was the adumbration. Giuditta is the real "witch of the wood" whom he had foreshadowed so long ago in the tragic note struck amid the gaieties of operette; and now, as Octavio picks up his *képi* to depart on his duty, she appears before him shimmering under the moon in her white night-gown, like a vision raised by an enchanter.

As soon as she learns that her Octavio means to leave her she overwhelms him with reproaches. What is the worth of a love that makes conditions, that sets any other loyalty before itself? That is not her creed, and she can believe in no passion of that faltering kind. Octavio, half conquered beforehand, now yields completely, and confesses to Antonio, who comes to fetch him away, that he intends to disobey his orders for Giuditta's sake. He stretches out his hand to bid his friend farewell, but the Lieutenant refuses to take it. He does not shake hands with a deserter. Octavio, as if struck by a whip-lash, recoils; then seizes cloak and cap again and rushes off with Antonio. Giuditta, left alone, cries in her desperation, "He has no heart!" and announces her resolve "to live . . . to dance for all . . . and forget all!"

So we are brought to the fourth Scene, where, amid the tawdry splendours of the Alcazar dance hall in a North African town, Giuditta has become a star of cabaret, expressing her recklessness and defiance in a waltz song of irresistible seduction, *"Meine Lippen, sie küssen so heiss!"* ("The kiss of my lips is a flame!"), with which she allures a rich English Lord, an *habitué* of the place. But, unseen by her, Octavio is watching in the crowd. Unable to endure life without Giuditta, he has deserted in face of the enemy, and stolen back in civilian dress to reclaim her. Now, as he sees her accepting a pearl necklace from the English Lord, and about to depart on his arm, he springs forward in jealous fury, feeling for the hilt of his sabre. . . . Then he realizes that he carries no sword now, that he is no longer an officer entitled to claim redress on the field of honour, but only a fugitive and a criminal. He falls back, and is left alone, his happiness, his life, destroyed.

The last Scene is one of the most moving that can ever have been put upon the musical stage. Four years have passed, and in a luxury hotel in a great capital waiters are preparing a private room for an intimate supper. The guests are the star of the Trocadero Theatre, *la bella Giuditta*, and a Duke, her latest capture. Everything has been thought of for her pleasure; even a pianist has been engaged to play soft music in an adjoining alcove during the meal. The Duke's Equerry sends for this musician to give him his last instructions. It is Octavio who enters in a well-worn evening dress; ruined and weary of existence, he has come down to this way of earning his living. The Equerry suggests a programme to suit the Duke's tastes. His Grace is very fond, for instance, of that popular waltz "The kiss of my lips is a flame". Does the pianist know it? "Yes, Colonel," replies Octavio impassively. . . .

Giuditta is the first to arrive, from her theatre. As she waits for her host she hears the piano behind the curtain, draws it and discovers Octavio. In answer to her questions he reveals that he was there and saw her the night the English Lord gave her the pearl necklace at the Alcazar. She assures him that her soul is his alone. "Have you what men call a soul?" he asks bitterly. In a passionate duet Giuditta tells him that she has never forgotten him, that it is not too late to renew their romance. But Octavio shakes his head sadly. Within him all is desolation and emptiness. He can endure the fate laid upon him, but love he no longer knows; and as the Equerry announces the Duke he retires to his alcove, and begins to play, as he is paid to do.

Giuditta cannot endure the situation. Pleading nerves and fatigue, she begs the Duke to excuse her; she will sup with him another night. Disappointed, the Duke offers her his arm to the door, and the waiters begin to dismantle the supper table. Behind the curtain the piano plays on. One of them pulls the curtain back. "What are you going on for? There's nobdy here." Octavio closes the keyboard and takes his hat. Before he departs he sings softly:

> *Schönste der Frau'n,*
> *Wo ist das Lied der Liebe,*
> *Es ist schon lang verklungen.*
> *Es war ein Märchen.*

"Where is the song of love? . . . It *was* a fairy-tale."

Such in stark outline (omitting the comedy sub-plot of the barrow-boy and his girl who give up fruit-selling in the Southern harbour-town in a disastrous attempt to become strolling players in Africa, and certain other minor characters) is the story of *Giuditta*. We have come a long way from the banalities of operettes like *The Count of Luxembourg* and *Frasquita*, and it is obvious what strong opportunities a plot like this gave to Lehár. Not only is there intense human drama in it; but the varied settings of the different scenes provided him with those openings for national and folk colouring in his score which he was always eager to seize. He set about his work with an enthusiasm that almost wore out his collaborators. Tauber, too, came to Ischl, to learn about his rôle of Octavio, and to offer valuable advice drawn from his stage experience. And it was Tauber who, when he was coming away with the authors of the libretto after a sitting that had lasted until 4 a.m., paused on the bridge over the Traun outside Lehár's villa and had an inspiration. "Boys!" he cried. "Do you know where I ought to sing Octavio? At the Vienna State Opera House!"

To his companions it must have sounded a wild dream. No Opera House in the world—not even Covent Garden—was, and is, so strict about the works it admits to its repertory as the Vienna State Opera. From the realm of operette Johann Strauss's *Die Fledermaus* is allowed within the sacred precincts, and beyond that . . . nothing. But could Lehár's works with any reason still be called operette? Yet, if not, what were they to be named? Herr Knepler told a group of enquiring journalists that *Giuditta* was a "typical Lehár (*ein echte Lehár*) in five tableaux"— and he could hardly have found a better definition. Actually it was to be called on the programme a "musical comedy", which is all wrong to English ears, since we use "comedy" almost exclusively in the sense of the laughable, and not in the broader continental significance that it bears in such a title as the *Comédie Française* or the *commedia dell' arte*.

But more important than the question whether the description of *Giuditta* on the programme was altogether satisfactory is the fact that the programme on which it was printed was . . . that of the Vienna State Opera. Lehár had at last won his recognition, and on Saturday the 20th January, 1934, *Giuditta* was produced there, at what were known as "Caruso prices", before a First Night audience of unusual importance, counting in its ranks several Cabinet Ministers, besides the leaders of the artistic and social worlds. Richard Tauber was the Octavio, and the heroine was played by a brilliant Czech singer, Fr. Jarmila Novotna, who had already appeared as Lehár's Frasquita in a film, and whose vivid beauty and expressive, speaking eyes made her an ideal choice for the rôle. The splendid scenic production under the direction of Hubert

Marischka gave great satisfaction to Lehár, who occupied the conductor's desk in person, presiding over the Vienna Philharmonic Orchestra.

The success realized all his hopes. The reception accorded by the First Night audience was a magnificent homage to *Giuditta* and to Franz Lehár; and forty-two performances were given by the State Opera, which represented a resounding triumph. Lehár's own view of this his last work was simple. "I gave my best," he always said, "in *Giuditta*."

CHAPTER NINETEEN

The Last Years

THE most important change in Lehár's private life during the early 1930's was his purchase of a new home in Vienna. At the beginning of the 19th century Schikaneder, the librettist of Mozart and founder of the Theater an der Wien, the playhouse that will always be linked with Lehár's fame, had built himself out of his profits a miniature *château* in a then rural suburb of Vienna, Nussdorf. It became known as the Schikaneder-Schlössl, and it was bought by Lehár in 1931. He was finding the house at 16 Theobaldgasse too cramped to contain all the spoils of his fame, and needed better safeguards of his peace and cherished privacy than a busy street in the heart of the city could supply. Two years were occupied in the renovation of the Schikaneder-Schössl and in the reconstructions necessitated by its new owner's requirements. A fresh attic story was built to house the "museum" of souvenirs, programmes, tributes, photographs, and so on, which had hitherto been housed at Theobaldgasse, and alterations were made to the communications by passages and stairs, so as to cut the Master off completely, when he wished, from visitors, from servants, and even from his family.

It was not until 1933 that he was able to transport himself to the charming Neo-Classical mansion, with its delicate Grecian frieze and sculptured pilasters, and its exquisitely wrought iron balconies, sheltered by the shrubberies and trees of the extensive grounds. The interior, when the decorations ordered by Lehár had been carried out, presented an even greater magnificence than the villa at Ischl. The tall salons of the Empire period were filled with furniture, both Gothic and baroque, on a scale to match their grandeur. Photographs[1] show us the great carved chests and cupboards, the vast oil-paintings and the statues, the giant vases and tall grandfather clocks with their decorative *genii* and cupids. Again we

---

[1] There are some fine ones in G. Knosp, *Franz Lehár* (Brussels, 1935).

are aware of the ecclesiastical note—a life-sized image of the Virgin and Child, a gilded *ambo*, once used as a desk for the reading of services in church, both lovely specimens of baroque art, and an embroidered vestment spread out upon the wall. Moreover, from the hall there opened a chapel, completely furnished, with a painted altar-piece in a rococco frame, and stone saints flanking it with waving draperies.

The beautiful grounds not only gave Lehár room for his solitary promenades (and care was taken that they were *kept* solitary, even the gardeners having orders to vanish at sight of him) but provided a happy haunt for the many pets of which both he and his wife were fond. He had aquariums and aviaries of goldfish and brightly coloured parrots, whose feeding was his own personal task, and the squirrels, too, leapt from the branches to eat out of his hand. *Schön ist die welt*—the animal kingdom, too, knew its admirer and its friend. There was the white angora cat, Kathi, and the famous little griffon, Lehár's favourite among his dogs, who had been trained to yawn when the "Merry Widow Waltz" was whistled to him—but once showed the bad taste (his master called it) to wag his tail with enjoyment at it! Besides these pets, friends tell of a canary that used to eat off his plate, a wild bird that fluttered into his bedroom for its food, a tame frog whose prodigious leaps after worms amused the Master highly, and a domesticated tortoise. . . . As for the goldfish, they grew so large with overfeeding that the tank would no longer contain them!

The first years at the Schikaneder-Schlössl, coinciding with the triumph all over the world of the Works of Lehár's last phase, were a kind of sunset glory shed on his life of successful endeavour. But Fortune has never yet stayed with any of her favourites until the very end, and now the shaking of her wings as she prepared to take flight began to cast a shadow upon Franz Lehár. A prologue to the bad days to come had been the ill-success of his later works in London already described. Another shock was the failure in 1935, under the stress of the growing inflation in Austria, of the music-publishing business which Hubert Marischka had taken over after the death of Karczag, involving heavy losses for Lehár. He parried this blow with his usual energy by immediately founding a publishing house of his own to issue his music at the premises he still possessed in the Theobaldgasse. This became in time the celebrated Glocken-Verlag, with branches all over the world, and still flourishes. Unhappily, not all the troubles that were to come upon Lehár could be remedied with such ease.

The world in which he lived was growing more and more unlike the world whose beauty had been the constant theme of his music. After the disaster of the inflation period in Austria came a worse threat still. The Germany of the "blood and iron" epoch had risen from the dust of defeat with a new and more terrible war-cry, "Race and soil!". It is impossible to think that Lehár, the incarnation of all that was sunniest, kindest and most beauty-loving in old Austria, a true citizen of the Vienna for whom a new waltz was as important as, if not more important than, a victory, could ever have found any attraction in the cold and brutal creed of Nazism. As for Anti-Semitism, not only was he married to a Jewess, but he had always liked Jews. So many of his artistic collaborators and performers had belonged to that race! His world had once been ravaged by war, and had scarcely recovered. The prospect of a new war must have appalled him.

Yet when, on the 12th March, 1938, Hitler's grey tanks rolled into Austria, and the swastika soon appeared in those ancient streets of Vienna down which Lehár himself had marched under the Double Eagle, he found himself placed in a peculiarly invidious position. If he did not want the Nazis, the Nazis wanted him; he who only desired to stand outside affairs and rule in his own world of music was in danger of being made a pawn in the shabby game of power politics.

It was known that Hitler adored Lehár's music, that *The Merry Widow* was his favourite among all plays. The way was open for Lehár to become a Court favourite of the new ruler of Austria (who had struck its very name off the map), but he had not the least desire to follow it. Even if he had, there was the fatal obstacle—his wife's Jewish blood. The wrath of tyrants is always close to their favour, and in refusing resolutely, as he did, to think of divorce or separation, in spite of the advice continually tendered to him by the Nazi authorities, Lehár was risking an explosion of fury on Hitler's part, spurned love so easily turning to hatred.

Nor was this the only way in which Lehár defied the régime and its tigrish vengeance. He was ordered to hand over the royalties due to one of his librettists, who because of non-Aryan blood was in exile, to the Nazi Government. He disobeyed, and found a way to get the money to his friend abroad. He was told that an elderly Jewish lady, mother of another banished friend of his, was in extreme destitution. Promptly he relieved her needs with a generous sum. These were not safe things to do in Nazified Austria, but they reflected that fundamental sense of justice and decency that Lehár could never in his life be induced by threats or by coaxings to swerve from. They needed courage of the difficult cold order, and they may be set in the balance against the charges of those who blamed him for not abandoning his art to become a leader of resistance, or for conducting, in the capacity of a simple musician, at a concert in aid of "Winter Help" patronized by high Nazi officials. Mme Peteani neatly sums up his position in these trying days as that of a man "defending two posts in danger, his work and his wife". He would neither prostitute the one to political ends nor forsake the other.

But the strain was great, particularly after the outbreak of the Second World War. Lehár began to show signs of age and nervous distress; his gait was enfeebled; and he was unable to do original work any longer. He busied himself instead with revisions of his old pieces, and in particular took an active part during February 1943 in preparing the new version of *Zigeunerliebe*, to be entitled *Garaboncias*, for the Opera House at Budapest. Artistically this invitation was a high tribute to the man who had made his name as a composer of operette, and Lehár gave all his energies to rehearsing the work in its glorified form and ensuring its success. He conducted at the First Night, which was a triumphant success, and then asked to be excused; he was worn out. He was prevailed upon, however, to take the baton for the second performance . . . and breakdown followed.

Suffering from the kidneys and also from eye trouble, Lehár, now seventy-three years old, returned to a Vienna which was already, as the fortune of war tilted against Hitler's Empire, evacuating and preparing to meet attack from the air. It was no place for an invalid, and Lehár and his wife retired to the villa at Ischl, which, with its principal hotels all turned into hospitals, was likewise wearing the melancholy aspect of war. And it was there in the spring of 1945 that the news reached him of the pillaging of the Schikaneder-Schlössl by Russian soldiers, aided by a mob, during the fighting in the suburbs of Vienna. All was destroyed, furniture, hangings, pictures, books, letters, tributes, documents, notes for work, and to nobody's profit, as Mme Peteani observes. When the bad news was broken to Lehár his reaction was characteristic. "What can the people who have lost their sons in the War feel like?" he said simply. As the trouble with his eyes was growing worse, and it could no longer be concealed from him that his wife, who nursed him devotedly day and night, was suffering from *angina pectoris*, he decided to withdraw to Switzerland, where he took a suite in the Hotel Baur au Lac at Zurich.

Here, in spite of malicious criticisms that percolated even to his retirement, he began gradually to mend in health, and to regain his spirits. As his sight gradually improved under treatment he was heard at the piano again in his rooms; he was seen at the theatre and out walking. In 1947 Tauber flew to Zurich from America to see his friend, a visit that must have been a tonic to Lehár's spirits. The two "brothers" did not know when Tauber took his leave that they would not see each other again; the well-loved singer and last great creator of Lehár parts died, as has been recorded in these pages, in London in the following January after an operation.

In spite of this bereavement, however, Lehár's strength continued to come back to him; his works were still holding the stage all over the world; his attendance at revivals in distant countries was pleaded for by Managements unable to believe in a Lehár who had grown old; his rooms at Zurich were a floral bower from the offerings of his faithful admirers. He himself felt that his powers were far from being exhausted yet, and in 1947 he wrote to his old friend and tried collaborator, Paul Knepler, to ask if he had perchance a libretto that might suit him. Herr Knepler replied to the effect that a Lehár libretto was not taken down from a shelf, but must be written with a due sense of its destination. Nevertheless he had a theme in mind and hoped soon to be able to show Lehár a scenario.

By the kindness of Herr Knepler we have been privileged to see this scenario, which bears the title *Louisa*. It is the groundwork of what might have been another *echte Lehár*. Laid in the period of the Second Empire in France its scenes include a revel of artists on Montmartre, a ball at the Tuileries, a harvest-home at a French country *château*, and a convent garden. There runs through it a touching love story, thwarted by diplomatic and Court intrigues, and ending on the note of renunciation. Moreover there is a haunting theme song for the heroine that one can imagine taking its place among the best loved of Lehár's melodies . . . if he had ever composed it.

For *Louisa*, which might have given Lehár the basis for a second *Giuditta*, was, so far as he was concerned, to remain a scenario and no more. On the 1st September, 1947, there fell upon him a blow that broke him. It has been said that when Mme Lehár went with him to Ischl in 1943 she was already suffering from a weak heart and from *angina pectoris*. When three years later the journey to Zurich was undertaken, her doctor, as he watched the car that was driving them to the Station, observed that "Frau Lehár is more ill than the Master." It was a fact that she concealed with magnificent heroism, in order that he might not be made uneasy and might continue to have the benefit of her nursing. But the consequence of this brave resolution was that the shock when it came was more terrible from its suddenness. On the evening of her death she and Lehár were sitting in the salon of their suite in Zurich after supper with two guests, one of whom happened to be the doctor attending her. Presently she rose and went for some purpose into the adjoining bedroom, without the least sign of distress. The next moment a cry came through to the salon, "Oh! my heart!", and by the time her husband reached her she had passed away.

For a time Lehár seemed a totally broken man; work on the scenario of *Louisa* was laid aside, and never resumed. The cords of the harp were broken, and it was never to be played again. But gradually, comforted by the loving care of his sister Mme Emma Papházay, and sustained by the sympathy of the people of Zurich, who seized every opportunity for paying him honour, especially by organizing a great concert of his works in the following February, he took up the task of living again—but with a difference. It seemed as if he were anxious to set everything in good order before his departure, and one of his first steps was to send a message to Mme Peteani, whom he had chosen to write his biography, with the suggestion that work upon it might be resumed.

This, however, could not be done effectively until he returned home to Bad Ischl, a move that had to be postponed for several months until his health permitted it. He left Switzerland at last in the middle of July and travelled by train to Salzburg, whence he reached Ischl by his own car. Silently on his arrival he traversed the rooms filled with so many memories, lingering long in his old work-room on the second floor, fingering the piano upon which so many of his inspirations had taken form. He could hardly be persuaded to leave this room and go to his accustomed place in the salon amid his treasures. Some of his beloved pets were there to welcome him—his old dog Jeani . . . some canaries. Then he inspected with feelings that could not be uttered the little house adjoining the villa in which, according to the strange marital arrangement accepted by both, his wife had used to live apart. It was now to be occupied by his sister and by Mme Peteani, in whose pages one must seek the account of his last days.

Lehár's return to Ischl was more than the return of an old and widowed man to the scenes of his former happiness, amid which he desired to pass his last days. It was, it could not but be, a public event for his fellow-citizens. Crowds thronged into the little town by coach, not to infringe his privacy, but to pay him such respectful homage as they could from outside his house; local associations in national costume, led by their bands, marched in to salute him. A reception to members of the Municipality was held in the salon of the villa, and toasts to the health of Ischl's most honoured citizen were duly drunk.

But Lehár did not belong to Ischl alone. Outside his doors stood the transmission coach of the Austrian radio, R.W.R., which was to send a message from him to his fellow-countrymen and to those in other lands within reach of his broadcast. In that affecting moment Austria, in her defeat and ruin, seemed to raise her head again, and to find a voice that could recall her ancient pride and the gifts she had given the world.

During these last months Lehár, Mme Peteani tells us, did not compose any longer, but talked. With the charming tyranny of an invalid too much beloved to be thwarted in any of his whims, he insisted on perching his biographer upon a high stool beside his bed, where it was almost impossible for her to keep her papers together or take notes, while he recalled the sunlit days of the past and the Europe of whose happiness he had been the singer. He was as strict as ever in excluding all disturbance while he worked; his mind was as keen as it had always been in detecting the smallest error in the notes he dictated.

Nor did he relax his scrupulous attention to his correspondence. If he was forced now to let his answers be typed for him, at least he could affix his signature to them—and the suggestion that some of the piles of letters that reached him might be ignored was met with the sharp retort, "That's not the way to behave!" The letters that he thus set himself to deal with were as varied and contained as many quaint surprises as ever. He had even a proposal of marriage from an unknown, who carefully explained that she was not interested in his money, having a pension of her own as a trained nurse, but that she felt suited to be his wife because of her prowess in cycling, ski-ing and dancing. . . . So it seemed that the tale of his conquests was not even yet ended!

But he was growing feebler instead of regaining strength. Blood transfusions were resorted to, without lasting benefit. He was reluctant to leave his bed, in spite of the advice of his doctors, and ate hardly anything, to the distress of his old and faithful servant Käthe, who had cooked for him for years and studied his tastes. It became plain that he was already half removed from this sphere, though so long as he lingered he was resolved that everything around him should be in fair and good order. A lady who called to visit him was surprised to receive an earnest remonstrance from him upon the way she was reputed to have behaved to her sisters. She had no ties with him to justify such a rebuke; simply he could not bear the thought of anything unworthy in his neighbourhood during these hours. He was watchful over every detail of household management; was anxious that every guest should have exactly what he or she liked best at meals; and was attended every morning by a girl from a manicurist's, that his appearance even in bed might show no slovenliness.

One night, Mme Peteani relates, she was woken by a knock at her bedroom door. It was Lehár's sister, come to give her the mournful news that the doctors had diagnosed impending paralysis of the stomach muscles, and that there was no further hope. Still he lingered, lying with closed eyes upon his bed, listening sometimes to the radio. One night his future biographer caught a glimpse of him through the open door of his room listening thus to a performance of Verdi's *Requiem* by Gigli and other famous singers. There was a look not of the earth upon his pale face and a smile of indescribable beatitude. Still living he had entered into his bliss.[1]

The anniversary of Sophie Lehár's death came, and that day he broke down and wept bitterly. But he regained mastery of himself, and when a few days later Mme Peteani came to tell him that she must go home (actually, it was to make room for his brother Baron Lehár and his wife in the villa) he begged her to remain. But when he was told that this was impossible he had a last talk with her, traversing once again in memory the episodes of his life, his griefs and joys, his failures and successes. Then he declared solemnly, "I did not come into the world to enjoy life, but to make others happy. That is what I have worked for." And he added that his greatest joy had always been the moment when one of his pieces was completed and he held the score in his hands. Afterwards when the Managers and the producers and the players took possession of it . . . it was not quite the same thing. When Mme Peteani at last took her leave he called after her through the doorway, *Auf Wiedersehen!*

During October letters reached her from Mme Papházay telling of his rapid decline. Another friend, a composer who had visited him, reported on the 14th October that the doctors gave him ten days more before the heart stopped. "He has made his peace with God," wrote the visitor, "and with the world." A few days later he was roused from somnolence by the trilling of his canaries in a sudden burst of sunshine. He had asked that their cage should be moved into his room, remembering that they would be cold downstairs. He smiled at the sound. "How beautifully they sing!" he murmured. It was the last music he heard; perhaps he could not have wished for any sweeter. On the 23rd October he told his devoted housekeeper, Frau Scaja, in spite of her protests, that his time had come, and having said it fell asleep, watched over by the sacred pictures surrounding his bed, not to wake again. At three o'clock in the afternoon of the next day, the 24th October, 1948, he passed over the river.[2]

[1] Peteani, p. 227.

[2] For the account of Lehár's last days the authors acknowledge a special indebtedness to Mme Peteani's biography, pp. 217–235.

Chord Off—For a Memory

LONDON, now that the trumpets and the scarlet of the Coronation have passed, is again the grey city that it has been since Hitler's War. The dust from the uncleared bomb sites covers it as with a penitential veil; the shop windows of Bond Street and Regent Street no longer display their Edwardian riches; at nightfall no laughter arises from a West End that has lost its animation. In Leicester Square the shuffle of the flat sandal replaces the exciting tap-tap of high heels; the democratic ugliness of female trousers has silenced the rustle of laced petticoats; white tie and waistcoat have yielded to jacket and soft shirt, lit only by the flamboyancies of modern neckwear; the whole neighbourhood seems flecked with ice-cream. And the reminiscent wanderer who seeks the spot where once stood delectable Daly's finds that a milk-bar carries the name, and realizes that, no doubt, nine-tenths of the young people who go in and out think it is the cognomen of the proprietor.

They see the big cinema next door, but they don't know—and probably couldn't care less for the fact—that this is where Daly's stood, the home of musical romance, the rose garden of feminine beauty, the temple of the Waltz, and the London shrine of the Master, Franz Lehár. The visitor may reflect, too, that of the other theatres associated with Lehár's name, the Shaftesbury is a riddled bomb ruin and the historic pillars of the Lyceum the portico to a dance hall. There remain, among the houses where Lehár's works were first heard in England, only the Palace and Theatre Royal, Drury Lane, and there are no memorials to him there.

Surely, on the site of Daly's at least, it would not be too much to ask for some sprig of remembrance? Vienna possesses a Lehár-Strasse and Bad Ischl a Quay Lehár. London might at least have a tablet to commemorate, in the land where he did so much, and which loved him and his works so well, the composer of *The Merry Widow* and *The Land of*

Smiles. It would not be to the point to object that Lehár was a "foreign composer". It was an essential part of his genius to have transformed Viennese operette into something universal.

There was justice in the complaint made by some of his compatriots that his works have not the true Vienna stamp. It was impossible for him so to confine himself. Is there any composer of musical plays who has drawn his subjects from so many lands and cities? Vienna, Paris, Alsace, Hungary, Russia, the Balkans, the Alps, Italy, Spain, Tangiers, the Far East—for all he has found the music that embodies their spirit. If it be true that a novel is (or should be) "a corner of Nature seen through a temperament", then these plays may be called a world felt through the soul of Franz Lehár. The sneer implied in the word "cosmopolitan" has no justification in his case, for it was at no cheap or superficial exploitation of foreign and exotic modes that he aimed. He had too much integrity for that; and if he had done no more than that he would not have been taken to the heart of the world as he has been.

It may well be found, as Time does its sifting of reputations, that Lehár will stand out above many of his forerunners and contemporaries who rivalled him in grace and gaiety and wit—an Offenbach, a Suppé, an Oskar Straus—by the depth and strength of the human feelings that find expression in his music. He demanded flesh-and-blood characters and real drama so insistently from his librettists because he could not write music that was divorced from the serious meaning of life. If he started (as he could scarcely avoid doing) on the beaten path of the operette, with its glorification of woman, wine and waltzes—and nobody has celebrated these pleasures with more infectious zest—he could not stop there. Prince Danilo was not content for ever with Maxim's, and his musical creator, always profoundly idealistic about love and life, could not bound his vision by the rim of the champagne glass.

So the first Lehár passed into the second, not by any abrupt break or "conversion", but by the steady development of his own nature. In the end it had become absurd to call his works "operettes"—though nobody has yet found a satisfactory alternative name for them. But the Opera Houses of the Continent showed understanding of the situation when they invited him to produce his later works on their boards. After that it hardly matters whether they are to be called "Operas" or not. "Music Drama" is perhaps the best title for them, for drama is their essence and their life.

Experience—some of it bitterly disillusioning—has shown that without interpreters of the right calibre Lehár's works cannot make their due effect. It is not easy, in the England of today at any rate, to find singers, or to afford orchestras, that can do justice to *The Land of Smiles* or *Frederica* or *Giuditta*. Even *The Merry Widow* cannot be satisfactorily treated as a cabaret show or a musical romp. For these reasons and others —among which may be counted the present popularity of "high-powered" American musicals—it may be some time before Lehár regains in the English Theatre the place which he once held, and which his songs and his waltzes have never lost in the affection of English folk. But it would be wrong to doubt that he will return in due course and with the military swing of his baton beat ghostly time to the triumphant revival of his plays. For London loved him—and he loved London well.

APPENDIX 1

Principal Works of Franz Lehár

1896. KUKUSCHKA. Book by Felix Falsari and Max Kalbeck.
(Revised Version, TATJANA, 1905.)
1902. WIENER FRAUEN. Book by O. Tann-Bergler and Emil Norini.
(Revised Version, DER SCHLÜSSEL ZUM PARADIES, by Emil Norini and
Julius Horst, 1906.)
DER RASTELBINDER. Book by Victor Léon.
1904. DER GÖTTERGATTE. Book by Victor Léon and Leo Stein.
DIE JUXHEIRAT. Book by Julius Bauer.
1905. DIE LUSTIGE WITWE. Book by Victor Léon and Leo Stein.
(English Version, THE MERRY WIDOW, 1907.)
1906. PETER UND PAUL REISEN INS SCHLARAFFENLAND. Book by Fritz
Grunbaum and Robert Bodanzky.
1907. MITISLAW DER MODERNE (One Act). Book by Fritz Grunbaum and
Robert Bodanzky.
1908. DER MANN MIT DEN DREI FRAUEN. Book by Julius Bauer.
1909. DAS FÜRSTENKIND. Book by Victor Léon.
(Revised Version, DER FURST DER BERGE, 1932.)
DER GRAF VON LUXEMBOURG. Book by A. M. Willner and Robert
Bodanzky.
(English Version, THE COUNT OF LUXEMBOURG. By Basil Hood, 1911.)
1910. ZIGEUNERLIEBE. Book by A. M. Willner and Robert Bodanzky.
(Revised Version, GARABONCIAS, 1943. *See below.* English Version,
GIPSY LOVE, by Basil Hood, 1912.)
1911. EVA. Book by A. M. Willner and Robert Bodanzky.
1913. DIE IDEALE GATTIN. Book by Julius Brammer and Alfred Grünwald.
1914. ENDLICH ALLEIN. Book by A. M. Willner and Robert Bodanzky.
(Revised Version, SCHÖN IST DIE WELT. By Ludwig Herzer and Fritz
Löhner, 1931.)
1916. DER STERNGUCKER. Book by A. M. Willner and Fritz Löhner.
1918. WO DIE LERCHE SINGT. Book by A. M. Willner and Heinz Reichert.

1920. DIE BLAUE MAZUR. Book by Leo Stein and Béla Jenbach.
(English Version, THE BLUE MAZURKA. By Monkton Hoffe, 1927.)
1921. DIE TANGOKÖNIGIN. Book by Julius Brammer and Alfred Grünwald.
1922. FRÜHLING (One Act). Book by Rudolf Eger.
FRASQUITA. Book by A. M. Willner and Heinz Reichert.
(English Version, FRASQUITA. By Fred De Gresac.
Lyrics by Reginald Arkell, 1925.)
LIBELLENTANZ. Book by Carlo Lombardo and A. M. Willner.
(English Version, THE THREE GRACES. By Ben Travers, 1924.)
1923. DIE GELBE JACKE. Book by Victor Léon.
(Revised Version, DAS LAND DES LÄCHELNS. By Ludwig Herzer and Fritz Löhner, from Victor Léon's book.)
1924. CLOCLO. Book by Béla Jenbach.
1925. PAGANINI. Book by Paul Knepler and Béla Jenbach.
(English Version, PAGANINI. By A. P. Herbert and Reginald Arkell, 1937.)
1927. DER ZAREWITSCH. Book by Béla Jenbach and Heinz Reichert, from the play by Gabryela Zapolska.
1928. FRIEDERIKE. Book by Ludwig Herzer and Fritz Löhner.
(English Version, FREDERICA. Book by Adrian Ross, Lyrics by Harry Pepper, 1930.)
1929. DAS LAND DES LÄCHELNS. *See* DIE GELBE JACKE, *above.*
(English Version, THE LAND OF SMILES. By Harry Graham, 1932.)
1931. SCHÖN IST DIE WELT. *See* ENDLICH ALLEIN, *above.*
1934. GIUDITTA. Book by Paul Knepler and Fritz Löhner.
1943. GARABONCIAS. Book by Innocent-Vincze Ernö from the text of ZIGEUNERLIEBE. *See above.*

NOTE

Of the above works, *Der Rastelbinder*, *Die Juxheirat* and *Frasquita* are published by Verlag Josef Weinberger; *Die Lustige Witwe* by Verlag Ludwig Doblinger (Bernhard Herzmansky); *Die Göttergatte*, *Der Mann mit den Drei Frauen*, *Das Fürstenkind*, *Eva*, *Die Ideale Gattin* and *Tangokönigin* by Doblinger and by Glocken-Verlag; the remainder by Glocken-Verlag, 3 Crawford Street, London, W.1. All English versions of Lehar's plays are published by Messrs. Chappell.

APPENDIX 2

Bibliography

PETEANI, Maria von   *Franz Lehár, Sein Musike, Sein Leben.* (Glocken-Verlag, London, 1950.)

CZECH, Stan   *Franz Lehár.* (Scientia Züich, n.d.)

DECSEY, Ernst   *Franz Lehár* (Drei Masken Verlag, Berlin, 1930.)

KNOSP, Gaston   *Franz Lehár: Une Vie d'Artiste.* (Schott Frères, Brussels, 1935.)

EIDLINGER, Karl, and
LIPP, Franz   *Lehár-Museum.* (Stadtgemeinde, Bad Ischl, 1951.)

HOLZER, Rudolf   *Die Wiener Vorstadtbühnen.* (Vienna, Staatsdruckerei, 1951.)

KELLER, Otto   *Die Operette in Ihrer Geschichtlichen Entwicklung.* (Stein-Verlag, Leipzig-Vienna, 1926.)

CRANKSHAW, Edward   *Vienna: the Image of a Culture in Decline.* (Macmillan, London, 1938.)

INDEX

A

About, Edmond, 128
Adair, Ronald, 170
Albert Hall, 202–3
All the World Turns on Love, 168
"Alone at Last" (song), 157–9
Alt Wiener Theater (Wertheimer), 25*n*
An der grauen Donau (waltz), 160
Andrews, Maidie, 174
Andrews, Tailleur, 123
Arkell, Reginald, 179, 205–7
Attaché, L', 42
Austrian Empire, 19, 21, 24

B

Bad Ischl, 41, 43, 152–3, 157, 215, 217, 222, 225
Barmen-Elberfeld Theatres, 23
Barnes, Winifred, 174
Barrett, Charles, 205
Barry, Norah, 122
Bates, Thorpe, 175, 179
Beaden, Phyllis, 181
"Beautiful Italy" (song), 207
Bekenntis (Lehár), 127–8, 206*n*
Bellamy, G. Somers, 170
"Beneath the Window of My Love" (song), 193
Berlin, 165
Berlintheater, 46
Berry, W. H., 60, 71, 87, 90–1, 96, 104–5, 111–24 (*pass.*), 130–2, 138–44 (*pass.*), 148, 175
Bishop, George, 191
Blue Mazurka, The (*Die Blaue Mazur*), 161, 180, 206
Bodanzky, Robert, 128, 129, 131, 150
Boosey, William, 47–9, 63–5, 70

Borthwick, A. T., 191
Boutall, Cathleen, 205
Bradfield, W. Louis, 57, 122
Brahms, Johannes, 22, 41, 152
Brisson, Carl, 170–1
Brooke, Maurice, 205
Brune, Adrienne, 122
Brunner, Beatrice von, 132
Budapest, 21, 34
Bullard, Renée, 191, 193, 194
Burke, Betty, 181

C

Caillavet, G. A. de, 150
Cannon, Charlie, 94
Carl Theater, 35, 37–40, 128, 135, 150
Carrington, G., 123
Casselli, George, 205
Chappell & Co., Ltd., 47
Christians, Mady, 168
Cingalee, The, 56, 60, 70, 90
Claremont, Arthur, 180
Cleather, Gordon, 90, 111
Cliffe, Clarina, 132
Clo-Clo, 162, 178
Cochran, Sir Charles B., 129, 204–8
Coleman, Charles, 132
Coliseum Theatre, 171
Collier, Beatrice, 132–3
Collins, José, 179
Comelli, 174
Confession (Lehár), 127–8, 206*n*
Conservatorium of Music, Prague, 22
"Coonah" (song), 176
Cooper, Dorothy, 191
Count of Luxembourg, The, 129–36, 140, 144, 150, 152, 175, 215
Country Girl, A, 55
Courtneidge, Robert, 83, 180

233